JAZZ MASTERS OF NEW ORLEANS

A Da Capo Press Reprint Series

THE ROOTS OF JAZZ

General Editor: Christopher W. White

JAZZ MASTERS
of
NEW ORLEANS

by Martin Williams

DA CAPO PRESS • NEW YORK • 1978

Library of Congress Cataloging in Publication Data

Williams, Martin T
  Jazz masters of New Orleans.

  (The Roots of jazz)
  Reprint of the 1967 ed. published by Macmillan,
New York.
  Includes bibliographies and discographies.
  1. Jazz musicians — Louisiana — New Orleans —
Biography. 2. Jazz music. 3. Jazz music —
Discography. 4. Music — Louisiana — New Orleans.
  [ML3561.J3W5315 1978] 785.4'2'0922 [B]
  ISBN 0-306-77541-7   77-9632

Published by Da Capo Press, Inc.
A Subsidiary of Plenum Publishing Corporation
227 West 17th Street, New York, N.Y. 10011

JAZZ MASTERS OF NEW ORLEANS

THE MACMILLAN JAZZ MASTERS SERIES

Martin Williams, General Editor

Jazz Masters of the Twenties
Jazz Masters of the Swing Era (in preparation)
Jazz Masters of the Forties
Jazz Masters of the Fifties
Jazz Masters of New Orleans

Also by Martin Williams:

Where's the Melody? A Listener's Introduction to Jazz

As editor:

Jazz Panorama
The Art of Jazz

JAZZ MASTERS

of

NEW ORLEANS

by Martin Williams

THE MACMILLAN COMPANY, *New York*
COLLIER-MACMILLAN LTD., *London*

FIRST PRINTING

The Macmillan Company, New York
Collier-Macmillan Canada Ltd., Toronto, Ontario
Printed in the United States of America

Acknowledgment is gratefully made to the following copy-
right holders for permission to reprint from previously
published materials:
For excerpts from Treat It Gentle *by Sidney Bechet.
Reprinted by permission of Hill and Wang, Inc.*
For excerpts from "Condition Red—Allen, That Is" *by
Martin Williams, which appeared in* Down Beat *maga-
zine August, 30 1962. Reprinted by permission of* Down
Beat *magazine.*

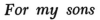

For my sons

ACKNOWLEDGMENTS

I KNEW the music of Sidney Bechet on records before I knew that it was New Orleans jazz. I owe further knowledge of New Orleans music to recordings reissued in the late Thirties and early Forties by Bluebird, U.H.C.A., Columbia, and Jazz Information. Therefore I owe a debt of thanks for this book to the men who made that music and to the men who kept those records available to listeners of my generation.

I owe my first knowledge of jazz history to *Jazzmen,* edited by Frederic Ramsey, Jr., and Charles Edward Smith. I also owe an early firsthand knowledge of New Orleans jazz to performances by Kid Ory's Creole Jazz Band, which I first heard in Los Angeles in 1944.

My special thanks to the following men who have given me their time and their knowledge over the years and especially for this book: Henry "Red" Allen, Jr.; Richard Allen; Rudi Blesh; Roy Carew; Mutt Carey; Natty Dominique; Harold Drob; Nesuhi Ertegun; Bud Freeman; George Hoefer; Frederick Ramsey, Jr.; William Russell; Elmer Schoebel; Boyd Senter; Zutty Singleton; David Stuart; Brian Rust, and Buster Wilson. And for special help I want to thank Don Heckman, Bob Wilber, and Danny Barker. I am likewise indebted to the many jazz scholars, researchers, and critics whose interviews and comments have contributed so much to this voulme.

My thanks also to Arthur Wang of Hill and Wang, the American publishers of Sidney Bechet's autobiography, *Treat It Gentle,* for permission to quote extensively from that book in these pages.

A portion of the "Henry Red" chapter appeared in slightly different form in *Down Beat* under the title "Condition Red— Allen, That Is." I would like to thank *Down Beat* and its editor, Don DeMicheal, for permission to include that material here.

M.W.

CONTENTS

Acknowledgments   vii

Introduction   xi

BUDDY THE KING   1

O.D.J.B.   26

THE ROLL   38

PAPA JOE   79

N.O.R.K.   121

SIDNEY   136

LITTLE LOUIE   162

ZUTTY   178

THE KID   205

BUNK   222

HENRY RED   251

Index   277

INTRODUCTION

As ANY HISTORY of the music will tell us, jazz started in New Orleans.

Surely it must have, for in 1917 a group of musicians from New Orleans suddenly found themselves a success in New York City, playing a music they had learned there. On their records, they were called "Dixie Jass Band" and later "Original Dixieland Jazz Band." And a few years earlier, it turns out, the Original Creole Orchestra, from New Orleans, had been playing the same style on the Orpheum Theater circuit.

Besides, pianist-composer Jelly Roll Morton declared that "jazz started in New Orleans," and that New Orleans was the city "where the birth of jazz originated." He had plenty of evidence because he could name hundreds of jazz musicians, men who played unlike anyone before them, and they came from New Orleans.

Then we have the towering figure of Louis Armstrong, who, between the mid-Twenties and the mid-Forties, changed the entire character of American popular music of all kinds—it's easy enough to prove that he did. And Louis Armstrong was from New Orleans.

And we have a legendary hero, a man who himself started jazz, according to the testimony of some of the oldest surviving players. He was a cornetist named Charles "Buddy" Bolden. And Buddy Bolden was from New Orleans.

More recently, a reaction set in to the idea that New Orleans was the "cradle of jazz." Some patent nonsense has been a part of that reaction (for example, the strange assertion that no New

Orleans musicians were of much importance *except* for Armstrong!), yet the reaction has some evidence on its side and calls for some cold reexamination. After all, it is New Orleans musicians who say that jazz started in New Orleans. Perhaps they say so because it was in New Orleans that they learned to play jazz.

The truth is that jazz started in New Orleans, depending entirely on what you mean by "jazz." Obviously, the word was first coined (or rather borrowed, and rather obscurely borrowed, it would seem) to describe a music that came from New Orleans. (Many New Orleans players detest the word, and Sidney Bechet, for one, continued to call the music "ragtime" all his life.) But, if we admit that this jazz music is clearly a kind of African-American music, then we are already in trouble. For all African-American music did not start in New Orleans. To put it another way, only New Orleans African-American music came from New Orleans.

Where did blues start? Nobody knows where or, for that matter, when. The most recent and persuasive suggestion is the Mississippi Delta country in the state of Mississippi itself. Ragtime was popular at the turn of the century. Where did it come from? Well, the centers during its great early period were Sedalia, Illinois, and St. Louis, Missouri. Even earlier there had been cakewalk and so-called minstrel music—clearly either African-American or strongly influenced by African-American music.

If we go back over the musical evidence that we have, we discover that there is a pattern of change in African-American music, and that as it has evolved, the music has become more and more complex rhythmically.

Perhaps that statement comes as something of a shock to the jazz traditionalist who speaks of the "purity" of early jazz and its closeness to its African origins. But it happens that African music is so complex rhythmically that it's beyond the ears of most Westerners, and that early jazz is relatively so simple (and for some players so unsure) rhythmically, as to be child's play by comparison, and that only in its most recent and still advanced guard developments does American jazz approach an African complexity rhythmically.

Personally I have no doubt that Missouri ragtime would have been the kind of music that it was whether or not there had been any New Orleans jazz; I don't think that ragtime was affected by the New Orleans idiom. But I do think that the New Orleans idiom was affected by ragtime.

We are right, no doubt, to consider the weekend celebrations in Congo Square as an important part of the background of New Orleans music. But what the music at these celebrations sounded like must remain somewhat conjectural. On the other hand, there can be no question of the influence of Sousa marches on both ragtime and on New Orleans jazz, and we know exactly what Sousa marches sound like—the evidence is concrete. Yet few historians, except for musicologist Leroy Ostransky, have had much to say about the relationship of ragtime and New Orleans jazz to the music of John Philip Sousa.

In any case, for New Orleans jazz we have documented on phonograph records a rhythmic evolution within the music itself. It begins with a phrasing, a melodic rhythm, rather close to ragtime but looser, and using rhythms ragtime only hinted at. And it ends with a percussion of four evenly spaced beats to a bar and a melodic rhythm as flexible and imaginative as Louis Armstrong's and Red Allen's.

It is probably hard for us to realize today how startling each of the styles in African-American music seemed in its own day. Ragtime's effect was revolutionary and national. People thronged to piano studios which claimed to teach them to play it properly. Yet today, to a casual listener, there may seem little difference between late minstrel songs and early ragtime. Or for that matter, between ragtime and early New Orleans jazz.

No, this fresh rhythmic character, and its difference from earlier African-American music, is not the sole characteristic of New Orleans jazz; and the music made several other important contributions—the durable so-called Dixieland ensemble style, for example, and a crucial emphasis on improvisation. But the rhythmic character of New Orleans music was fundamentally important, and it was in part the greater rhythmic resourcefulness of the music that helped give it its greater emotional range. Thus in New Orleans jazz, African-American music underwent an all-important change which redirected its course and gave it a way to continue and to grow. Of that much we can be certain.

And, as I say, we know a great deal about that change; its

background and sources, its nature as it gradually evolved, and about the players who brought it about.

The story of New Orleans music is fraught with romanticism. A colony, originally settled by French and populated by Spanish, Caribbeans, Africans. The juxtaposition of the castes by color. A world-fabled tenderloin district. Mardi Gras Carnival. A tradition of surviving African musical culture in the Congo Square ceremonies. A legendary hero, crowned King Bolden by his admirers, who went berserk reputedly from sex and drink but who supposedly founded a music. A diamond-toothed dandy who played piano in the houses and said he invented jazz, and had the colorful name of Jelly Roll. A fallen king, noble in adversity, Joseph Oliver. But these are only the beginning. And there are heirs, successors, usurpers.

It is sometimes hard for us to focus. Jelly Roll Morton may be an entertaining or exasperating man. But if he were not an important musician, we might as easily look elsewhere for our colorful braggarts. And if Oliver were not a musician to be honored, his personal nobility would surely be less honored by the hundreds of jazz followers who never knew him.

We would do such men wrong to make them the victims of our own romanticism or nostalgia. Yet the music itself has been the victim of romanticism. A player considered an amiable amateur by his elders is dug up by the more exclusive partisans of New Orleans jazz, who go into verbal ecstasies when he executes a major triad. A ditty originally written in New York City for comedian Bert Williams is hallowed as a "traditional New Orleans piece." A trumpeter adds a few obvious pick-up notes and some doublings to an old blues theme, and his work is transcribed and picked over like variants in a Shakespearean text. Dozens of men who stayed at home, simply because they were not good enough musicians to undertake Chicago or New York, find themselves more prolifically recorded than an important player like Jimmy Noone.

"Jelly Roll Morton's importance in jazz music cannot be overrated," wrote a commentator in the late Thirties, in the kind of giddy hyperbole that was sometimes found in the jazz writing of the time. Well, if it could be, Jelly Roll himself was the man to do it. So rather than blame the journalists and historians, it might be best to go back to the sources. And at the core of those sources is the music.

I have tried in this book to use musical achievement as the basis for what I have included, and that, by and large, means musical achievement that has come down on phonograph records and occasional sheet music. I have not tried to write a handbook on New Orleans jazz, and you may find some capable players unmentioned in these pages. My perspective on the music is, I hope, that of the Nineteen Sixties; that is, I have tried to rehear it in the light of both subsequent research into its history and of subsequent developments in jazz.

Of course we cannot leave out Bolden, although as of now we have no recordings by him. But we are left with only a footnote on cornetist Buddy Petit and only a mention or two of Chris Kelly, a player who has been highly praised by all those who heard him, because there is a dearth of recordings.

As I say, New Orleans jazz has been sifted, resifted, and re-searched again. We even know what kind of music was favored in a certain Storyville bar in a given year. And we know a great deal about a trombonist, let us say, who happened to play a job with a well-known musician, or who happened, perhaps by chance, to appear on a record made by the touring representa-tives of a New York company who were scouting the South in the Twenties.

Still, I hope I have been able to fill in some gaps in previous histories. I have included accounts of the appearance and career of Henry "Red" Allen, Jr., and of the important drummer, Zutty Singleton, who arrived in New Orleans as a teen-ager and began to participate in its music. Also, I have covered the careers of more players than my chapter headings indicate, including Freddy Keppard, Jack Laine, Tony Jackson, Johnny and Baby Dodds, Clarence Williams, Spencer Williams, Jimmy Noone, and others.

Here you will find Louis Armstrong only as "Little Louie," in a chapter which includes more personal and nonmusical exposition probably than any other. In this book we leave this giant of a musician as he departs from King Oliver's band and joins Ollie

Powers. The rest of his story is told in other books in the series, in Richard Hadlock's *Jazz Masters of the Twenties* and in Hsio Wen Shih's forthcoming *Jazz Masters of the Thirties*.

One encounters frustrations and contradictions in jazz research. On verbal and historical evidence one cannot doubt the musicianship and importance of a man like Fate Marable and the instruction he gave to several New Orleans players. Yet one of his two surviving recordings, *Frankie and Johnny*, when recently reissued, proved to be a grim disappointment—having heard it once, one can imagine only a scholar or antiquarian wanting to hear it again.

There is an abiding necessity in a book like this to give material on the city of New Orleans and its history. What I have tried to do in these pages, beyond the necessary preliminary exposition in the first chapter, is to spread out such matters and reveal them gradually as they come up in the particular careers of the musicians I have discussed. Similarly I have tried to approach the music and the recordings from several points of view, from appreciation through a kind of layman's analysis.

For my errors, I apologize, and hope that I have not made too many. For example, I tend to confuse the various Storyville cabarets and bars in my own mind and perhaps some of that confusion has crept into these pages. I have tried to make the proper distinction between cornet and trumpet (cornet being the instrument that most men use in New Orleans and trumpet being the one most took up later and elsewhere in the late Twenties) at least until Red Allen's generation. I have also tried to exercise some care in using the terms *heterophonic* and *polyphonic*, explanations of which appear later in these pages, as applied to New Orleans music.

Whatever the success of my own book, as a summary of years of research and as a new look at the music, it is my conviction that the next word to be said about New Orleans jazz should be said by Danny Barker, who is a Negro, a musician, a devoted researcher, and a writer of insight and grace, and the love of the musical achievements of his home city. I trust also that William Russell and Richard Allen will soon be giving us the results of their research, and that Russell will soon put together his trunkful of notes and write Bunk Johnson's full story, and also that of

Manuel Manetta, who knew Bolden and gave instruction to Red Allen.

As a final preliminary to my own account, I ask you to glance with me at two aspects of New Orleans and its traditional music today. First, there is a local jazz appreciation club. It is Jim Crow.

Second, as I write there are a couple of halls in the city hiring the older musicians. They function as tourist attractions, they are shrewdly operated, and some players feel they offer conditions that are awful for performance and in backstage facilities. They frequently hire honest but third- and fourth-rate players—"ham-fat musicians" the better performers call them because they grease their instrument valves with ham fat. Some of them, for all their robust charm and admirable energy, can't keep steady time or play in tune. And some of them are apt to find themselves with a local following and, as a result, get recorded. When they do, they may very well get glowing national reviews as the noble bearers of the great tradition.

It is not so much that King Oliver turns in his grave when such pronouncements are made. It is that a skillful and knowledgeable musician in New Orleans today, now in his late fifties, sixties, or even seventies, is apt to be turning in his tracks.

After emancipation . . . all those people who had been slaves, they needed the music more than ever now; it was like they were trying to find out in this music what they were supposed to do with this freedom: playing the music and listening to it—waiting for it to express what they needed to learn, once they had learned it wasn't just white people the music had to reach to, nor even to their own people, but straight out to life and to what a man does with his life when it finally *is* his.

—SIDNEY BECHET

JAZZ MASTERS OF NEW ORLEANS

BUDDY THE KING

*He'd take one note and put two or three to it. He began to teach them—
not by the music—just by the head. . . . They had lots of band fellows
could play like that after Bolden gave 'em the idea.*

—WALLACE COLLINS

*Bolden cause all that. . . . He cause these younger Creoles, men like
Bechet and Keppard, to have a different style from old heads like Tio
and Perez.*

—PAUL DOMINGUEZ

IN NEW ORLEANS in the 1890s, there was a man named André
Porée, a drayman, a keeper of mules and wagons, chiefly for
hauling garbage. He was a good businessman. Porée stabled his
mules in a large open city block uptown, and he was not the
only one using this space. It had become a gathering place for
the city's Negroes.

White New Orleans had been bitter over its defeat at the end
of the Civil War and angry at the humiliations of the occupation
and the opportunism of Yankee scalawags. One of its responses
had been to retaliate against its Negro population, and thus began
post-Civil War Jim Crow in the city. One of the first acts was to
prohibit Negroes from gathering in any public park. This meant
the end of a unique cultural tradition in New Orleans—the open
Sunday gatherings of Negroes for worship and celebration, music
and dance in Congo Square. The end of gatherings in public
parks, however, did not mean the end of all gatherings for the

city's Negroes. The Sunday festivities moved to the open area uptown where Porée kept his animals and his wagons. By the 1890s the people were flocking in, and Porée noticed both the size of the crowds and the business being done by those who set up stands and wagons to sell food and refreshments.

Porée decided to invest his money in the future of the area. He set up an amusement ground with a large, barnlike main hall containing several smaller halls and rooms, and an open pavillion. He staged all the amusements that turn-of-the-century America enjoyed on a Sunday outing: baseball, balloon launchings, picnics, greased pig chases, music, and dances. He allowed private clubs and benevolent associations to put up their own structures in the area. He named it Lincoln Park in honor of the emancipator, and it was a huge success.

For public dancing, Porée hired a band led by Charles "Buddy" Bolden, a local barber, and thereby established an American legend. Bolden was, according to Bunk Johnson, "one fine looking brown-skinned man, tall and slender and a terror with the ladies." As a terror with the ladies, Bolden made plenty of scandal himself, but as publisher of a little gossip sheet called *The Cricket,* he exposed scandal. (His main method for obtaining his news was simplicity itself: a friend who was a paid police informer also informed *The Cricket.*)

Bolden became a great local celebrity. People flocked close to the bandstand at Lincoln Park merely to listen to his music—as many as danced to it. He was pursued by women, admired and envied by men, idolized by children. He pleased them all. He swaggered and strutted, but he tossed out favors to the men and the children, as well as the women. Most of all, he played a music which must have in some sense expressed what the people felt, and probably he gave the lowest and most downtrodden of his listeners an image of themselves that was at once realistic, mocking, humorous, forlorn, and accepting of a life few of them had any hope of escaping. Primary of course was his irreverence. On the surface Bolden seemed to have a hedonist's complete disrespect for any propriety. But it went deeper than that. With his eyes on the white policemen at the door, but not loud enough so that they could hear him, Bolden's singer, Lorenzo Stall, would offer these words to the melody known (still known) traditionally along the Mississippi as *Funky Butt*, known commercially as a theme in *St. Louis Tickle*, and known in New Orleans as *Buddy Bolden's Blues:*

> I thought I heer'd Abe Lincoln shout,
> "Rebels, close down them plantations and let all them niggers out,"
> I'm positively sure I heer'd Mr. Lincoln shout.

> I thought I heer'd Mr. Lincoln say,
> "Rebels, close down them plantations and let all them niggers out,"
> "You gonna lose ths war; git on your knees and pray,"
> That's the words I heer'd Mr. Lincoln say.

Obviously, Buddy Bolden did not pop out of Zeus's head. He and his band had been there, playing their horns before there was any Lincoln Park. And just as obviously there was some kind of musical tradition behind him. Still, Bolden was "King" to the populace by their own proclamation, and "a man who started it all" in New Orleans jazz to the musicians. So what he did was give the music a dramatic, secular focus, both for his audiences and for its present and future practitioners.

To understand Bolden, we should at least glance at his own traditions. And to glance at them, as is conventional in studies of New Orleans jazz, we must go back to the gatherings at Congo Square.

In talking about jazz, we are talking about Negro-American culture and its enormous influence, direct and indirect, on all American culture. Therefore we are talking about the culture produced by people who were partly cut off from (and sometimes systematically robbed of) their own traditions, their own leadership, their own religion, their own culture and lore, and who built up a new one. Of course, there was still a memory of the African past and its culture in the beginning, even though members of the same tribe and the same family were often deliberately separated and traditional worships and beliefs were sometimes forbidden. But the Africans were not entirely cut off from the white man's culture. Indeed, black men were encouraged to believe in the white man's god and follow his form of worship. (And what self-justification the white man must have felt when he persuaded the black man to acept his god!)

A commentator in 1868 in *Lippincott's Magazine* reported that slaves' music included religious songs; river songs; plantation songs; songs of longing, dreamy, sad, and plaintive [the blues?]; songs of mirth; and descriptive songs—all influenced variously by both African and Western traditions.

In New Orleans, through the presence of the freed "Creoles of color"—the independent and sometimes wealthy mulattoes who embraced European culture—there was a rather different and more complex exposure on the part of their blacker brothers to European and American traditions.

Harold Courlander's remarks on Haiti are also enlightening about Louisiana:

"The Catholic Church regarded every slave as a soul to be saved, as a complete and finished man except for salvation. . . . The Church did not insist on washing out of the African mind everything that was there. It regarded its mission as that of supplying the single quality that was lacking—salvation. . . .

"The Protestant churches in Haiti, on the contrary, have demanded that their converts become new people. They have forbidden their adherents to take part in non-Christian rituals or other activities—including even the dance. They have presented them with a simple and painful choice.

"These were the essential attitudes that prevailed during slavery days in the United States. In the beginning, while plantation owners fought against church activities among the Negroes, the church and the plantation owners were largely united in their war against 'heathen' practices. Africanisms which might have either died in due course or persisted were stamped out with Puritan fervor. Significantly, it was in French-Catholic Louisiana that African-style drumming, singing and dancing survived in the United States to the beginning of this present century."

New Orleans was originally a French city, but it became a city not so much in the manner of its namesake as in the manner of, say, a southern French port like Marseilles. Also, as the result of migrations of both Creole colonials and slaves, it became French also in the manner of Haiti, Santo Domingo, and Martinique.

New Orleans was founded in about 1718 and remained a colony of France, under the influence of the mother country, until about 1755, the time of the Seven Years' War, which largely ended direct French influence in the New World. Early New Orleans settlers were thieves, prostitutes, and vagabonds.

France officially ceded New Orleans to Spain in 1762, but Spain did not take possession for nearly seven years. In 1800, Napoleon took Louisiana back but France did not take possession and there was a period of three years with weak government and much lawlessness. Then France sold New Orleans and its territory to the United States. As Marshall Stearns points out in *The Story of Jazz*, the city's population was then about 10,000, half of it white. It had doubled ten years later, and more than doubled ten years after that. By 1900, the population was 287,000.

In 1791, Santo Domingo experienced slave rebellions and many whites fled to Cuba. In 1809–1810, when France and Spain were at war, these same refugees fled to New Orleans. According to Herbert Asbury, they brought with them an influential regard for luxury and display, and soon the modest cottons of the Creole ladies had been replaced by boldly colored silks and taffetas. During the same period, about 3,000 free blacks, also refugees from the Domingan rebellions in which they had not taken part, arrived in New Orleans.

With the migrations following the Domingo insurrections, also came the queens and doctors of vodun (or voodoo), the best known being Marie Laveau, Dr. John, and Sante Dédé, who was a quadroon. The grand vodun festival was June 23rd and it lasted until St. John's Day, an occasion sacred to both vodun and the Church. The most important vodun ceremonies, which of course featured drums and music, took place at Dumaines Street, adjacent to Congo Square.

The growth of the city of New Orleans was due chiefly to the western expansion of the United States. The settlers needed materials and supplies; the Mississippi and its connecting rivers could transport them. And near the mouth of the Mississippi, protected on the river's navigable delta, was New Orleans.

Thus, with its basically French culture, the city had West Indian culture, African culture, Spanish, and—with the coming of its posterity—British-Protestant.

At various times, beginning with the "Black Code" of 1724, the colony, and subsequently the city, attempted to supress all religion and all religious rites except Catholic. But by 1817, the municipal council made legal the Sunday dances in the Congo Square.

Historian Herbert Asbury comments:

"The slaves in Louisiana had no freedom of movement whatsoever until the coming of the Americans, who brought to bear upon the whole question of slavery a new viewpoint, entirely different from that of the French and Spanish, which gradually compelled the liberalization of the laws and customs regulating the life of the black man. Recognizing the value of recreation and a measure of social intercourse in keeping the Negro contented with his lot, the American authorities, soon after the Louisiana Purchase, began to allow the slaves to gather for dancing. These assemblies appear to have begun about 1805 and at first were held in various places in and near the city, among them an abandoned brickyard in Dumaine Street. The most celebrated . . . however, was a large open space at Rampart and Orleans Streets, part of which had been indicated on the maps as a public square (the early maps) . . . called Congo Square, and is still so known among the Negroes of New Orleans. Its official name, however, was never anything but Circus Square until after the Civil War, when it was changed to Beauregard Square in honor of General P. G. T. Beauregard. . . . The weekly concourse of slaves in Congo Square reached the height of its popularity and renown during the fifteen years which preceded the Civil War. . . .

"The favorite dances of the slaves were the Calinda, a variation of which was also used in the VooDoo ceremonies, and the Dance of the Bamboula, both of which were primarily based on the primitive dances of the African jungle, but with copious borrowings from the contre-danses of the French."

The ceremonies were perhaps somewhat secularized at this point, and they did serve as a tourist attraction. Still, one should not make too much of a distinction between sacred and secular even at this date, because, for the worshipers probably no such distinction yet existed. A mating dance could be as much a religious rite as a wedding ceremony was to a white Christian. And dance and chant invoked and gave homage to the dieties, as much as the recitation of the Creed to a Protestant congregation.

There is in jazz literature a tradition of the early descriptions of the drum and stringed instrument ceremonies of Congo Square, going back to those of Benjamin Henry Latrobe, an architect, who set down his impressions in 1819, through those of "Henry Didimus" (a pseudonym for Henry Edward Durell) written in 1853, to that of George W. Cable, not set down until 1886.

Durell wrote his description as a part of his biography of composer Louis-Moreau Gottschalk, and his effort was to recreate the scene as Gottschalk had witnessed it as a child, a memory which became the basis for Gottschalk's piece, *La Bamboula*.

"Let a stranger to New Orleans visit of an afternoon of one of its holydays, the public squares in the lower portion of the city, and he will find them filled with its African population, tricked out with every variety of a showy costume, joyous, wild, and in the full exercise of a real saturnalia. As he approaches the scene of an infinite mirth, his ear first catches a quick, low, continuous, dead sound, which dominates over the laughter, hallo, and roar of a thousand voices, while the listener marvels at what it can be doing there. This is the music of the Bamboula, of the dance Bamboula; a dance which takes possession of the Negro's whole life, transforms him with all the instincts, the sentiments, the feelings which nature gave to his race, to sleep for awhile, to be partially obliterated by the touch of civilisation, but to remain forever its especial mark.

"Upon entering the square the visitor finds the multitude packed in groups of close, narrow circles, of a central area of only a few feet; and there in the center of each circle, sits the musician, astride a barrel, strong-headed, which he beats with two sticks, to a strange measure incessantly, like mad, for hours together, while the perspiration literally rolls in streams and wets the ground; and there, too, labor the dancers male and female, under an inspiration of possession, which takes from their limbs all sense of weariness, and gives to them a rapidity and a durability of motion that will hardly be found elsewhere outside of mere machinery. The head rests upon the breast, or is thrown back upon the shoulders, the eyes closed, or glaring, while the arms, amid cries, and shouts, and sharp ejaculations, float upon the air, or keep time, with the hands patting upon the thighs, to a music which is seemingly eternal.

"The feet scarce tread wider space than their own length; but rise and fall, turn in and out, touch first the heel and then the toe, rapidly and more rapidly, till they twinkle to the eye, which finds its sight too slow a follower of their movements."

It was through Gottschalk that New Orleans music—or at least an impression of New Orleans music—was heard throughout the Western world. The following possibly romanticized comments about *La Bamboula* were made in 1848 in *La France Musicale:*

> Who does not know the "Bamboula"? Who is there who has not read the description of that picturesque, exciting dance, which gives expression to the feeling of the negroes? Joyful or sad, plaintive, amorous, jealous, forsaken, solitary, fatigued, ennuied, or the heart filled with grief, the negro forgets all in dancing the "Bamboula". . . .
> Gottschalk has composed several pieces, among others, one which is a chef d'oêuvre. This piece he calls "Bamboula". . . .

Gottschalk, a sensualist, something of a hedonist, and a performer of great personal magnetism, was perhaps an ideal man for destiny to have chosen to make both Europe and America aware of the important musical amalgamation taking place in the United States. Of course, by the time he was performing, there were already familiar minstrel songs which reflected an African-American idiom, but Gottschalk was a "serious" musician. He was born in 1829. His father was of German-English and half-Jewish ancestry, and his mother was French, the titled daughter of Santo Domingan refugees. He was sent to Paris at thirteen to study piano, having shown talent as a player and a composer; he was refused by the Paris Conservatoire (because he was American, apparently), but he was highly praised by Liszt, Chopin, and Berlioz. The source of the praise is significant, for what Gottschalk attempted to do in his own composing was use the "folk" idiom of his youth as a basis for concert composition, much as those men were doing. And the idiom that meant most to Gottschalk was, often, what he heard in Congo Square or a Latin American idiom he recognized as its kin.

Gottschalk's *La Bamboula* sounds like a complex cakewalk, with a hint of the syncopated tango of later New Orleans. *The Banjo* (1851) is perhaps a little closer to later New Orleans jazz rhythmically. *La Bananier* uses an African ostenato bass, and

Suis-moi, to music historian Wilfred Mellers, "fuses habanera with cakewalk—a more refined version of a style later to be explored by Jelly Roll Morton."

Gottschalk, for all his "serious" intentions, survives today in most music criticism as an outstanding "popular" artist. He toured the United States, to great success in frontier towns and logging camps, interpreting (it seems clear in retrospect) future American popular culture in a "concert" style that was then acceptable to his listeners as serious.

The original French colonials of Louisiana, the white Creoles, and the succeeding Spanish immigrants had intermarried so that the Creole population of the Vieux Carré, the old quarter of the city, had largely become a French-Spanish mixture. Successive waves of immigration gave New Orleans a large Italian population. And soon there were Irish communities, German communities, English communities, even a new, lately arrived, French community.

Obviously New Orleans was a city with cultural traditions very different from either the Anglo-Saxon Puritan culture of the northeast or the Anglo-Saxon Cavalier culture of the mid-Atlantic states. One telling reflection of this difference was the existence of the colored Creoles.

A provision of the Louisiana "black code" of 1724, which we referred to above, was that slaves could be freed by their masters. Children shared the status of their mothers, and when a white Creole aristocrat died he frequently provided in his will that his mistress, African or part-African, would be free. This, plus the fact that high-born whites continued to take "colored" mistresses, had created a class of colored Creoles with traditions going back to the early eighteenth century. As free men and women, they were of course allowed to own property—which was sometimes willed along with freedom—and some became wealthy land-owners or prosperous small businessmen who sent their children to France for their education. And their pride in their somewhat unstable social status and position at times took on all the aspects of snobbery.

A mulatto was half white, half Negro. A quadroon was one-quarter Negro, three-quarters white. An octaroon was one-eighth Negro. A griffe was three-quarters Negro, one-quarter white.

And Dr. Edmond Souchon believes that "the self-imposed color line between light and dark Negro is much more marked than is the Jim Crow line between white and colored."

Emancipation hit the colored Creoles rather hard. From the time that Louisiana became a part of the United States, the influx of Southern whites, with rather different ideas about color and race, became even more marked. And after the Civil War, there was an influx of ex-slaves from nearby sugar and cotton plantations, whose economy, by the way, had been wrecked by the war and its aftermath. The colored Creoles found themselves caught in the middle, and as segregation and prejudice grew they found themselves more and more in the black world. And while there was still a downtown Creole community, separate from the uptown Negro community, there were orchestras in New Orleans with faces from light brown to near black.

The Creole musicians had found themselves with no choice. But at the same time, many of them were intrigued by the kind of music their darker cousins were making. It has been said that New Orleans jazz resulted from the juxtaposition of the Creoles' musicianship and the freed slaves' passion and feeling. Downtown sophistication plus uptown blues. To the downtown sophistication belongs a transplanted European musical tradition, ranging from the opera house to the folk ditty. And to the uptown tradition belongs work song, spiritual, field holler—an already developed African-American idiom. Put them together and an old French quadrille becomes *Tiger Rag*.

Buddy Bolden was seven years old when the dances at the Congo Square were stopped. We can assume that, like nearly everyone else, he was present at the first outings in the area that was to become Lincoln Park. Marshall Stearns conjectures that he attended "underground" vodun meetings. We know he was a Baptist and that Negro Baptist musical culture was well established. He grew up with brass bands and parades all around him. (And it is worth remarking here that "cutting contests" between local "star" cornetists are traditionally a part of American Sunday afternoon band concerts.) Mutt Carey has declared that Bolden took basic musical lessons from hearing the celebrations at "a holy roller church."

Gottschalk had women tearing his clothes off and fighting their way into his bedroom. So did Bolden. Gottschalk was by intention a "serious artist" who became a popular success. Perhaps we are quite wrong to make such distinction between "popular" and "serious" culture. Surely we are in making such distinctions in Negro American culture in 1900. In any case, to Bolden there was *no* success except in pleasing his audience. But he was aware that by his time there were two musical traditions for his own people, a sacred and a secular. His name, notice, is not French or Spanish, his worship was not Catholic, and to him—as to everyone by his time, particularly since Protestantism had come to New Orleans—there was a conflict between the two musics.

Bolden's career was short—incredibly short in view of its importance. He was born, in 1868, a child of Emancipation, and he had become a celebrity at least by 1895.[1] He did not die until 1931, but he was committed to the East Louisiana State Hospital on June 5, 1907, eventually diagnosed as a paranoid, and he stayed there the rest of his life.

Bolden's band, which played the dances at Lincoln Park on Fridays, Saturdays, and afternoons and evenings on Sundays, was a small group, three horns and three rhythms, no piano, a sort of cut-down brass band. Other groups, bands of twelve or fourteen pieces, played in the other halls, performing waltzes, quadrilles, schottisches. Bolden's band played some such pieces too, by ear, and played the blues most of all. The master of ceremonies, Buddy Botley, danced, sang, and announced. Bolden's musicians—particularly the leader, trombonist Frankie Deusen, and banjoist Lorenzo Stall—arrived for work "playing the dozens," and hurled enough scatalogical insults at each other to gain themselves the reputation of the nastiest talking men in the history of

[1] There is controversy among some followers of New Orleans jazz over the exact date that Bolden formed his first band. Bunk Johnson said that he joined Bolden in 1895. The only known picture of Bolden does not show Bunk as a member of his band, and had therefore been labeled as a picture taken "before 1895." There might be any number of obvious and plausible reasons why Johnson did not appear in the particular picture that we have, but which would still allow the picture to have been taken after 1895: the picture was taken a month before Bunk joined; or, Bunk didn't play the particular job at which the picture was taken; or, Bunk was not feeling well that day and was home in bed; or, Bunk arrived ten minutes late, after the photographer had gone, etc.

New Orleans. Bolden "drank all the whiskey he could get ahold of" and had all the women he wanted, but he could go out of his way sometimes to flatter the fattest and ugliest woman in the crowd with a kiss or a dedication of a tune, and with that he won the crowd. In his numbers, he spelled out the conditions in which many of his most avid fans lived: *If You Don't Like My Potatoes Why Do You Dig So Deep?*, *All the Whores Like the Way I Ride, Make Me a Pallet on Your Floor.* If the middle-class audience of druggists, dentists, doctors, and lawyers, meeting in another part of the building, would ask him to tone it down, Bolden might respond with his loudest and dirtiest songs—and he had a reputation for a cornet volume that could be heard for miles through the still, quiet air of the delta. But Bolden could play quietly and prettily on the Sunday matinees, that is, until around 9 o'clock, when the pimps and whores and gamblers would start arriving. He loved nothing better than a pressing mass of sweating humanity, gathered around the bandstand, so he could shout, "My chillun's here. I know it 'cause I can smell 'em." And then he would sing *Funky Butt* with its original words or admonish the band to play quieter so he could hear the whores dragging their feet.

For all its apparent vulgar simplicity and honest directness, there must have been in Bolden's music, and in its hold on his audience, an implicit emotional complexity. So there was in the man it seems. His friends knew that Bolden's mind was going. It became particularly apparent when he ceased to be able to take the amiable, salacious kidding about his prowess that was a part of his daily life. Also, he began to take on more and more jobs for his band, more and more for the same night, and he showed less and less responsibility toward remembering them, toward bringing his own band to them, or toward sending a standby group until he perhaps made a token appearance himself.

Bolden began verbally abusing himself in the mirror, and he began threatening, and on one occasion beating, his women. He broke down one afternoon after shaving one of his former cronies, Tom Pickett, who had been kidding him about his love life. Slowly and carefully, Bolden went over Pickett's face with his razor several times. As soon as he could escape the barber chair, Pickett fled into the street, yelling. Then Bolden was in trouble with the police, with his friends, and with the members of his band.

Frankie Dusen took over the group, called it the Eagle Band and had Bunk Johnson playing cornet in Bolden's place. The first night that Bolden saw the new billing and Bunk on the stand at Lincoln Park, he looked, turned, and slowly made his way out of the hall, alone and silent, with the crowd separating to let him pass. Dude Botley followed him home to try to look out for him. He peeped through a crack in the door to the rear of the barber shop and saw Bolden sitting in a chair with his head in his hands, apparently crying bitterly. Then he saw him walk out of the room, get a bottle and his cornet. He tried a drink but began crying again. "The tears came to my eyes too," Botley remembered, "and I got to thinking about how many thousands of people Bolden had made happy and all them women who used to idolize him and all of them supposed to be friends. 'Where are they now?' I say to myself. Then I hear Bolden's cornet. I look through the crack and there he is, relaxed back in the chair, blowing that silver cornet softly, just above a whisper, and I see he's got his hat over the bell of the horn. I put my ear close to the keyhole. I thought I had heard Bolden play the blues before, and play the hymns at funerals, but what he is playing now is real strange and I listen carefully, because he's playing something that, for a while sounds like the blues, then like a hymn. I cannot make out the tune, but after awhile I catch on. He is mixing up the blues with the hymns. He plays the blues real sad and the hymn sadder than the blues and then the blues sadder than the hymn. That is the first time that I had ever heard hymns and blues cooked up together. A strange cold feeling comes over me; I get sort of scared because I know the Lord don't like that mixing the Devil's music with his music. But I still listen because the music sounds so strange and I am sort of hypnotized. I close my eyes, and when he blows the blues I picture Lincoln Park with all them sinners and whores, shaking and belly rubbing. Then, as he blows the hymn, I picture my mother's church on Sunday, and everybody humming with the choir. The picture in my mind kept changing with the music as he blew. It sounded like a battle between the Good Lord and the Devil. Something tells me to listen and see who wins. If Bolden stops on the hymn, the Good Lord wins; if he stops on the blues, the Devil wins."

It was not quite the end for Bolden, but he did not bring his Lord's music and his devil's music together. He and the band tried to patch things up, and they did for a while. But Bolden was never the same again. He was sullen, usually quiet, usually brooding. Things were building up in him, and on an afternoon in 1907, while playing a parade with Henry Allen Sr.'s Brass Band, he went berserk in the street.

Exactly how did Buddy Bolden play? We don't know, and unless the records he is supposed to have made are someday found, we may never know. Louis Armstrong heard him when he was about five or six at the nearby hall nicknamed Funky Butt. He remembered that he would look through big cracks in the wall of the building to see what was going on. "It wasn't no classyfied place, just a big old room with a bandstand. And to a tune like *The Bucket's Got a Hole in It,* some of them chicks would get way down, shake everything, slapping themselves on the cheek of their behind. Yeah! At the end of the night, they'd do the quadrille, beautiful to see where everybody lined up, crossed over—if no fights hadn't started before that." But to Louis Armstrong, Bolden's playing was too crude and did not move him.

To Sidney Bechet, "he could play, that was true, but he was mostly a hell of a good showman. Musical showman too: if he made a mistake he'd make up something and throw it in and if it didn't fit, well, it was powerful and emotional and probably loud and most people didn't notice." To Bechet, Manuel Perez was a much better musician and cornetist.

Even Mutt Carey, whose style was older than Armstrong's or Bechet's and presumably closer to Bolden's, when giving due credit to Bolden's importance, seemed to give it with a note of reluctance. "When you come right down to it, the man who started the big noise in jazz was Buddy Bolden. Yes, he was a powerful trumpet player and a good one, too. I guess he deserves credit for starting it all."

When Bunk Johnson recreated Bolden's style, he probably did it in something of his own way rhythmically; but he showed Bolden taking a very logical and orderly approach to theme and variations. He gave an opening theme statement followed by a chorus with one or two basic variational ideas (say a pick-up note or an added doublet or triplet here and there), then another chorus which used and followed through on another idea for variation (say a rhythmic displacement or an added syncopation), then another using several triplets, then another with more pronounced heavy accents, etc. The same sort of thing one hears in Bunk, or one hears in Jelly Roll (most extendedly in his piano version of *Hyena Stomp*, say), or, for that matter, in Gottschalk.

Probably we can get closest to Bolden's style through the surviving records of Freddy Keppard, for according to the testimony of several men, Keppard's style was a more musical and sophisticated extension of Bolden's. It was still rugged and forceful; it was clipped and more staccato, rhythmically closer to ragtime, than later New Orleans jazz.

Keppard's recordings were made relatively late in his active musical life, which is not to say that he was very old when they were done but is to say that when he made them (most men attest), some hard living and some hard drinking had diminished his former power and abilities. But the recordings by Keppard that we have, sometimes flawed as some of them are, offer us a compelling, forceful musician, as well as an historically important figure.

By Bolden's later days, and during Keppard's heyday, there was Storyville, And Storyville the world over is a romantic, nostalgic name. It has been romanticized as man—and particularly American man?—can romanticize the vices of his past. All that is left of the area today is Basin Street—a grim, institutional housing development now rises on the land where once there were rowdy saloons, luxurious whore houses, and shabby cribs.

New Orleans was a seaport town and prostitution was almost inevitably big business in New Orleans. Some of the most expensive property in the city was devoted to it; it gave direct employment to thousands and indirect employment to others who worked in cabarets, dancehalls, gambling joints, bars.

According to Herbert Asbury, prostitution was always a close associate with the politics of the city. It expanded after the Louisiana Purchase when its main customers were the flatboat crews and its areas were along the river. It expanded again when the American politicians gained control of the city, beginning in about 1836.

For about twenty-two years, after 1869, New Orleans was under the thumb of the mafia—a control which ended with the shooting and lynching of mafia leadership, acts largely condoned by the rest of the city.

Storyville came about in 1897. An alderman named Sidney Story decided to segregate the already booming vice in New Orleans into two more or less "open" districts, where prostitution would be allowed, one in the French Quarter and the most famous above Canal Street. For his pains, the latter came to be popularly called Storyville. Whores, pimps, gamblers, bouncers, and occasional dope pushers were of course not the only people one found in the area. There were doctors, dentists, tradesmen, and various middle-class businessmen scattered throughout as well.

Jazz historian George Hoefer wrote:

"The New Orleans *Blue Book*, a directory of red lights, listed Lulu White's Mahogany Hall, Gypsy Schaeffer's and Madam Tonia's. The latter, a mansion operated by Antonia P. Gonzalez, had the inscription 'Gonzalez, Female Cornetist' printed on the glass of the front door according to the reminiscences of Storyville written by former Crescent City resident Roy Carew in the *Record Changer* of February 1943. Another regular advertiser was Tom Anderson's Annex on Basin Street, a large saloon that functioned as the District's city hall, where 'Mayor' Anderson wielded a semblance of control over the worldly pleasures offered in the limited area north of Canal Street and west of Basin.

"A pleasure-giving aspect of the nightly gaiety was music furnished by ragtime piano 'professors,' string trios, and small jazz bands. The music most frequently heard was jazz, an expressive sound derived from combining European melody with pure African rhythms.

"The great ragtime pianist Tony Jackson, who could play a thousand songs ranging from the blues to operatic arias, used his slow blues for the Naked Dances at Madam Tonia's. These dances, used as 'come ons,' were performed by pretty Creole girls."

But let's make no mistake about it, for a Negro male who was a musician, Storyville was the place where he could find work. So it was for a female of mixed blood.

Dude Botley told Danny Barker: "Them Monday nights at Lincoln Park was something to see, when them madams and pimps brought their stables of women to hear Bolden play, each madam had different color girls in her stables. For instance, Ann Jackson featured mulatto girls; Maud Wilson featured high browns; and so forth and so on. And them different stables was different colors just like a bouquet."

It was the upper end of the district that made it world famous. And so elegant was this upper end—and so widely accepted as part of the life of the city—that the guide to its houses, the *Blue Book* of the Tenderloin 400, was widely distributed throughout the city. At the upper end of the upper end was the Mahogany Hall of Miss Lulu White. *The Blue Book*, complete with pictures of Miss White, read this way:

THE NEW MAHOGANY HALL

A picture which appears on the cover of this souvenir was erected specially for Miss Lulu White at a cost of $40,000. The house is built of marble and is four story; containing five parlors, all handsomely furnished, and fifteen bedrooms. Each room has a bath with hot and cold water and extension closets.

The elevator, which was built for two, is of the latest style. The entire house is steam heated and is the handsomest house of its kind. It is the only one where you can get three shots for your money—

> The shot upstairs,
> The shot downstairs,
> And the shot in the room.

Introductory

In presenting this souvenir to my multitude of friends, it is my earnest desire to, in the first place, avoid any and all egotism, and, secondly, to impress them with the fact that the cause of my successes must certainly be attributed to their hearty and generous support of my exertions in making their visits to my establishment a moment of pleasure.

While deeming it unnecessary to give the history of my boarders from their birth, which would no doubt, prove reading of the highest grade, I trust that what I have mentioned will not be misconstrued, and will be read in the same light as it was written, and in mentioning the fact that all are born and bred Louisiana girls, I trust that my exertions in that direction will be as appreciated as yours has been to me.

Yours very socially,
Lulu White

This famous West Indian octoroon first saw the light of day thirty-one years ago. Arriving in this country at a rather tender age, and having been fortunately gifted with a good education it did not take long for her to find out what the other sex were in search of.

In describing Miss Lulu, as she is most familiarly called, it would not be amiss to say that besides possessing an elegant form she has beautiful black hair and blue eyes, which have justly gained for her the title of the "Queen of the Demi-monde."

Her establishment, which is situated in the central part of the city, is unquestionably the most elaborately furnished house in the city of New Orleans, and without a doubt one of the most elegant places in this or any other country.

She has made a feature of boarding none but the fairest of girls —those gifted with nature's best charms, and would, under no circumstances have any but that class in her house.

As an entertainer Miss Lulu stands foremost, having made a lifelong study of music and literature. She is well read and one that can interest anybody and make a visit to her place a continued round of pleasure.

And when adding that she would be pleased to see all her old friends and make new ones. What more could be added?

Louis Armstrong revealed in a *Life* interview in 1966: "Storyville was mostly for white people. Most of the whores were white or light creoles or mulattoes. Lulu White had the biggest house. All those rich men used to come there from all around. Jelly Roll Morton played the piano there and that's how he could pay for that gold tooth with a diamond in it. I don't know if they had colored maids in Lulu White's, but Lulu was colored. It was a crazy deal."

Besides, *The Blue Book, The Mascot* and the *Sunday Sun* were devoted to affairs of the red-light district. An item from *The Mascot* for as early as January 5, 1895, reads:

> Miss Bessie Lamothe, 9 South Franklin Street, wishes her friends to understand that she did not announce that she received in a pink dress on New Years, but she desires it to be understood that she receives every night in Un Robe, blanc de nuit. . . .

And from *The Sunday Sun:*

> Nina Jackson, who keeps the swell mansion, 1559 Customhouse Street, and who is herself one of the jolliest girls in the bunch, has gotten rid of those two tid-bits, May and Mamie, and in their stead she has two of the finest and most charming ladies to be found anywhere. Queen Emmette, known as the Diamond Tooth, is one of the girls, and Etta Ross is the other.

Nostalgic? Colorful? Quaint? Perhaps. But where there are pleasure palaces there are madams and pimps and, behind them, politicians and policemen. For them, "everything in the line of hilarity" means money. And what it takes to bring it in is girls, plus sidelines like alcohol, gambling, and dope. Virgins are best. Get them hooked on dope, on sex, on sadism, and when the bloom is gone (by the early twenties, say) toss them out into the alley. Maybe they can set up a bed or crib in a space between two buildings and stay in business. Or maybe they walk the streets and alleys with their mattresses on their backs and go down for a quarter, for anyone fool enough or drunk enough to forget about venereal disease. Sure, colorful.

In any case, we shall, of course, hear much of Storyville prostitutes, and of Vodun, in this book, and particularly as we look at the career of Jelly Roll Morton.

Jelly Roll Morton said of Freddy Keppard that he "had the best ear, the best tone, and the most marvelous execution I ever heard." But Morton was capable of exaggerating the talents of his associates—his remarks on trombonist Roy Palmer (for one) are not borne out by the recordings we have. However, Mutt Carey, while giving King Oliver his due, also spoke glowingly of Keppard as the king, as having New Orleans "all sewed up," and calling him the very best cornetist before Louis Armstrong. He continued, "Freddie had a lot of ideas and a big tone too. When he hit a note you knew it was hit. I mean he had a beautiful tone and he played with so much feeling too. Yes, he had everything; he was ready in every respect. Keppard could play any kind of song good. Technique, attack, tone, and ideas were all there. He didn't have very much formal musical education but he sure was a natural musician. All you had to do was play a number for him once and he had it . . . he was a natural! When Freddie got to playing he'd get devilish sometimes and he'd 'neigh' on the trumpet like a horse, but he was no freak man like Joe Oliver. Freddie was a trumpet player anyway you'd grab him. He could play sweet and then he could play hot. He'd play sweet sometimes and then turn around and knock the socks off you with something hot."

Freddy Keppard was born in 1889, which makes him Bolden's junior by thirteen years and Armstrong's senior by eleven. He was raised on Villere Street, and when he was still a boy he and his older brother Louis, who was already playing guitar, would disguise their age from the police by putting on long pants and going down to shine shoes along Basin Street for a nickel a shine. Freddy was playing mandolin by the time he was ten years old, and performing in duo with his brother around the neighborhood. He began on cornet when he was sixteen.

Keppard's Olympia Orchestra, which he organized around 1905, and which had Alphonse Picou on clarinet, could play "legitimate" enough to get society jobs, and "hot" enough to get jobs in uptown dancehalls a few years later.

In late 1911 or early 1912, Bill Johnson, the bass player, who had been living and playing in Los Angeles since 1909, became interested in organizing an Original Creole Ragtime Band to play the New Orleans style and sent back home for his horn players. He got Keppard, Eddie Vinson on trombone, George Baquet on clarinet, Leon Williams on guitar, Dink Johnson on drums and Jimmy Palao on violin. (Keppard's Olympia Orchestra, meanwhile, was taken over by A. J. Piron, who used King Oliver on trumpet.) Thus Keppard became the first cornetist to take New Orleans ensemble style out of the city.

The group, minus Dink Johnson, went on the Orpheum Theatre circuit out of San Francisco in 1913 as the Original Creole Orchestra. The tour took them to Chicago the following year and then to New York, first in 1915 for a Winter Garden show called *Town Topics*, billed as "That Creole Band."

We know that the band also appeared at a Sunday concert on December 5, 1915. They were reviewed by the New York *Clipper* (the writer spoke of "a rather ragged selection" and the "comedy effect of the clarinet"). There was another New York performance at Loew's Orpheum during April of 1917. And there was a return to the Winter Garden that same month, plus jobs at the Lexington Opera House and the Columbia Theatre.

Meanwhile, their clarinetist, George Baquet, had settled in Philadelphia. He was at first replaced by a piccolo player, Bab Frank, and then by the New Orleans clarinetist "Big Eye" Louis Nelson (De Lisle) who joined in Boston with high hopes.

In their book *Jazz: A History of the New York Scene*, Samuel B. Charters and Leonard Kunstadt relate the following incident:

> After a week at the Keith the band was to return to New York. In the Boston terminal De Lisle, still confused by the hustle of northern cities, lost track of the others. He finally rode the train alone into New York. He waited for them in Grand Central, then decided he'd better find a place to stay. Keppard had given him a card for Lottie Joplin's boardinghouse, so Louis went up to Harlem. Scott Joplin had been dead only a few weeks and the house was shrouded in sadness. The next afternoon Louis started walking the streets, trying to find someone from the band. The first person he ran into was Keppard, leaning against a lamp post. Keppard laughed and said he didn't know where the others were either. He ". . . just never could keep a bunch together." Then he shook his head and walked down the street.

Down home in New Orleans, the musicians began to get clippings forwarded by members of the Creole Band. They saw that journalists and the public alike (who were quite familiar with St. Louis ragtime by this time) wondered where on earth this music came from.

The Creole Band received offers to record, particularly it seems from Victor Records, but Keppard, musical leader of the group, refused. The traditional explanation is that Keppard did not want to put his music on a phonograph record because that would make it too easy to steal. (Keppard, as a kind of joke, was the player who in New Orleans began the stunt of covering his fingering with a handkerchief whenever he played; the public loved it, but a good musician would steal by ear, of course, not eye.)

Another version of Keppard's refusal, popular for a while in older New York circles, was that Keppard, afraid of being cheated, wanted to know the fees paid to Victor's best selling artist of the time, Enrico Caruso, and demanded the same.

Sidney Bechet was probably closest to the truth. He said that Keppard had explained that he simply didn't want to make the records. The men from Victor acted like businessmen, and Keppard felt that if he and the Creole Orchestra recorded for them, the music wouldn't be for pleasure any more.

In 1959 the British discographer Brian Rust made an interesting discovery. In doing research in the Victor files in New York, he came across a listing for an unnumbered test recording, made on December 2, 1918, of *Tack 'em Down* with an instrumentation of cornet, trombone, clarinet, alto saxophone, piano, mandolin, bass, and drums, by "Creole Jass Band." That date is nearly two years after Keppard's first New York opening.

More recently, Rust has commented, "I may have been somewhat overimpressed in that I assumed that the band was Keppard's; but it certainly could have been Bill Johnson's, as his Creole Jass Band was playing in New York at that time, as an advertisement I once had—but alas! I have lost—proved. (It was from the entertainment pages of one of the New York dailies if I remember rightly.) I don't say categorically that Keppard was in the band then, but it is obvious there was some connection between it, the one that did the Victor test, and the one that opened in New York (with Keppard) on March 7, 1917."

When the Creole Band finally broke up in 1918, the Original Dixieland Jazz Band had already had its sensational success with its first recordings. Keppard himself settled in Chicago. Very soon, however, King Oliver became Chicago's cornet king and could attract the crowds by thrusting his horn out of a window and "blowing Keppard down."

Keppard, however, was still doing well, first with his own group with Jimmy Noone on clarinet and Paul Barbarin on drums. It seems, however, that Keppard wanted to get rid of Barbarin, and Noone, who was the drummer's brother-in-law, quit and joined Doc Cook at the Dreamland in retaliation. Barbarin went back to New Orleans. Bill Johnson went with King Oliver. It was the beginning of a long succession of sideman jobs for Freddy Keppard, some of which resulted in his first and only recordings.

Keppard went with Doc Cook too and made several records. Reedman Jerome Don Pasqual has said of the move, "Keppard really gave the band a lift and then we really went to town. Later, Andrew Hilaire and Johnny St. Cyr joined the band. Doc Cook seldom wrote out any special parts for Freddy Keppard but would just give him his head and while we were playing the arrangements Keppard would do anything he wanted." Later Keppard worked with such locally celebrated bands as those of Ollie Powers, John Wycliffe, and Erskine Tate. He was still playing in Chicago in the early Thirties, still loud but, according to those who heard him, no longer very well. He died in 1933.

Freddy Keppard was a dedicated player. For him, there was no illness or discomfort to keep a man from playing the best he could if he was a real musician. However, he was apparently a reluctant businessman as a leader. And as he told Bechet, he did not really want to turn this communal music of New Orleans into a commodity. The trouble was that by the time he said that, he already had. Probably the preliminary step along that path was taken when the first band played for entertainment and entice-ment in Storyville. But in bringing his music to the rest of the country in 1912, Keppard had also brought it into the entertain-ment and show business of the nation at large. Once Freddy Keppard had played his music on the Orpheum Theatre circuit, to the acclaim that it received, there was no turning back either for himself or for New Orleans jazz.

Recordings

Bolden's augmented brass band made at least one cylinder recording, a copy of which has not survived, or at least so far been found. At least one scholar of New Orleans jazz believes that Bolden's band also made disc records, recorded and sold locally in New Orleans, but no copies have turned up so far.

A rare 10-inch LP "This is Bunk Johnson Talking . . ." issued on William Russell's American Music label (No. 643) offered Bunk John-son's re-creations of Bolden's playing.

Currently Freddy Keppard's recordings are rather hard to come by. Two sides by "Cookies Gingersnaps," a small ensemble from Doc Cook's orchestra, with Keppard and Jimmy Noone, are in Columbia albums: *Here Comes the Hot Tamale Man* in "The Sound of New Orleans" (C3L 30), and *Messin' Around* in "The Sound of Chicago" (C3L 32). Together they give a clear evidence of Keppard's style, his ensemble lead, his solo approach, his breaks.

A now-rare Riverside 10-inch LP, "New Orleans Horns" (RLP 1005) had Keppard's forceful blues *Salty Dog* and *Stock Yard Strut*. *Salty Dog* was also included in Riverside's "History of Classic Jazz" (SDP 11). Riverside's RLP 1015, "Johnny Dodds, Vol. 2," had a different version of *Messin' Around* and *Adams Apple;* the latter also appeared on 12-inch on RLP 12-123, "Johnny Dodds in the Alley." A rare "Take" of the Keppard "Messin' Around" is on Milestone 2002.

References

Armstrong, Louis, *Satchmo: My Life in New Orleans*. Signet, 1955.

Asbury, Herbert, *The French Quarter*. Knopf, 1936.

Barker, Danny, "A Memory of King Bolden." *Evergreen Review,* September 1965.

Bechet, Sidney, "The Road North." From *Treat It Gentle*, Hill & Wang, 1960.

Blesh, Rudi, *Shining Trumpets*. Knopf, 1946; revised edition, 1950.

Borneman, Ernest, "Creole Echos." *The Jazz Review,* September and November, 1959.

Charters, Samuel, "Keppard, Freddy." From *Jazz: New Orleans 1885–1957*, Jazz Monographs No. 2, Walter C. Allen, 1958.

————, and Leonard Kunstadt, "That Creole Band." Chapter 4 in *Jazz: A History of the New York Scene*, Doubleday & Co., 1962.

Courlander, Harold, *The Drum and the Hoe*. University of California Press, 1960.

Driggs, Frank, and Thornton Hagert, "Jerome Don Pasqual." *Jazz Journal,* April 1964.

Goffin, Robert, *Jazz from the Congo to the Metropolitan*. Doubleday, Doran, 1944.

Gottschalk, Louis-Moreau, *Notes of a Pianist*, edited and annotated by Jeanne Behrend. Knopf, 1965.

Hoefer, George, liner notes to "Kid Ory! Storyville Nights," Verve V/V68456.

Jackson, Preston, "King Oliver." From *Frontiers of Jazz*, edited by Ralph de Toledano, second edition. Ungar, 1962.

Mellers, Wilfred, *Music in a New Found Land*. Knopf, 1965, pp. 250–257.

Meryman, Richard, "An Interview with Louis Armstrong." *Life*, April 15, 1966.

Ostransky, Leroy, "New Orleans Style." Chapter 6 in *The Anatomy of Jazz*, University of Washington Press, 1960.

Russell, William, and Stephen W. Smith, "New Orleans Music." From *Jazzmen*, edited by Frederic Ramsey, Jr., and Charles Edward Smith, Harcourt, Brace and Co., 1939.

————, and Gene Williams, "Zue Robertson—King of the Trombone." *Jazz Information*, March 15, 1940.

Rust, Brian, *Jazz Records A–Z 1897–1931*. Published by the author, 1962.

Stearns, Marshall, "Past Two: New Orleans." From *The Story of Jazz*, Oxford, 1956.

Twain, Mark, *Life on the Mississippi*. Chapters XLI-XLVII.

O. D. J. B.

BUDDY BOLDEN started New Orleans jazz, we may assume, in the sense that his strong personality gave focus to a musical activity that existed around him. But Bolden was a bluesman—clearly so from the tunes he played in his early years—so perhaps he gave a more meaningful emotional character to the music than it had before him.

By the turn of the century, Missouri ragtime was a national craze. We tend to forget, in glorifying the New Orleans tradition, that its players, as popular performers, played the popular music of the day as well as their own local repertory. Therefore New Orleans musicians—Negro and colored Creole—played ragtime, although, perhaps from the very beginning, they played it in their own way. And for what their own way was, Jelly Roll Morton's transformation of Scott Joplin's *Maple Leaf Rag* will amply demonstrate. Similarly, they had been playing a music analogous in form, popular marches, before they played ragtime, and no doubt they transformed the marches too. And they built their own pieces, putting together several themes, on the model of rags.

At the same time that the colored musicians were playing ragtime, so of course were the white players of New Orleans. In their own playing, the white players were undoubtedly influenced by the transformations that the Negroes and colored Creoles were making in the ragtime style. All of which is fairly obvious but is, I think, a sound way of looking at the basis of white New Orleans jazz and the so-called "Dixieland" style, which first swept the country in 1917, and has often reswept it since.

Traditionally, the father of white New Orleans popular music (which inevitably means an African-influenced music) was a man named George Vitelle Laine, known as "Jack" or "Papa" Laine. He was born in the city in 1873 and was still alive and reminiscing in the mid-Nineteen Sixties. He began on string bass and alto horn and finally settled for drums. He formed his first band in 1888, and soon he was leading a Reliance Brass Band for parades and concerts and, with several of the same musicians, a Ragtime Band for dances.

Due to the popularity of his music, Laine became an organizer and contractor of groups, and he had the talent for it. If someone in the white community wanted music for a party, a picnic, a dance, a parade, an advertising wagon, he would usually hire a Laine band. Laine would gather his musicians along "Exchange Alley," at Exchange Place between Canal and Bienville Streets, where the players who wanted a job would hang out.

Laine's groups did use some improvisation. Some of the men could read; some could not but learned the pieces by ear. Guitar players, incidentally, were pivotal in such groups. They called out chords to unfamiliar pieces, thus giving valuable ear training to the reading and nonreading musicians alike.

Sooner or later, almost all of the important white players of New Orleans passed through Laine's organizations, from the members of the early Tom Brown band through the Brunis Brothers. But let it be noted that two members of Jack Laine's Ragtime Band, clarinetist Achille Baquet (note the French origin of his name) and trombonist Dave Perkins (note the Anglo-Saxon origin of his), were of mixed blood, light-skinned, blue-eyed, part Negro and, on occasion, passing. Perkins even played in Bolden's group.

In 1913, "Joe Frisco," later famous as the stuttering comedian and colorful character, was a member of a vaudeville act billed as Frisco and McDermott, which played New Orleans. To accompany a dance team on the bill, local musicians were hired, and trombonist and leader Tom Brown put together a spirited small group. Frisco talked about their music when he returned to Chicago, and in June of 1915, Tom Brown, Ray Lopez on cornet, Gus Mueller on clarinet, Arnold Loyocano on guitar and piano, Steve Brown on bass, and William Lambert on drums headed north for an engagement at the Lamb's Café.

There is some dispute still as to who first applied the name "jass," or later "jazz," to a dance band; Brown's version of how his group got the name begins with the fact that he didn't have local musicians' union clearance for the Chicago job. The origin of the word, actually, is still in doubt, but there seems little question about the connotations it had acquired by 1915. So Brown says that the Chicago union spread the word that his group was playing jass music, implying whorehouse music, as a retaliation. But rather than try to live down the rumor, the group embraced it and billed itself as "Brown's Dixieland Jass Band, Direct from New Orleans, Best Dance Music in Chicago." The public came to find out what on earth "jass music" might be and exactly how one danced to it in public.

Brown had originally wanted to bring a clarinetist named Larry Shields with him, and when he heard that Bert Kelly's orchestra in nearby White City had an opening on clarinet, he got Shields the job. Later Brown was able to switch players, sending Mueller over to Kelly's group, and getting Shields for himself.

Early the following year a man named Harry James, who was running the Booster Club in Chicago, wanted a jazz band too, and he went down to New Orleans to search one out. He found one, and thus did cornetist Nick LaRocca, clarinetist Alcide "Yellow" Nunez, trombonist Eddie Edwards, pianist Henry Ragas, and drummer-leader Johnny Stein head for Chicago.

Dominic James LaRocca was born in New Orleans in 1889, the son of an Italian immigrant shoemaker. He grew up in the tough Irish Channel section of town. The elder LaRocca played cornet as a sideline but considered professional musicians penniless wanderers and drunks, and had decided that his fourth child, Nick, was going to be a doctor. Indeed, when the youngster took to his father's cornet and began teaching himself to play it, his father smashed the horn to discourage him. Later, he smashed a second cornet that Nick had procured on his own.

Nick persisted in his self-taught pursuit of music with quite a bit more freedom after his father's death, both on the cornet and on the family phonograph, where Sousa march records were a favorite. He was soon playing in public, and by 1908, one of his first associates was a local fifteen-year-old clarinetist, Larry Shields. A day job as a maintenance man at a print shop brought together LaRocca and Eddie Edwards, a visitor who played trombone, who subsequently joined with the young cornetist in a small electrical contracting business. On their off-evenings and off-days the young musicians hung out at Exchange Alley, picking up jobs through Papa Laine's contracting.

It was on a later job, with drummer Johnny Stein, that the club manager, Harry James, heard LaRocca and brought the group North. A postcard which clarinetist Nunez mailed back home from Chicago indicated some success, but also the frank expectation that the group would be returning to New Orleans and its members expecting to rejoin the Laine fold. However, the success was apparently enough so that a better offer came from a rival cafe, the Del'Arbe. Stein was reluctant but LaRocca, Edwards, Nunez, and Ragas left him, sent back to New Orleans for drummer Tony Sbarbaro (later Spargo), and took the job.

Meanwhile Tom Brown's band had gone on tour, an excursion which began with eleven weeks at the Century Theatre in New York. The group, called the Five Rubes for the occasion, had worked up an act, a comedy presentation which is still echoed in the funny hats and wild blazers which seem permanently a part of the neo-dixieland band.

When Brown returned to Chicago, Shields was apparently discouraged and he traded places with Nunez in the LaRocca group, which was by now appearing at the Casino Gardens as the Dixie Jass Band.

Soon after, a booker approached Brown for another New York job, but his group had dissolved by then and he recommended the LaRocca group. Thus on January 15 the "Dixie Jasz (sic) Band" opened in a club called the Paradise in New York at Eighth Avenue and Fifty-eighth Street in the Reisenweber Building. At first business was hardly sensational. Apparently, the management had trouble persuading the public that the music was supposed to be danced to, but it hung on. It had two other ballrooms in the building offering waltzes which helped to pay the freight. And by the end of the year nightclubbers were flocking to Reisenweber's third floor; the Paradise club had become fashionably "in," and had raised its prices and the band's pay. Soon an electric sign outside read "The Original Dixieland Band—Creators of Jazz."

The group was also in demand for private parties and, perhaps more notable, the vaudeville stage, where Edwards and LaRocca blew into the bells of each others horns, Shields put a false tincan mute on his clarinet, Edwards moved his slide with his foot, and the numbers were delivered at increasingly breakneck tempos.

The group was recorded first by Columbia, then Victor, then Aeolian, but the Victor record of *Livery Stable Blues* and *Dixie Jass Band One-Step* (later *Original Dixieland One-Step*) was the seller. The former title was apparently responsible for its huge success. It featured rooster effects from Shields' clarinet, cow moos from Edwards, and horse whinneys (out of Freddy Keppard's lighter moments, the old-timers say) from LaRocca. The public thought the music hilarious. And so, in a sense, it was. But to any who knew its sources, the effect of its reception and popularity must have been painfully ironic. And it is Keppard's Creole Band, by the way, that Jelly Roll Morton offered as the direct origin of the O.D.J.B.'s style.

The recordings put the O.D.J.B. repertory on wax. The tunes were each made up of several parts or strains, a form modeled on ragtime pieces but played differently, and many of them, according to most of the musicians still down home, borrowed from the repertory of the colored bands of New Orleans. They were *Ostrich Walk, Tiger Rag, At the Jazz Band Ball, Fidgety Feet, Sensation Rag, Bluin' the Blues, Jazz Me Blues, Clarinet Marmalade.*[1] The last, like *Tiger Rag* and *Sensation,* of course featured Shields, and the licks and breaks the clarinetist used on the piece became standard, either literally or as models, for subsequent performances.

Before the Reisenweber job was up—and it lasted into 1919— pianist Henry Ragas had pneumonia, apparently brought on by

---

[1] It might be further noted that the melody of *Barnyard Blues* or *Livery Stable Blues* is taken from Stephen Adams' hymn, *The Holy City;* that the first strain of *Fidgety Feet* echoes *At a Georgia Camp Meeting* (1897); that the third strain of *Dixieland One-Step* echoes *That Teasin' Rag* (1909); that the main strain to *At the Jazz Band Ball* uses the chords to *Shine On Harvest Moon,* and that *Tiger Rag* has the same chords as Sousa's *National Emblem March.*

fast living, late hours, and heavy drinking, an early victim, perhaps, of what was soon to be called "the jazz age."

Ragas died a month before the band was to leave for a job at
Rector's Café in London. His eventual replacement was J. Russell
Robinson, who soon contributed the best-selling *Margie* and
Singin' the Blues to the repertory. Eddie Edwards, who had be-
come the band's business manager, was drafted before the trip,
and he was replaced by Emil Christian from New Orleans.

In London, Robinson left in a dispute over a dancehall booking
and the group picked up Britisher Billy Jones. The London reception was, again, a mixture of puzzlement, controversy, and
delight, and included a stiff but apparently polite Command Performance before King George V.

The confused, confusing, and, to us today, highly charged comments of a reporter from the London *Daily News* are worth
quoting:

> As to the word "jazz," the bandsmen rejected both the current
> explanations. They will not have it that the word is of Red Indian
> origin, or that "jazz so" is a term of praise in the dialect of the
> Negroes in the southern states. The word was invented by someone
> in Chicago . . . it is possibly a purely onomatopoeic expression. . . .
> In view of the unkind and disrespectful things which have been
> said about Red Indians and Negroids and West African savages, it
> should be stated that the players are all white—as white as they can
> possibly be.

Back in New York, Edwards and Robinson rejoined, and the
first important job was at a New York café named for the Folies
Bergère and located on top of the Winter Garden Theatre. But
soon the life of the O.D.J.B. was one of touring theatres and
clubs and one-night dances. And the touring and "jazz-age" high
living were beginning to wear on its members, particularly Larry
Shields, who left in December 1921. One would like to believe
that Shields, as the most naturally gifted musician in the group,
was pulled two ways by the clowning and the shallow nature of
the music's success.

By this time, of course, the band had long had its imitators.
It is not difficult, after all, to imitate the dixieland style—amateur
bands by the hundreds, probably the thousands, formed by everyone from high-school kids through middle-aged businessmen, are

still doing it. The first had been the Earl Fuller Jazz Band in
1918. Its clarinetist was Ted Lewis, and thus did some of the
worst aspects of Shields' clarinet style achieve a sort of immor-
tality. Jimmy Durante had a jazz band for a while and used
drummer Johnny Stein. And as one looks through a jazz discography, he finds the Original Dixieland Jazz Band entry followed
by several "originals," Original Indiana Five, Original Memphis
Five—the latter was a capable group actually, with trumpeter
Phil Napoleon, trombonist Miff Mole, clarinetist Jimmy Lytel, and
pianist Frank Signorelli, the latter two of whom served as replacements in the O.D.J.B., but none of whom had ever been to
Memphis or even the South.

Louis Armstrong has written of the way that in 1917 and 1918,
he and everyone else in New Orleans was listening to the first
recordings of the Original Dixieland Jazz Band. He singled out
their *Tiger Rag* as the first record of the piece, adding "between
you and me it's still the best." But Sidney Bechet, who had given
clarinet lessons to Larry Shields, described their music quite differently, feeling that it was pat and derivative and hence a kind
of aesthetic blind alley, and declaring *Livery Stable Blues* a
burlesque of the blues. Put those statements together and, I think,
one is close to the truth. The band caught the light side of the
music, some of its rhythmic excitement, and a great deal of its
jocularity, mockery, and irreverence—but not much of its deeper
substance.

Music historian Wilfred Mellers put the case in extreme terms
in comparing the O.D.J.B. records to those of Jelly Roll Morton
and King Oliver. And, at the same time, he touched on a psycho-
logical truth that most white Americans have still to deal with:

"The wildness of the blues, the tension of the heterophony,
have vanished, leaving only a eupeptic jauntiness. Oliver makes
something positive, even gay, out of a painful reality; the Dixieland Band, purging away both the passion and the irony, leaves
us with the inane grin of the black-faced minstrel. The brassy,
reedy sonority of the Negro band—which can be simultaneously
hard as nails and warmly sensitive—becomes a footling tootle; the
perpetual jigging of the dotted rhythm becomes a jerking of

puppets. All that comes over as genuine is an element of pathos beneath the merriment. If there was pathos in the vivacity of the Negro rags, it is sadder still to find white men, with or without blackened faces, wearing the same mask. The pathos is for the most part extra-musical."

Mellers is speaking of the music's effect, of course, and a comparative effect at that, which (for Oliver's group at least) is out of historical order and context. But perhaps one is not right to hurl personal recriminations at the members of the O.D.J.B. Perhaps they did not deliberately "purge away" anything. They may have played honestly what they felt, understood, and could play, by and large. If their music had the social function of sentimentalizing an urgent Negro idiom for the benefit of whites, how far can one go in blaming them personally?

In any case, it is perhaps difficult for us today to be completely fair to LaRocca, difficult for us even to estimate what the musical contributions of LaRocca and his musicians might actually have been. That is because of a book, *The Story of the Original Dixieland Jazz Band,* published in 1961 by the Louisiana State University Press, and written by H. O. Brunn with LaRocca's cooperation. It is a slickly written show-biz success story whose tone echoes many a Hollywood backstage musical. The book begins with the strange assertion that the role of the O.D.J.B. has been neglected in jazz history, passes on to the perfectly reasonable statement that it was "the first to popularize the radical new music," but then makes the pronouncement that "they introduced a music of their own creation—jazz."

Brunn even asserts that there was no jazz being played in New Orleans or anywhere else in 1908! He describes the musics of the city as favoring Irish celebrations and Italian feast days, and he speaks of German bands roving the streets. He mentions no French or Spanish or Caribbean festivities, and, by his account, there were apparently no Negroes or colored Creoles, much less Negro or colored Creole music. In the streets of New Orleans the colored were indeed the invisible men to LaRocca and Brunn.

True, there is quoted late in the book a tribute to the O.D.J.B. taken from Louis Armstrong's "ghosted" early biography, *Swing*

That Music. There is a mention of A. J. Piron as having requested the O.D.J.B. to record *Sister Kate.* And there is a mention of Jelly Roll Morton—LaRocca wanted to reclaim composition of the *Tiger Rag* from him. But LaRocca does not answer Morton's more important claim that *Tiger Rag* was transformed by the colored bands many years before from an old French quadrille. One does not have to answer the evidence about the Negro origins of jazz if one does not mention it, apparently.

Other white players of LaRocca's generation have been franker about the inspiration of their music, but to be sure not all of them. Was it sheer ignorance or unconsciousness on LaRocca's part? Had he gotten so much of the music at second-hand that he simply did not know? [2]

Thus it is that Negro Americans have long considered the Dixieland style an Uncle Tom music, to be played only when it was a question of getting or not getting a much-needed job. It is a music identified for them both with white men and with an early popularization. But this of course has meant also that the reputations of the magnificent ensembles of King Oliver's Creole Jazz Band and Jelly Roll Morton's groups have suffered.

It is interesting that Paul Mares, leader of the white New Orleans Rhythm Kings, who was quite open about the origins of his music as we shall see, should have been able to catch something of its deeper side and play it—if not exactly creatively, then at least respectfully.

Yet one must not deny LaRocca his important influence. With the help of his records, young Bix Beiderbecke, for one, growing up in Davenport, Iowa, glimpsed an emotional and human essence in the music, and in LaRocca's work, a cornet style that was for him full of musical implications. But Beiderbecke did not imitate. He did not imitate LaRocca nor his later guides and favorites like King Oliver, Bessie Smith, and Louis Armstrong.

[2] Such may be the ways of Jim Crow, of course. One wonders how many Americans knew in 1900 (or, for that matter, in 1967) of the Negro origins of ragtime. I can recount the story of a white pianist friend who was rehearsing with a Southern band in 1940 and was ordered by the leader to "stop playing so colored." The tune they were running down was the Count Basie blues *One O'Clock Jump!* Jim Crow requires a constant supply of the ignorance that is born of repression of the facts. No wonder the white man's repression seems completely willful to those who know the facts, even though it may be unthinking or unconscious.

Beiderbecke played like himself. And thereby gave jazz the deepest and most abiding respect that he could have.

By January 1925, Nick LaRocca found keeping the band together and keeping up a fairly fast life had become too much for him. He collapsed and was advised to give up music. By then, incidentally, only Edwards and Spargo of the original group were still with him.

In 1936, the ex-trumpeter (he had switched from cornet in the Twenties) was working at house building in New Orleans. Someone from the William Morris office approached him for a sort of novelty appearance in a movie, *The Big Broadcast of 1937*. He turned the offer down, but he sensed the possibility of a comeback. He learned that Larry Shields was working in a Bible house in New Orleans not too far from his own home. They began to practice together. Eddie Edwards, who ran a newsstand across from Carnegie Hall in New York during the depression, was found coaching a boys' baseball team at the West Side YMCA. Robinson, as the composer of the by-then standard *Margie,* was not hard to find. Tony Spargo had remained a professional drummer, working in and around New York. The reassembled O.D.J.B. played on Ed Wynn's national radio program in July 1936.

Then, in the February 17th issue of the *Saturday Evening Post,* an article appeared by J. S. Moynahan on the Original Dixieland Jazz Band. The country had its new musical fad called swing, and, to the public at least, Benny Goodman was its king, although Bob Crosby's Dixieland group wasn't doing badly. LaRocca and his men were out to prove that swing was nothing new, but "another name for jazz," and, in Moynahan's exposition, the "real" jazz was vastly superior and swing something of a flawed, pale echo of the truth. The "March of Time" film series produced a short that was more or less faithful to the early career of the Dixieland Band, but it clearly implied that they were responsible for "creating" jazz. They toured theatres with a Ken Murray vaudeville package, and on their own.

Most interesting perhaps, the group made some more recordings for Victor, with both an expanded "big band" and with the five-piece group redoing *Original Dixieland One-Step, Barnyard Blues, Tiger Rag, Skeleton Jangle, Clarinet Marmalade, Bluin' the Blues.* The recordings make interesting comparisons to the earlier versions. Although the ensembles seem somewhat mechanical and stilted, LaRocca particularly, whose first efforts probably echo the eariest manifestations of the New Orleans style, shows, in a greater looseness and flexibility of phrase, that he has not been insensitive to subsequent developments in jazz.

There was dissension in the ranks, however, and most of it was directed at the trumpeter-leader. Earlier, the ensemble had been a cooperative one—by intention at least—but this time LaRocca was not only in charge but receiving double salary. And after a couple of years back in the limelight, LaRocca quit again, taking up his building business once more, until he retired in 1958. Edwards, Shields, and Frank Signorelli on piano continued for a while with Sharky Bonano on trumpet, but before long most members of the group had drifted out of music once more. All but Tony Spargo; he was still a professional drummer in the 1960s.

Recordings

A now-rare 10-inch LP on label "X" collected the early Victor recordings of the Original Dixieland Jazz Band. The group's English recordings of 1919 and 1920 were collected in the Riverside album RLP 156/157. It is now rather difficult to come by in this country but it may be available in certain British and continental record stores specializing in jazz.

The O.D.J.B.'s first recording, *At the Darktown Strutter's Ball,* can be heard on Columbia's "The Sound of New Orleans" (C3L 30) as can a selection by the "Louisiana Five" with Alcide Nunez on clarinet.

References

Brunn, H. O., *The Story of the Original Dixieland Jazz Band.* Louisiana State University Press, 1961.

Charters, Samuel B., and Leonard Kunstadt, "That Creole Band." From *Jazz: A History of the New York Scene,* Doubleday & Co., 1962.

Gillis, Frank, "Biography of a Jazz Tune, *Livery Stable Blues/Barnyard Blues.*" *Jazz Journal,* June 1963.

Kunstadt, Leonard, and Mike Zaccagnino, eds., "Tony Spargo Photorama." *Record Research,* July 1963.

Mellers, Wilfred, *Music in a New Found Land.* Knopf, 1965, pp. 288–289.

Smith, Charles Edward, "White New Orleans." From *Jazzmen,* edited by Frederic Ramsey, Jr., and Charles Edward Smith. Harcourt, Brace and Co., 1939.

(Unsigned) "Larry Shields." *The Record Changer,* February 1954.

THE ROLL

According to the *Congressional Record of the United States Senate* on August 31, 1959, Kenneth Keating (Rep., N.Y.) arose and spoke as follows:

> Mr. President, I should like to offer a small historical footnote to the current debate with respect to the Lake Michigan water-diversion bill. .
>
> I do not anticipate that this offering will change any votes, but it may be of interest at least to those Senators who are students or connoisseurs of early American jazz.
>
> The late Jelly Roll Morton, one of the great pianists which New Orleans gave to the Nation, used to sing a 12-bar blues song not long after the turn of the century, and the title of that song was *Michigan Water Blues*.
>
> The first chorus went as follows
>
> > Michigan water tastes like sherry wine,
> > (I mean sherry wine):
> > Mississippi water tastes like turpentine,
> > Michigan water tastes like sherry wine.
>
> Frankly, I do not know at this point whether Michigan water
>
> tastes like sherry wine, but even if it should, that would still be no justification for diverting it to the Chicago sewer system.

Although he acknowledged that the copyright of *Michigan Water Blues* belonged to Clarence Williams, Jelly Roll Morton said it had actually been written by New Orleans pianist Tony Jackson, and on occasion hinted that he had a hand in it himself. And Jelly Roll Morton, who once asserted that he had "invented jazz," would surely have conceded it his due to appear in the

Congressional Record, although being dragged in by his heels during a discussion of the Chicago sewer system might not have been his idea of the way it should have been done.

This Jelly Roll Morton is a man who has been discussed and evaluated in many, many ways by musicians and close observers other than himself, and the contradictions abound.

—You don't think Jelly got all those diamonds with what he made in music? What do you think that nickname means?

—I was on one of his first record dates. He had good tunes, good arrangements, good men, and everybody played well, including Jelly. But the whole time he kept jumping around telling everybody, the record company guys and us, we were all going to be millionaires from that one record.

—Sure he bragged, but he could back up everything he said.

—I remember once I was driving to make a gig with him and somehow we got on the subject of marksmanship. Jelly said "when I was with Wild West shows I could shoot with the best marksmen and sharpshooters in the world." A couple of miles down the road we passed a shooting gallery, Jelly pulled the car over, got out, walked up and damned if he didn't knock down every target.

—When he got excited, he stammered. His mouth was full of diamonds and his big voice could frighten you.

—Bragging was his only talent. I've heard amateurs play better piano.

—He was a hustler and a pool shark. He only used music to cover up and make people think he was some kind of hick.

—Jelly lived music. Music was what really mattered to him, whatever else he did and however much he tried to run away from it.

—You think he was a Creole? He couldn't even speak the language, but he sure pretended he could.

—He came from New York around 1911 and for that time he was a very good piano man. Everybody listened to him. But he didn't start recording until 1923, and by then he had lost his touch and his music was out of date.

—It was in the late Twenties when he started making those records in Chicago with his Red Hot Peppers that he really hit his stride. On the basis of that music he is still a great jazz musician, and there is some things on those records nobody has been able to steal yet.

—Piano player? Leader? Well, I used to know him on the riverboats in the early Twenties and he said he was a singer.

—He was a genius. He was a fine accompanist in a band, an excellent leader, and the first great jazz composer. If he had had one ounce of business sense or the right management, he would have been a rich man because his music was very very popular.

—No, he never played piano in New Orleans. He used to hang around a lot and I think he had a girl he was, you know, sort of hustling for. I heard he played a little guitar and tried a little trombone for awhile, and I know he hung around musicians because people gave musicians free food.

—Sometimes. when we'd finished playing a New Orleans dance, I'd go by Hattie Rogers' place and play with him. Her girls really went wild for his piano.

—He could play very good piano back in New Orleans. And he was writing good pieces then too. Do you know that blues he called *New Orleans Joys* when he recorded it? He wrote that in New Orleans, and everybody learned it.

—Pimp? Well, he sold fake patent medicines, tried to sing and dance and tell jokes on stage, and he shot pool. But he was a musician really. He just couldn't get away from it. He always talked like he was going to be the biggest deal in the world and the richest man. But most of all he wanted to be a musician. If you ever heard him talk about music you'd know that. And he was a great musician—just listen to his records.

—Jelly Roll Morton stole all his tunes and he couldn't play *nothing!*

Perhaps we had better let Morton finish it himself with a direct quote, "Man, no matter what you're playin', you're playin' Jelly Roll music." ". . . As I can understand, my folks were in the city of New Orleans long before the Louisiana purchase, and all my folks came directly from the shores of France . . . and they landed in the New World years ago. . . . My grandmother bore sons named Henri, Gus, Neville, and Nelusco—all French names; and she bore the daughters Louise, Viola, and Margaret—that was the three daughters. Louise, the oldest daughter, so fair she could always pass, married F. P. La Menthe, also an early settler and considered one of the outstanding contractors and demolishers in the entire South. Louise happened to be my mother, Ferd (Jelly Roll) Morton.

"Of course, I guess you wonder how the name Morton came in, by it being an English name. Well, I'll tell you. I changed it for business reasons when I started traveling. I didn't want to be called Frenchy."

An elegant beginning, at least the way Morton told it to folklorist Alan Lomax in the music room of the Library of Congress in 1938. It has been put another way, a bit less elegantly. "The family into which Ferdinand Joseph Morton was born," wrote Arna Bontemps and Jack Conroy, "lived at the corner of Frenchman and Robertson in New Orleans. . . . Young Ferdy was given guitar lessons at the age of six. His teacher was a Spaniard. . . . How long Ferdy's formal music training continued is not known, but the indications are that he never gave it his undivided attention. For a while he was employed in an uncle's hairdressing shop. Later he learned to make barrels and worked at this end of the wine business. . . ."

One gets the image that a young man named Ferdinand Joseph Le Menthe was born in about 1885 into a well-to-do colored Creole family in New Orleans (La Menthe had been a contractor, according to most reports). Perhaps the truth is a bit different. Alan Lomax's research turned up a man named Morton who did portering and who married Ferdinand's mother after La Menthe had taken his leave. And the young musician did receive a press notice or two in the Twenties as William "Jelly Roll" Morton.

Morton was as exasperating as he was enchanting. And for every occasion when he sounded like an inflated has-been of small time show biz, there were occasions when he sounded like a perceptive theorist about jazz music—an excellent jazz critic the like of which the music itself has not produced since. And often the braggart, the exaggerator, and the liar turn out to be just the Falstaffian, extreme kind of liar who more than half expects to be disbelieved.

What he did not expect to be, clearly, was his own worst enemy. Alas, he was also sometimes offensive enough to be just that, too.

Morton was asked by Alan Lomax to sing an old New Orleans

song about Robert Charles, a song with a strange underground reputation. At first, he refused, and most New Orleans men— Negro, colored Creole, even white—would have refused to perform it in public or even for the archives of the Library of Congress. By suddenly berserk, homicidal behavior, a previously mild-mannered newsdealer named Robert Charles, soon after the turn of the century, had set off a series of riots in New Orleans. It was apparently a case of a final goading and the last straw of humiliation—Charles had been arrested by a policeman who refused to let him return to get his hat. Those riots are traditionally said to have encouraged the final step in the gradual imposition of racial segregation by law in that city. In the late Thirties, Morton apparently remembered them vividly; some still do.

Dr. Edmund Souchon remembered the racial situation in his youth this way: "In New Orleans the self-imposed color line between the light and the dark Negro is much more marked than is the Jim Crow line between white and colored." And he exclaimed, "Jelly Roll's attitude was in no small measure due to his complete rebellion against the strict Jim Crow laws of the South, but he also presented a very interesting subject for investigation by a psychoanalyst. Jelly Roll was the victim of his particular 'cult' or 'social group,' if you will."

Perhaps any changes in this situation, even today, are more superficial than real. Louis Lomax wrote in 1961, "And while in New Orleans segregationists were bringing public education to a lamentable halt because of the school integration issue, subdued laughter was pulsating throughout the Negro community. Fact of the matter is that New Orleans' schools have been integrated since the turn of the century. The white schools are peppered with light-skinned Negroes passing for white. They pass during the school day and then go home to social life among their Negro friends and relatives. Fear of detection caused them to join the white boycott of the integrated schools, and when segregationist Judge Leander Perez of nearby St. Bernard Parish threw open the doors of that community's all-white schools to accomodate the boycotters, the light-skinned Negroes were among the first to go over and register."

At the turn of the century New Orleans had three classes and with the arrival of "the prejudice," the colored Creoles were sure

that they had suffered the most. They were proud families, cul-
turally identified with the French community; they were petit
bourgeois or landowners, and many of them, or members of their
families, had been educated abroad. Their status came about, because as we have mentioned, there was in the so-called Louisiana
"Black Code" of 1724 a provision for freeing of slaves. All children shared the status of their mother, and when a white slave
owner died he frequently had provided that his colored mistress
should be freed. The children of their union were automatically
free too.

A kind of social snobbery came naturally to this class of mixed
French, Spanish, and African forbearers, and there is no doubt
that Ferdinand La Menthe, or William Morton, or Jelly Roll, carried that snobbery with him. Morton's defenses were even more
complicated: His family had apparently not been so prosperous
as he wanted the world to think. And, in several senses, not all
of them of his own making, he was not a member in good standing of that family. Young Ferdinand moved around rather freely
on the fringes of New Orleans sporting life when he was still
quite young, and his associations were not only with the musicians but decidedly with the gamblers, the pool players, and the
pimps. The inevitable talk about the big money fell on his ears
quite early, and it must have been a wonderous parody of the
American success story that he heard there in Storyville, New
Orleans.

There is a tale that in the late Teens of the century, in California, a white hotel owner told Morton to play a waltz. Morton
replied haughtily, 'Waltz? Man, these people want to *dance* and
you talkin' about a waltz. This is the *Roll* you're talkin' to. I
know what these people want!" It wasn't a matter of waltzes to be
sure; he even played some jazz waltzes. He just wasn't taking
orders. And why? Because he was being spoken to wrongly. Was
he Negro? A colored Creole? Not white exactly . . . he was the
Roll!

Neither of Morton's parents make more than shadowy appearances in his own telling, and one gets the impression that his
grandmother had the strongest influence on his childhood. But
high life in New Orleans had a deeper effect on his youth. And
no matter how much Creole pride clung to the face he so often

showed the world, he had long since—perhaps without really knowing it—rejected his bourgeois heritage. "My grandmother gave me that Frenchman look," he told Lomax, "and said to me in French, 'Your mother is gone and can't help her little girls now. She left Amede and Mimi to their old grandmother to raise as good girls. A musician is nothing but a bum and a scalawag. I don't want you around your sisters. I reckon you better move.'

"My grandmother said all this and she walked up the path to the white columns of the front porch, went inside, and shut the door."

Was it really music that made his grandmother turn him out? Or was it the pool? Or was it the lure of the Storyville houses and bars, which he knew at fifteen?

"There were about three things in New Orleans that any young colored man could be, unless he inherits a business," an old player has remarked, "a musician, a pimp, or a dockworker. Jelly was too weak for the docks. But he was the other two."

Morton described his experience on the levees this way in Rudi Blesh and Harriet Janis's *They All Played Ragtime*:

> I trucked cotton in a New Orleans levee camp. The fellows who trucked it were called longshoremen. The fellows who put bales in place were screwmen. These were permanent people. Made tremendous salaries. Around $18 a day, and that is way back.
>
> Another class on the levee are on river boats. Handled all kinds of things. They were called roustabouts. Weren't treated like other fellows. Had a captain over them with a whip or lash in their hands. I had never seen them whipped, but I have often heard they whipped them to keep them going. They would carry on their backs all kinds of things, big boxes of lard. Carried this stuff up the gangplanks. Looked like a man couldn't carry so much. Singing and moving to rhythm of songs as much as they could. People who works on a levee called levee camp people. There is nothing to do on a levee except when the city is in danger.
>
> Roustabouts would never dream of striking on river boats. They were just like in slavery. And on the other boats they were getting big money. Longshoremen didn't get as much as screwmen. I never heard of those guys quitting.

What did Morton think about it as his grandmother shut the door—that he was about to become a pianist in one of the houses, or a pianist with certain lucrative sidelines, or were the sidelines the real point? Does it really matter what he may have thought? For long before that door shut, Ferdinand La Menthe or William Morton had actually become Jelly Roll Morton, musician. His real destiny was the music that had already captured him. "Morton," wrote Whitney Balliett, "gave the American dream an awful pummeling before it finally cut him down," but even as he pursued the diamonds and the Cadillacs, as he wandered, gambled, pimped, the music was always there, the thing actually leading him on, the thing having its own triumph throughout his life. And hearing his music, we know that it can tell us much more about the man and his inner feeling than his boasting and his proud face could ever reveal.

"You see, my young friends have brought me into the Tenderloin district at a very young age. . . ." And he came to know the life in this borderline world of Storyville intimately. He remembered it all his life and he could talk about the dress, the swaggering gaits of the "swells," and the "really tremendous sports" and the hangers-on by the hour. His elaborate vocabulary and sentence structure could be enagagingly pretentious, and it has been suggested that he learned it from the purple rhetoric of the New Orleans *Blue Book* directory. "Within the walls of the Arlington," goes one *Blue Book* entry, "may be found the work of great artists from Europe and America. Everybody must be of some importance, otherwise he cannot gain admittance. . . ."

Another says, "If it were in my power to name Kings and Queens, I would certainly bestow the title 'Queen of Smile' on Bertha. Her 'Chateau' is grandly equipped and lacks nothing to make it the finest in the world. Pretty women, good times and sociability has been adopted as the countersign of Miss Weinthal's new and costly home."

Or, " 'Snooks' has the distinction of keeping one of the liveliest and most elaborately furnished establishments in the city, where an array of beautiful women and good times reign supreme. A visit will teach more than pen can describe. 'Snooks' also has an array of beautiful girls, who are everlastingly alert for a good time."

And finally this passage about Gypsy Schaeffer:

"To operate an establishment where everyone is treated exact is not an easy task, and Gypsy deserves great credit. Gypsy has always made it a mark in life to treat everyone alike and to see that they enjoy themselves while in her midst.

"There are few women who stand better with the commercial people than Gypsy, who has always kept one of the best and most refined houses in which a private man may be entertained by lots of handsome and well-cultivated ladies. A visit once will mean a long-remembrance and friendship forever.

"What more can any sane person expect?"

Still, there was an undeniably poetic quality about Morton's speech, and on the Library of Congress records, his sentences sometimes roll with the cadence of verse.

He was talking about the Storyville hangers-on who, when they couldn't live off their women, might have to go to work as gardeners in the white section of town:

> They got something when they could,
> And when they couldn't,
> They would work out
> In the yards.

Or (and note his nice irony too):

> Well every night
> The boys would hang around
> Some of 'em would even go so far
> To meet their sweet Mammas.
> St. Charles Street was quite a way off,
> But sometimes they would brave it and walk
> To where their sweet Mammas were working.
> And of course sometimes
> It was okay for them to go into the house.

Among the musicians, the pianists who played in the houses in Storyville made the money. There were no pianists in the early bands in New Orleans, and this was partly because the bands usually doubled as marching ensembles in parades, and partly because no leader could afford to pay a pianist what he would make in a sporting house, or even in a Storyville bar.

"I was the first one in New Orleans to employ a jazz pianist in the red-light district . . . in those days jazz was associated principally with dance halls and cabarets . . . jazz didn't start in sporting houses . . . [but] it was what most of our customers wanted to hear," so said Countess Willie Piazza, "the first lady

of Storyville." And the pianists were following the development
that the New Orleans musicians were giving to jazz. They did
not originate style, but because they were likely to have a superior musical knowledge, and needed to know both harmony
and melody, they made important contributions.

We should not romanticize, of course. Audiences were as sus-
ceptible then as now to all sorts of musical grandstanding. Roy
Carew recalls a piano contest held in the Dauphine Theatre,
about 1916 he believes, among white players, some of them well
known in the Storyville district. Kid Ross played some genuine
Basin Street honky-tonk music. And Erwin LeClerc played some
things that were quite advanced musically. But the man who
walked away with the applause and consequently the prize was
a man who did *Dixie* with one hand while playing *Yankee
Doodle* with the other.

Morton says he learned the guitar at seven and piano at ten.
He says he sang in close harmony with a group of young gallants
who crashed parties and sang for their supper. He says he played
drums and trombone in street parade bands—and no one who
has heard his left hand on piano should be much surprised at that.

Who were his influences? Probably, as with most musicians, his
influences were anyone and everyone he heard both within New
Orleans and during his later travels. Musicians say his most important influence was Albert Cahill. But there was one man whom
Jelly Roll Morton himself praised with something like consistency—indeed his admiration for him was unbounded—and that
was Tony Jackson.

Morton once told Roy Carew, with great pride, that he had
beaten Jackson in a piano contest. He usually claimed he won
almost every contest he entered, but beating Jackson was something of a stunt. "Jelly Roll said that, as the other contestants
were seated on the stage while Tony was playing, he (Jelly)
was seated near enough to the piano to keep telling Tony *sotto
voce,* 'You can't sing now. . . . You can't sing now.' I don't know
if that affected Tony's playing any, but Jelly Roll won the contest.

"It would have been strange if Tony Jackson could have been
bothered by Jelly Roll's reverse coaching while he was playing
the piano," Carew felt. "I remember that at the last place I
heard him in New Orleans, Frank Early's café, I believe, the

piano was in poor repair; among other defects, there was a key in the bass that would stay down every time it was hit, but that never seemed to bother Tony. He would keep going just as smoothly as a well-oiled machine, and when the key would go down, Tony would pull it up without the slightest interruption to his playing and singing. To me he was always remarkable. One night I sat there listening to the man who 'knew a thousand songs' putting out his usual high-class presentation of good rags and late songs, when a stranger stepped over to the piano and requested Tony to sing *Everybody's Doin' It,* which in my estimation is about the poorest effort Berlin ever put forth, even if it did get very popular. 'I don't know that one,' replied Tony, and the stranger walked away and out of the café. I looked at Tony in surprise, and said, 'You certainly ought to know that song, popular as it is.' Tony grinned at me and replied 'Oh, I know it all right—but I hate the damn thing!' "

Tony Jackson was one of the players who early carried New Orleans music—or at least his own early version of it—outside the city. He was born in 1876, and apparently he never took music lessons of any kind, but taught himself. As a young man, he worked is some pretty high-class bordellos including Lulu White's Mahogany Hall. Bunk Johnson remembers playing with him after work at the Big 25 bar, a favorite musician's hangout around 1894, and preserved a piece called *Baby, I'd Love to Steal You* which they worked up together at the time. Until late in his life, no means of publication was ever made available to Jackson, apparently, unless he sold his compositions outright, sometimes for about five dollars. The exception to this rule was first made in 1916 when he sold a melody and shared composer credit with one Egbert Van Alstyne. The piece was called *Pretty Baby,* and when Gus Kahn outfitted it with lyrics for Fanny Brice, who used it in the "Passing Show" of that year, it became a hit and has of course remained a standard. A few other Jackson publications followed, but to no such popular success.

Morton hinted rather broadly that Jackson finally left New Orleans because he was a homosexual and looking for a place where he would find less social pressure. One wonders, all things considered, why New Orleans would care. At any rate he started to travel in 1905 and soon settled in Chicago. He worked mostly as a solo pianist and singer, already billed as "The World's Greatest Single-handed Entertainer." Judging from his surviving work, and a Morton re-creation like *The Naked Dance,* Jackson's piano was strongly influenced by ragtime. Sidney Bechet described his work as "dicty," and said he was no real blues man, as Morton was. After 1917 he occasionally led a band which might include trumpeter Freddie Keppard, clarinetist Lorenzo Tio, bassist Wellman Braud, clarinetist and soprano saxophonist Sidney Bechet. Bechet remembered:

"About that time I took another job, too, at the Pekin, sort of after hours—about one to four—with Tony Jackson, who was playing there at that time. Tony was a wonderful entertainer, a wonderful composer, and a wonderful piano player; he was the onliest man I know who could entertain an audience for two hours by himself alone. We'd played together at the DeLuxe, and then he had this band at the Pekin and asked me to join him there. Oh, I really went with Tony. He wrote several songs— you remember *Pretty Baby, Some Sweet Day* and *Such a Pretty Thing;* he certainly was a great entertainer. But when I was all booked to go to London with Will Marion Cook, like I'll tell you in a minute, I couldn't figure why Will wouldn't take Tony along with him. I was a young fellow, you know, and he just wouldn't say; but finally he tole me, because Tony had some kind of venereal disease and had sores back of his neck, and so that's why the old man didn't want to take him."

He was, above all, a cabaret entertainer, and Jackson himself was undoubtedly as proud as were his friends and followers of the fact that he could deliver an operatic aria, a light classic, or a sentimental popular ditty of the day, as well as his own specialties. Singer Alberta Hunter remembers, "Tony was just marvelous—a fine musician, spectacular, but still soft. He could write a song in two minutes and was one of the greatest accompanists I've ever listened to. Tony was always jolly, but he had bad teeth, just terrible! He had mixed gray hair and always had a drink on the piano—always! It was only beer, but he drank plenty of that. Tony wrote *Pretty Baby,* which he dedicated to a tall skinny fellow, and another song that everybody sang at that time, *When Your Troubles Will Be Mine.* . . . There would be so many people around that piano trying to learn his style that sometimes he could hardly move his hands—and he never played any song the same way twice."

Jackson lived in Chicago on South Wabash Street with his sisters, quietly from all reports, and his death at forty-five in April 1921 was rather bizarre, the result of a seizure of eight weeks of the hiccups which the efforts of doctors and nurses could not relieve.

We should not leave Tony Jackson however without mentioning one famous Chicago club at which he worked, the Elite No. 1, especially because of the description of the place once given by Jelly Roll Morton. "The most beautiful place on the South Side and the most famous place throughout the history of America of cabaret land. The trade was the finest class of trade, millionaires, and good livers." Incidentally, Jelly once said of the later Elite No. 2 that the manager, a former partner in the No. 1, ruined his club because he insisted on using symphony musicians, "which was considered obsolete since the invasion of Tony Jackson and Jelly Roll Morton in the city of Chicago."

Morton remembered the place from about 1912. Both he and Jackson were playing in the bars of the "Section" which was along State Street, and near Thirty-fifth. Jackson was there to stay. Morton was between New York and California, on his first trip to Chicago. The men might play by the hour and attract an audience that spilled out into the street, and apparently sometimes jam up traffic. "More than one old timer," John Steiner writes, "remembers that the special police were assigned to an opening of the likes of Jackson and Morton."

Jelly Roll Morton worked as a pianist in Storyville, entertaining that fantastic cross section of life, of people from every class, every race, and every economic group, mingling so freely—except in the high-class houses—yet so momentarily, tentatively, and precariously, in the New Orleans night. Did he have the kind of celebrity that he claimed for Tony Jackson, Albert Cahill, Albert Carrol, Albert Wilson, Kid Ross, and the others?

Perhaps it would not matter if Morton had not been a real piano "king" in the top houses. Beginning in 1904, he traveled constantly east and west and north of Louisiana, along the Gulf

Coast and up the great river. At first, he used New Orleans as a kind of base of operations, but later he no longer needed its havening influence and cut himself loose from his home town forever.

Morton met some of the important second-generation ragtime players in St. Louis like Artie Matthews, but mostly he recites the names of characters like Jack the Bear, Benny Frenchy, and Bad Sam. And he constantly registers his disgust with the shoddy brothels and bars he had to put up with—shoddy compared to New Orleans anyway. Besides, in Storyville, a shabbily dressed laborer could retaliate for his lot by surreptitiously dropping a louse down the neck of a silk-hatted *bon vivant* who was standing next to him.

As I say, in music, Morton's delusions, his arrogant pride, and his unstable snobbery frequently fall away. On the recordings he made for the Library of Congress, he re-created a scene, a card game of "Georgia skin." The players were a sharp bunch and he admired them both for their skill and for the vagabond life they claimed to lead. The game climaxes as one of the players sings encouragement to the cards themselves. The piece is like a work song, and the slap of the card play is the stroke of the hammer. ("I'm gonna get one and go, directly, *slap*/ My baby is down and out, *slap*.") The melody has something of the incantive movement of *Sometimes I Feel Like a Motherless Child*. It is "folk music," at the roots, and a music the sophisticated Morton was sure he had gone quite beyond. But he sings the plaintively beautiful blue notes with a reverence that shows us how deeply he apprehended the men involved in that game. No matter what his grandmother might have said, no matter what the colored Creole in him might say, he re-creates the scene with dramatic vividness and with a passionate and wondering appreciation of the human beings who played it. If his art can help us see this way, a way his deeper self could see, Morton served all men well.

"I went to Memphis about 1908. At that time I was very shy about playing the piano any place." A mere three years later, he wasn't so shy. James P. Johnson remembered him in New York. "I was taken uptown to Barron Wilkins' place in Harlem. Another boy and I let our short pants down to look grown up and sneaked in. Who was playing there but Jelly Roll Morton! He had just arrived from the West and he was red hot. The place was on fire! We heard him play his *Jelly Roll Blues.*

"I remember that he was dressed in full-back clothes and wore a light brown melton overcoat, with a three-hole hat to match. He had two girls with him.

"Then I was just a short-pants kid in the back of the crowd and I never saw him again until ten years later in Chicago. I was able to appreciate him then, but I couldn't steal his stuff. I wasn't good enough yet. . . .

"I've seen Jelly Roll Morton, who had a great attitude, approach a piano. He would take his overcoat off. It had a special lining that would catch everybody's eye. So he would turn it inside out and, instead of folding it, he would lay it lengthwise along the top of the upright very solemnly as if that coat was worth a fortune and had to be handled very tenderly.

"Then he's take a big silk handkerchief, shake it out to show it off properly, and dust off the stool. He's sit down then, hit his special chord (every tickler had his special trademark chord, like a signal) and he's be gone! The first rag he'd play was always a spirited one to astound the audience."

The years 1917 to 1922 saw Morton's second and most important California trip. He worked in San Diego and in Los Angeles; he participated in the last days of the "Barbary Coast" joints in San Francisco, at a place called the Jupiter. He went as far south as Tampico, Mexico, and as far north as Vancouver, B.C.

Shep Allen, who knew Morton on the Coast, has described his attitude then as happy-go-lucky. "It was all right if it broke good, and it was all right if it broke bad. He just took it in his stride. Any way, it would come was all right with Jelly Roll. He always did carry a lot of money. I don't know about that one thousand dollar bill story, but he saw a lot of money in his hands or in his pockets, all the time, every day. And the diamond in his tooth— that's a fact."

In Los Angeles, he worked in Central Avenue cabarets like the Cadillac, the Newport Bar, and the Penny Dance Hall upstairs at Ninth Street. Later he led a six-piece band at Leek's Lake and Wayside Park and at the latter place he entertained King Oliver one night in April 1922.

Critic William Russell believes that "the period was one of Jelly's happiest and most prosperous. He could have his big car, his diamonds, and could keep his music just as a sideline for special kicks while he made his real money from the Pacific Coast 'Line.' As one friend put it, 'You don't think Jelly got all those diamonds he wore on his garters with the $35 a week he made in music.' But whether Jelly was really 'one of the higher ups,' as he claimed, or just a procurer, is immaterial, for Jelly's real interest undeniably was always music."

Singer Jimmy Rushing, then a twenty-year-old, had his first job at the Quality Night Club, where the stars of the then small community of Hollywood would come (and drink gin by the case, according to Rushing). Morton would come in, listen to someone play piano for a bit, and then announce, "Whenever you see me walk in, get up off that piano."

According to saxophonist Jerome Don Pasqual, who was visiting from St. Louis with the Charlie Creath band, Morton was then known simply as *the Roll*. "He didn't have a band though every so often he would come over and sit in with us. He was a sensational pianist and he had a terrific style with much originality. In fact in those days I thought he had the trumpet style on piano that Earl Hines was soon to make famous."

It is from his 1917–1922 stay out West that another of the well-known and characteristic Morton legends comes. When he needed a band for a job at Baron Long's Café in Watts, in south Los Angeles, he sent back to New Orleans for cornetist Buddy Petit—the man who Louis Armstrong, Red Allen, Lee Collins, and others all praise as an influence. Petit arrived with clarinetist Wade Whaley and trombonist Frankie Dusen. Their provinciality, their awkwardness, their dress—these were just too much for the Roll. When they arrived at the job with instruments wrapped in newspapers or homemade sacks, his criticism was harsh. And when they insisted on cooking a pan of red beans and rice on the bandstand, Morton's ridicule of the hicks from down South was merciless. Petit left for home, and he said if Jelly Roll ever showed up again in New Orleans he was going to get killed.

Also from this period comes a story that is succinctly revealing of Morton's pride, of his strength as well, and of how the two sometimes came together. After the trip to the Regent Hotel in

Vancouver, Morton fell onto very hard times. He played briefly
in Casper, Wyoming, where the temperature was 45° below
zero. He rode out of Denver, Colorado, "blind baggage," as they
say, and jumped off at Colorado Springs to drop in at joints and
play for tips so that he could eat. When he finally got back to
the Coast, he thought he had landed a good job at a hotel in
San Diego. But then he discovered that the group playing opposite him, a white orchestra, was being paid twice what he was
getting, and he simply pulled his group out and left.

I think it was probably during the California years that Morton came to understand that music was his real calling, and his
composing there seems to have been prolific. In Los Angeles, he
entered into a music publishing venture with the vaudeville team,
the Spikes Brothers, whom he had known with McCabes Min-
strels on the Gulf Coast and in St. Louis in 1911, and who wrote
Some Day Sweetheart. (Morton said that *he* had actually helped
adapt it from an old song, a streetwalker's lament called *Tricks
Ain't Walkin' No More*.) From this time also dates Morton's
earliest music manuscript, a lead sheet for *Frog-i-more Rag*—the
odd title apparently comes from the fact that he originally wrote
it to accompany a vaudeville contortionist named More who
performed in a frog costume. *Wolverine Blues* (not a true blues,
by the way) also apparently dates from this period. And down
in Tijuana, Morton dedicated the *Kansas City Stomps*, not to
the midwestern town, but to a local bar.

Jelly Roll Morton left California in 1922, not to return for
almost twenty years. He had set his sights again on Chicago.
He had been there briefly in about 1912, as we have seen. In
1915 the *Original Jelly Roll Blues* had been published by Will
Rossiter, one of the first men to promote songs by having them
sung in retail stores and advertising them in trade journals.
But perhaps 1915 was a bit early for Morton's music. At any
rate, by the mid-Twenties, things had changed—so much so that,
some say, the center of jazz had moved there from New Orleans.

However, Chicago high life by the 1920s was no product of free
enterprise, nor would it welcome a free-lance maverick like Jelly
Roll Morton. The cabarets, the whisky, and the vice were a part
of hoodlum enterprise, which soon turned into a gangster empire,

ruled by Al Capone. One catered to the hoods, or one did not work. Jelly Roll Morton did not cater to the hoods. In fact, he catered to nobody.

He did find some work there, to be sure. He had a job at one café in 1922, with a group that included the New Orleans trombonist Zue Robinson, and because of his stay in the windy city, Morton began his career on phonograph records the following year. However, in 1923, he is also reported in Kentucky. And in St. Louis, working in the riverboat bands of Fate Marable. ("When you get to New York, say hello to Jelly Roll for me. He used to work in my band," the highly successful Marable told Henry "Red" Allen some years later. "*Work* for him?" was Morton's retort in New York. "He had some little old band that wasn't doing nothing, so I let him use my name.")

Harrison Smith, who was an off-and-on business associate of Morton's later in New York, tells this story from the early Chicago days: "W. C. Handy utilized Jelly Roll's Incomparables for a broadcast out of Chicago in 1924. The announcer said 'Ladies and Gentlemen, you have just heard W. C. Handy and his famous Memphis Band.' Jelly Roll, standing by disgusted and thinking that the broadcast was terminated, yelled out 'modestly' for the world to hear—'Like hell you have!' " It was one of several battles with Handy—not the first, for Morton says that in 1908 in Memphis he had asked Handy's band to play the blues, only to be told that a full orchestra could not play a blues (Jelly proved differently by distributing copies of his *New Orleans Blues*)—and not the last fight with Handy, as we shall see.

So Jelly Roll Morton's Chicago years were largely spent in and out of Chicago, often in St. Louis. But what he did while in Chicago is much more important for the Morton who survives today, for before those years were over, he had formed an alliance with the Melrose Brothers Music Company out of the music shop of Walter Melrose and Marty Bloom, and soon he was publishing and recording.

Melrose has described the first meeting this way: "When we first met Jelly Roll he walked into our music store—it was in 1928 —wearing a cowboy hat and a big bandanna 'round his neck. He announced: 'I am Jelly Roll Morton.' He talked constantly for two hours and we didn't get a word in edgewise. All of the monologue concerned how good he was and damned if he didn't prove it, as he helped a great deal in pulling us out of the red."

After he found Melrose and Melrose found him, Jelly Roll Morton became, for about five years anyway, the kind of success and celebrity he always claimed to have been.

Drummer Zutty Singleton remembers him. "He was livin' high then. You know, Jelly was a travelin' cat, sharp and good lookin' and always bragging about he wrote this and that and the other thing—in fact, everything! And let me tell you this—no one ever won an argument with Jelly either!

"Once I was walkin' somewhere with Louis and Lil Armstrong (they were together then), and Lil had got herself a brand new baby grand piano. We all went to Louis' place and Jelly sat down at that piano and really gave us a serenade. He played and played, and after each number he'd turn around on that stool and tell us how he wrote each number and where it came from. It was a real lecture, just for the benefit of me and Lil and Louis."

Pianist Lil Hardin, later to be Lil Armstrong, also remembers Jelly Roll's deportment in those days. "Mrs. Jones ran an employment and booking agency at the store, so all the musicians and entertainers hung out there. They'd rehearse, sit around, and gossip for hours. Almost every day there was a jam session and I took charge of every piano player that dared to come in.

"But one day the great Jelly Roll Morton from New Orleans came in and I was in for a little trouble.

"I had never heard such music before. They were all his original tunes. Jelly Roll sat down, the piano rocked, the floor swayed while he ferociously attacked the keyboard with his long skinny fingers, beating out a double rhythm with his feet on the loud pedal. I was thrilled, amazed, and scared. Well, he finally got up from the piano, grinned, and looked at me as if to say, 'Let this be a lesson to you.'"

Clearly the swaggering didn't start with the Melrose alliance and the success on records, however. Trumpeter Lee Collins was working with King Oliver as a replacement for Louis Armstrong in 1924, and ran around a bit with Morton—"One day I went

over to see him . . . at his room at Thirty-fifth and Grand Boulevard (now South Parkway). There he was—in bed with two
women, one sitting on each side of him. I tell you, he was some
character! . . . He asked me to come work with him. 'You know
you will be working with the world's greatest jazz piano player
. . . not one of the greatest—I am *the* greatest.'

"Jelly finally got dressed and we went in his car to see the
manager of a big-name ballroom out on the South Side. But he
and this man could not come to any agreement on the price
Jelly wanted for playing there.

"Jelly told the manager, 'You bring Paul Whiteman out here
and pay any price he wants because he has the name of 'King
of Jazz.' But you happen to be talking to the real king of jazz.
I invented it and I brought it here.'

"Jelly was a peculiar man—if he liked you he liked you too
much, and it was the same way if he hated you. He was also
very prejudiced and liked nothing but Creoles."

His first recording date was apparently the one which took
place in June of 1923, for a label called Paramount, one of the
first companies to record jazz regularly for what was then called
the "race market." He assembled a band consisting of trumpet,
trombone, clarinet, alto sax, and rhythm, with himself on piano,
and they recorded *Muddy Waters Blues* and *Big Fat Ham*. The
group played with a rare unity, confidence, and swing. The
unknown trumpeter leads the ensemble with something of the
firm, clipped authority of Freddy Keppard, and Jasper Taylor's
percussion (on wood blocks, his drums and cymbals wouldn't
record on the acoustical equipment) shows a wholly infectious
awareness of Morton's particular rhythmic ideas. The orchestration outlines the best qualities of his later work; the horns play
in unison and harmony, and veer into separate, interweaving
heterophonic melody. The solo clarinet and trumpet on *Muddy
Waters* play with particular lovely and moving blues feeling.

Beginning in July 1923, Morton was recording for the Gennett
company, chiefly as a piano soloist. He did some of his best
pieces: *King Porter Stomp, New Orleans Joys* (*New Orleans
Blues*), *Grandpa's Spells, Kansas City Stomp, Wolverine Blues,
The Pearls*, and the following year he did *Shreveport Stomp* and

Original Jelly Roll Blues. (He also participated in the first "mixed recording date; with the white New Orleans Rhythm Kings, he did *Mr. Jelly Lord, Milenberg Joys, London Blues.* George Brunis, trombonist with the NORK, has reported, "We thought it best to say that he was Cuban, so that's what we did.")

For the Rialto Music Shop's own label he did a wonderful version of *Frog-i-more* which lay unissued and unknown until it was rediscovered on a junk heap in a "test" pressing in 1944. In 1924, he made a duet date with King Oliver, and a kind of tour de force of momentum for both men resulted on *King Porter Stomp.* The following year he did a duet with clarinetist Volly de Faut on *Wolverine Blues.*

These are the best records that Morton had made before September 1926, but they are not the only records. And the poorest records he made must have made it seem that his talent had largely spent itself on a handful of piano solos, a duet or so, and two good sides with a band. But on September 15, 1926, Morton did his first Chicago session for Victor, and thereby began one of the most remarkable series of recordings in jazz history.

The Victor Morton records are beautifully conceived, beautifully played, and (undoubtedly most important) they were carefully rehearsed. Probably no jazz records before or since have received more preparation and care.

Preparation, incidentally, wasn't the only thing involved. When Morton contributed *Jackass Blues,* Melrose hired a mule, hung some advertising signs across his flank, and the Roll rode him down State Street.

Banjoist-guitarist Johnny St. Cyr is on all but four of Morton's Chicago Victor titles, and he has said, "Jelly was a very, very agreeable man to cut a record with. . . . He'd leave it to your own judgment . . . and he was always open for suggestions." The late Omer Simeon, who was Morton's choice for clarinet on most of his best records, wrote of them this way: "Walter Melrose brought all the music down from his music store. Morton was working for Melrose then and the pieces we played were mostly stock arrangements Jelly had made up and published by Melrose. Jelly marked out parts we liked and he always had his manuscripts there and his pencils and he was always writing and changing little parts. . . . Jelly left our solos up to us but the backgrounds, harmony and licks were all in his arrangements. He was easy to work for and he always explained everything he wanted. . . .

"We would have a couple of rehearsals at Jelly's house before the date and Melrose would pay us $5 a man. That's the only time I ever got paid for a rehearsal. . . . Technicians set the stage for the date—Jelly had to take orders there for a change. . . .

"Melrose spared no expense for a record date—anything Jelly Roll wanted he got. Melrose worshipped him like a king. Jelly was great for effects, as on *Sidewalk Blues* and *Steamboat Stomp* and later on like the opening on *Kansas City Stomp*. . . . For the second date he got Darnell Howard and Barney Bigard in for the trio effect he wanted on two of the sides [*Sidewalk Blues* and *Dead Man Blues*]. I played all the clarinet part and Howard and Bigard just sat there and held their clarinets except for the few strains Jelly wanted them to play. . . .

"He was fussy on introductions and endings and he always wanted the ensemble his way but he never interfered with the solo work. He'd tell us where he wanted the solo or break but the rest was up to us. . . . I remember on *Dr. Jazz*, the long note I played wasn't in the stock arrangement. Jelly liked it and had Melrose put it in the orchestration. . . ."

The care and the preparation were necessary because Morton was attempting a delicate balance between arrangement and improvisation, between soloist and group, between part and the whole. He was attempting to give both discipline and spontaneity to jazz performance, and he was concerned with the over-all shape and movement of the performance as well as of each of its parts.

The evidence of his care has further testimony from drummer Baby Dodds who with his clarinetist brother Johnny played on two of the Chicago sessions. "On all the jobs with Jelly Roll it was he who picked the men for the session. He went around himself and got the men he wanted to record with him. We weren't a regular band. . . . But when Jelly Roll gave us a ring we met for rehearsal and we all knew what was expected of us. Of course we all knew each other from New Orleans but those record sessions were the only times we all got together to play music. But there was a fine spirit in that group and I enjoyed working with Jelly Roll immensely. . . .

"At rehearsal Jelly Roll Morton used to work on each and every number until it satisfied him. Everybody had to do just what Jelly wanted him to do. During rehearsal he would say, 'Now that's just the way I want it on the recording,' and he meant just that. We used his original numbers and he always explained what it was all about and played a synopsis of it on the piano. . . . You did what Jelly Roll wanted you to do, no more and no less. And his own playing was remarkable and kept us in good spirits. He wasn't fussy, but he was positive. He knew what he wanted and he would get the men he knew could produce it. But Jelly wasn't a man to get angry. I never saw him upset and he didn't raise his voice at any time. . . .

"And the records we made with Jelly were made under the best of recording conditions. They were recorded in the Chicago Victor studio on Oak Street near Michigan Avenue, and the acoustics there were very good. It was one of the best studios I ever worked in."

Finally, here are the words of George Mitchell, the fine trumpeter on all of Morton's Chicago recordings, "I don't know how I was picked for the records with Jelly Roll. I had heard plenty about him but hadn't met him and was playing regularly at night when those record dates came up. I always had an idea that I was included because they knew they could depend on me. A lot of the New Orleans cornet men were hitting the bottle—like Freddie Keppard—and they wanted someone they knew would show up.

"We rehearsed the tunes for three or four days right in the record studio before recording. Both rehearsals and recordings were in the afternoon, since most of us had regular night jobs.

"Jelly Roll was sharp, always in good humor, and was always talking. The music parts were always ready for us. Jelly Roll wanted you to improvise a lot, and if anyone went dry on ideas, he would help you out by playing some figures on the piano. I wish I could tell you more about Jelly Roll, but at the time I didn't think too much about those records. I was so busy with my regular jobs."

Even a casual description of the typical Morton performance can give some idea of why such careful preparation was necessary. *Black Bottom Stomp,* one of the more successful fast pieces, is played by three horns (the usual trumpet, clarinet, and trombone) plus rhythm, and it lasts less than three minutes. It has three different themes, variations on some of them, sometimes has a pronounced 2/4 rhythm, sometimes a stomping 4/4. It has stop-time rhythmic patterns, horns in harmony, horns in heterophony (in several melodies at once), antiphonal call and response patterns among the horns, and solos with rhythm accompaniment.

That summary account may make *Black Bottom Stomp* seem impossibly cluttered, disparate, perhaps even pretentious. Yet on hearing, one realizes that its details fit unobtrusively in place and that *Black Bottom* flows from beginning to end with rare order and direction. There are patterns of musical and rhythmic echo: heterophony, fragmented and split melodies, stop-time, recur at key moments in ways that give a sense of order. But most of all there was one guiding musical intelligence in charge. No other New Orleans musician—and few other jazzmen—have had the conception of form that Jelly Roll Morton had.

To be a bit more detailed about *Black Bottom*—for it may serve as an introduction to so much of Morton's orchestral music— the performance begins with an introduction (which we later realized is a kind of pre-echo of the second theme) stated as a "call and response" by the horns. The first theme begins with the horns in close harmony. But the trumpet breaks away in a solo "call" momentarily and the clarinet and trombone answer in a variational "response." The second melody is played polyphonically with a more pronounced rhythmic momentum, with Johnny Lindsay's string bass heard strongly, and this rhythmic momentum is tantalizingly suspended at certain points for breaks. Next Omer Simeon's clarinet delivers a variation. Then Morton's piano solo—unaccompanied, by the way. Then George Mitchell's trumpet against intermittent "black bottom" variants of Charleston rhythm, banjo playing against string bass. Then the three horns interweave over very light rhythm. And in a final "stomp" chorus Lindsay's bass again leads the way, and Kid Ory's trombone takes the momentary breaks in rhythm. The strongest climaxes on *Black Bottom Stomp* come not when volume or mass increase, but when Lindsay's bass and Andrew Hilare's bass drum enter and swing the group in a very special way. Obviously, Morton's musical thinking was far ahead of that of most of our contemporary "Dixieland" groups and the banal frenzy of the "out-chorus" that often ends each piece.

A recording like *Jungle Blues* is in the strongest contrast to *Black Bottom Stomp*, almost its opposite in every respect. *Jungle Blues* is deliberately simple and archaic; basically it is a primitive blues bass line and it has a simple riff as its melody. But in about three minutes, Morton forms and reforms the riff into three melodic sections; he handles the regular, not to say monotonous, accents of the bass line with some variety; and when he has brought the performance to the brink of monotony, he ends it exactly at a moment too soon. Between the complexity of his best stomps like *Black Bottom Stomp* or *Grandpa's Spells* and the simplicity of *Jungle Blues* or *Hyena Stomp* we encounter the range of an artist.

Probably the masterpiece of the whole Victor series is *Dead Man Blues*. It begins with an exchange of dialogue between two voices which are supposed to be comic, but which—like a great deal of Morton's comedy—is rather forced. (There is one area of agreement among all men about Jelly Roll Morton: he could have charm and good spirits and he could be an engaging man, but he did not have much sense of humor.) Musically, *Dead Man* begins with an echo of the Chopin "Funeral March," played on trombone with just the merest hint of breathy humor.

Dead Man undertakes a touchy combination of spriteliness and seriousness. On one level, it offers three very good themes by the composer, and otherwise belongs to the players—to the easy swing of George Mitchell's trumpet ensemble lead and solo; the strength of Omer Simeon's clarinet melodies in ensemble and solo; the poignancy of Kid Ory's simple ensemble trombone lines.

Mitchell's two solo choruses are beautifully constructed and they provide a fine transition into the trio as well (this trio theme, incidentally, was not used in earlier versions of *Dead Man*; King Oliver had recorded the same melody in 1923 as *Camp Meeting Blues*).

There are three choruses on that trio section, and they develop with a beautiful simplicity. In the first, three clarinets state the melody. In the second, the clarinets repeat their theme, but the trombone sings a quiet blues counter-melody beneath them. This prepares for a more complex texture of the final chorus, heterophony by trumpet, single clarinet (Simeon), trombone, and rhythm. Here, the semi-improvised lines interweave so delicately that they seem the final fruition of the New Orleans ensemble style. But this final chorus has a further function of balancing the heterophony of the opening ensemble. (The version of *Dead Man* currently available on LP is a tape splice of two different "takes" of the piece, and George Mitchell's trumpet solo is from an obviously inferior version wherein Mitchell made a mistake. Nevertheless, one can gain from it an idea of the artistry of the best version of this fine piece.)

In his later years Jelly Roll Morton found himself incensed at a radio broadcast, a Robert Ripley "Believe It or Not" show, which implied that W. C. Handy had originated jazz music. Morton wanted to set the record straight about New Orleans and about Jelly Roll Morton. He was also ready for a comeback. His blasts at Handy led him to bragging once more. Before long he was saying that he himself had created jazz in 1901.

"In 1912, I happened to be in Texas, and one of my fellow musicians brought me a number to play—*Memphis Blues*. The minute I started playing it, I recognized it. I said to James Milles, the one who presented it to me (trombonist, still in Houston, playing with me at the time), 'The first strain is a Black Butts strain all dressed up.' Butts was a strictly *blues* (or what they call a boogie-woogie) player with no knowledge of music. I said the second strain was mine. I practically assembled the tune. The last strain was Tony Jackson's strain, *Whoa B-Whoa*. At that time no one knew the meaning of the words jazz or stomps but me. This also added a new word to the dictionary, which they gave the wrong definition. The word *blues* was known to everyone."

Morton had earlier accused Handy of using guitar player Guy Williams' *Jogo Blues* as the basis for his *St. Louis Blues*.

Handy was by his own admission a kind of folklorist, working with indigenous and often traditional material, writing it down, refining it, and often incorporating several themes into quite well-wrought, varied compositions. Morton frequently did the same sort of thing with folk-blues melodies. The question of plagiarism is a knotty one when we are dealing with artists who form their material from folk sources, and a charge of tune lifting of this kind might be leveled against almost any major jazz musician.

Especially with Morton, the question of plagiarism and collaboration is—like nearly everything else in his career—puzzlingly complex. On the one hand, when he recomposed Santa Pecora's *She's Crying for Me* into *Georgia Swing*, he gave Pecora credit. Charles Luke is fully credited with *Smoke House Blues*. Mel Stitzel with *The Chant*. King Oliver with *Doctor Jazz*. Morton always acknowledged that Porter King had at least collaborated on *King Porter Stomp* and that King was at that time a better musician.

On the other hand, Dick Hadlock recently discovered the introduction to *Shreveport Stomp* note for note in Rudy Wiedhoft's earlier *Saxophobia*. Lee Collins recorded his *Fish Tail Blues* with Morton in 1924, but Morton's later *Side Walk Blues* is clearly the same piece with a new trio section, probably developed by Morton. Morton acknowledged his early debt to New Orleans pianist Frank Richards, but in such a way as to hint that Richards was perhaps the author of *New Orleans Blues*—or at least of an earlier piece that inspired it.

In the early Sixties, I noticed a Twenties recording by clarinetist Boyd Senter of *Steamboat Stomp*, a piece Morton also recorded and took credit for. Writing to Senter about it, I got this friendly reply: "First let me say this, in Jelly Roll's book, he must have been kind of cracking up. His story about Walter Melrose and myself about my tune *Sugar Babe* said that the Melrose Music Company was going on the rocks, and we were pushing *Sugar Babe* to try and stay on our feet. Here is the real story on that:

"I was making records for Pathe & Perfect, on my first session I made a tune, and had no name for it. Lew Gold was waiting to take the recording studio over after I was through and asked me the name of the last tune I made. I said I had no name as yet. He said, 'I just won some money on a horse named Slippery

Elm' so that is where I got the title. That was my first tune with the Melrose Publishers. My second was *Bucktown Blues*. While in Chicago with Walter Melrose, he said 'When do you make some records,' and I told him as soon as I was in New York again, so we wrote *Sugar Babe*. Then I made a trip through the South on the RKO Circuit, and when I got back to New York I did some more recordings, and at that time they were calling everything stomps, so I had an old tune that I had been playing around Denver called *Just Jazz*, so made it and called it *Steamboat Stomp*. Now here is where the catch comes in, if you can look up in some way the recording dates of mine (my records on a lot of things were lost in Chicago) along with the publishers' date of my tunes, you will find out that all my tunes were recorded before they were ever published. But you won't have to go to any trouble like that, all you will have to do is get in contact with ASCAP and they can tell you that it is my tune along with many more, and all on the second copyright. They are still being published by the Edwin H. Morris Company, Inc., 31 West 54th Street, New York.

"I might add that someone in Europe has recently made some recordings of *Steamboat Stomp*, *Sugar Babe*, and my *Bucktown Blues*."

It is also undoubtedly true that Morton did, as Harrison Smith contends, deliberately steal some songs in retaliation over business arguments. Smith even names Ben Garrison as Morton's later ghost writer. Smith recalls, "It was a sad day for Jelly in January of 1930 when the finance company grabbed his $6000 Lincoln car because of the matter of a $1000 loan on it a year previous had slipped Jelly's memory. With no car to transport his band, he was really hot and since the gang at the Rhythm Club—Chick Webb, Jimmy Harrison, Kaiser Marshall, Fess Williams, Ben Garrison, Bill Robinson—and all the others gave him the horse laugh 'cause he was hoofin' and no longer on 'rubber,' he stole twenty-eight songs . . . and got $700 which redeemed his car. Then it was his turn to laugh at the gang because he was on 'rubber' again. The way he got the compositions was: he proposed to be president, nominal head and editor of the new 'Morton Music Corp.' Pending the incorporation of the new concern, several people submitted compositions for recording con-

sideration but the finance company bursted up that dream. So
when the party who lent Morton $700 for which the composi-
tions were securities, heard that he purchased stolen property,
he confiscated the car for his loan. So there were two confisca-
tions in one month and Jelly was again without 'rubber' and the
gang had the last laugh. Webb used to call him corny to get his
goat. They called him a Chicago foreigner invading their territory. Jelly Roll hated all of them and none of them would work
for him and that's why the recording personnels at this time
were so different."

Then, there is a question of collaboration. Some men have
even hinted that Morton's technical knowledge of music was so
limited that he had to get help, especially for his orchestrations.
The names of Tiny Parham and Elmer Schobel show up on
several of the Melrose "stock" arrangements of his pieces.
Schoebel says that he merely "worked with Jelly on his tunes
and did the arrangements." Some of these stocks predate the
recordings of the same pieces; some do not, and the stocks are
clearly taken from the records.

Perhaps Morton did need some technical help. But it is evident that a single musical mind is at work during Morton's
career and that it refined and evolved a style carefully—a style
very different in its intentions from Rudy Wiedoff's or Boyd
Senter's or most other people's. No one should accuse him of
scrupulous honesty as a composer, but probably no one should
accuse him of deliberate dishonesty as an artist either.

Roy Carew has written me a letter on Morton's technical
abilities: "As to Morton's ability to arrange, I'm sure it was ade-
quate to anything in the jazz field in his time. There were a few
passages, as in *Creepy Feeling, Sweet Jazz Music,* and an elaborate version of *Winin' Boy* in the Library recordings, on which
he would have been hard put, but on the general run of material,
he was perfectly competent. He told me that he could arrange
jazz orchestrations for ten or eleven instruments and know how
they were going to sound. For more instruments he said there
would be spots that would have to be worked on. For the N. O
Jazzmen records made in 1939, he made studio arrangements
geared to the ability of the men, being aware of what they
could do. He told me that, when the party in charge asked for

lead sheets for copyright purposes, and he replied that Tempo-Music Publishing Company owned the numbers, they said, 'All right, someone else will be leader on the next session.' 'That meant,' said Jelly, 'that I will have to do the arranging, and someone else will get leader's salary.' I don't know if it worked out that way or not. I suggested later that orchestrations of the Tempo tunes might be desirable, and a short time later he sent me an orchestration of *Good Old New York*. I took it to the group at a supper club here, and to me it sounded very good when they played it over."

Carew further says, "As to Morton's love of music, he loved any good music. I think he wrote a waltz, as a matter of fact. One evening when I strolled into the Music Box, he was at the spinet playing *The Angel's Serenade* from the music. He said 'I was just trying this over. It's a beautiful thing, isn't it?' He once told me 'Good music doesn't get old.'

"I have heard a good deal of jazz and near-jazz in the last twenty years, and feel very sure that for real ability Morton belongs with the real top-notchers. He could compose, arrange, direct, play, and sing more than acceptably. I don't know of any *one* musician in that field can equal that standard. But of course, I'm prejudiced."

Changing the titles on his pieces was almost a standard practice for Morton. Thus *Frog-i-more Rag* (or *Froggy Moore*) became (when words were added) *Sweetheart O' Mine*. *Fickle Fay Creep* was once *Soap Suds*. *London Blues* and *Shoeshiner's Drag* are the same piece. And when Louis Armstrong recorded *Chicago Breakdown* it was actually *Stratford Hunch*. *Big Fat Ham* (or *Big Foot Ham* on some record labels) became *Ham and Eggs*. *Black Bottom Stomp* was once published as *Queen of Spades*. Jelly's later theme song, *Winin' Boy Blues*, was once a part of his *Tomcat Blues* and his *Midnight Mama*, the last two actually the same piece. *New Orleans Blues* into *New Orleans Joys* was made obviously to indicate a happy blues, but the piece Morton did with Johnny Dunn as *Buffalo Blues* was later called *Mister Joe*. A section of *Milenberg Joys* shows up in the piece Morton did with Dunn called *Dunn's Bugle Call Blues*. And so forth.

The Chicago-made Victor records sold, and the diamond tooth

dandy with the thousand-dollar bills pinned to his underwear was at last making it as a musician. But in several senses the center of musical activity was moving. It was moving artistically in that at almost the very moment that Morton began recording, Louis Armstrong was giving jazz a renewed musical language. And Don Redman and Fletcher Henderson, with three brass, three saxophones, and rhythm, were giving the jazz orchestra a new format and style. Artistically Morton was superb. Modishly, he was almost out of date before he started. Then, geographically, the center of commercial musical activity had moved to New York. So did jazz move too, and in late 1927 so did Jelly Roll Morton.

But, in New York, Wilbur de Paris has said, Fletcher Henderson and McKinney's Cotton Pickers were the bands, and "Jelly was just another leader making gigs."

Morton did a couple of not particularly distinguished recording in New York in late January of 1928 under the name "Levee Serenaders" and another four sides in March, working with plunger trumpeter Johnny Dunn. His first important job however was at a place called Rose Danceland, and happily the event led him back to the Victor studios.

Uptown Rose Danceland (not the downtown Roseland its name apparently traded on) was a tough and typical taxi dancehall. It was on the third floor at 125th Street and Seventh Avenue. "We'd play for fifty minutes in a row and rest ten," said Omer Simeon, whom Morton found again in New York, who could stand the job only for a week (he was replaced by Russell Procope) but who came back for the recordings. Other players included Ward Pinkett on trumpet and Julius "Geechy" Fields on trombone.

The group made Morton's first artistically successful New York recordings in a return to Victor—for two more years as it turned out. They made *Georgia Swing, Kansas City Stomps, Shoe Shiner's Drag, Boogaboo,* and the lovely quartet recording of *Mournful Serenade,* an acknowledged adaptation of King Oliver's *Chimes Blues.* It was Morton's last date fully done in his older style, and one reason for its success is surely that the material was carefully rehearsed on the stand at Rose Danceland.

Guitarist and banjoist Danny Barker, younger than Morton

but also from New Orleans, recalls, "Jelly Roll spent most of the afternoons and evenings at the Rhythm Club and every time I saw him he was lecturing to the musicians about organizing. Most of the name and star musicians paid him no attention because he was always preaching, in loud terms, that none of the famous New York bands had a beat. He would continuously warn me: 'Don't be simple and ignorant like these fools in the big country towns.' I would always listen seriously because most of the things he said made plenty of sense to me.

"Jelly was constantly preaching that if he could get a band to rehearse his music and listen to him he could keep a band working. He would get one-nighters out of town and would have to beg musicians to work with him."

At first Morton had swaggered a bit too much perhaps. Harrison Smith reports that the ex-champion boxer Jack Johnson asked Morton in 1928 to let him front his band. "Jack played great bull fiddle. Jelly just laughed it off." And that "Bill McKinney, of Cotton Pickers fame, begged Jelly Roll to make arrangements for the band. Jelly just laughed it off."

But all too soon, the work got scarcer and scarcer and Morton tried other things. One man even remembers him toward the end peddling hair straightener on street corners, using Creole clarinetist Albert Nicholas's straight, silken locks as an unauthorized testimonial for his product.

At the Rhythm Club, Morton fought constantly with Chick Webb and his musicians, and they enjoyed needling him. "It was hard to keep up with him," Simeon reported, "he could talk twenty-four hours in a row."

At first, he would come in and say to the pianists, "Get up. You don't know what you're doing." Actually, the musicians thought he was good, but, compared to their favorites like James P. Johnson and Fats Waller, a little old fashioned.

What was all the fighting about? Was it Jelly Roll Morton, a man whose career was somewhat on the skids and whose style was going out of date, bragging his head off to bolster his ego? Not entirely, I think. Morton's day was an earlier day, but in several ways he advanced jazz and he had several strong ideas about the nature of the music. The subsequent history of jazz has not always proved him right (although surprisingly often, it *has* proved him right), but he did have a sincere dedication to the integrity of the music.

His theories were usually put forth as attempts to explain what he did, and also to defend jazz against public misunderstanding and exploitation. At times one feels he believes his music was for anyone, and he certainly did not want it to be esoteric or cultish. But at the same time, he offered his music in its own terms, to say what it had to say and not what the public wanted to hear.

Many of his theories about jazz are obviously intended to balance the kind of prudish ignorance which thinks the music is loud, fast, and disorderly. After all, one popular American dictionary at the time actually defined jazz as blatant, loud, cacophonous, nonmusical noises. His famous "always keep the melody going some kind of way" is an acknowledgment that melodic variation and embellishment is his way. And it is also a part of his insistence on continuously proper and interesting harmony.

A great deal has been made of Morton's remark that riffs, short repeated melodic figures, are only for backgrounds. Actually he did not always use them that way, for the melodies to several of his pieces are reiterated riff figures. But history could hardly have borne him out better, for a riff accompaniment to a solo is one of the continuing facts and exciting resources of jazz orchestration and background.

Morton also insisted that a pianist should imitate an orchestra, and again he has complete historical confirmation, for almost every piano style in jazz has been derived either from the imitation of the jazz orchestra or of the solo hornman. Pianists are the great refiners and synthesizers of jazz—the horns originate.

"Breaks," he said, "are one of the most effective things you can do in jazz." And these momentary suspensions of a stated pulse continued to be effective. Charlie Parker's break on *A Night in Tunisia* is a fable; breaks are a cornerstone in Horace Silver's style. But Morton's subtle sense of time and dramatic suspense in making breaks is not even approached by his direct imitators.

Similarly, Morton's insistence that jazz can be soft, sweet, and slow, "with plenty rhythm," is another way of saying that swing is not the same thing as loudness or emotional frenzy. A jazz group cannot swing unless it can swing quietly, and the problem of swing at slow tempos has plagued jazz men in all periods. Morton put his finger on the basic issue.

He argued with ragtime players who preceded him; he accused them of speeding up and of various other rhythmic failings. In his later years especially, Morton certainly had his own rhythmic failings. However, one could easily say that his own best music was an adaptation of ragtime form, but with greater rhythmic and emotional variety, and with blues feeling.

When Morton insists that jazz should have "Spanish tinge," whether a piece is directly a jazz tango or not, I think he is acknowledging that much of the rhythmic character of his music comes from a syncopation of the tango—"New Orleans was inhabited with maybe every race on the face of the globe. And, of course, we had Spanish people, plenty of them. . . ."

Emotionally? Undoubtedly the blues are the source—the blues, church music, work songs and the rest—folk sources which the simple optimism of ragtime left emotionally untapped, however much it may have borrowed from their melodies.

There was more to Morton's life in New York than street-corner bragging. He continued to record for Victor until late 1930. Looked at in one way, the records are Morton's efforts to keep up with the times. But in another sense they are a refusal to stand still and repeat himself.

By June 1928, Morton had already stated and developed his orchestral conception on a beautiful series of records, and he had done solos, duets, trios, quartets. He had added an extra voice to the ensemble (the alto sax that is sometimes so successful on the *Pearls* and *Beale Street Blues*). In the next two years he tried larger bands with more harmonized writing for the various sections, and small bands with more emphasis on solos. Sometimes he succeeded. *New Orleans Bump* is a very good example of more or less the same kind of big-band writing Don Redman and Duke Ellington were also working on. *Burning the Iceberg* is one of the few really successful examples of a big-band expansion of the New Orleans style on records. Morton used the old shifting textures of harmony, polyphony, and solo with a group consisting of three brass, four reeds, and rhythm. And

Blue Blood Blues depends on its soloists (Ward Pinkett, clar-inetist Albert Nicholas, Geechy Fields) for its effectiveness, and it is as good as any similar, small-group, string-of-solos record until the late Thirties.

In October 1930, Morton made his last Victor record date for nine years. His contract was up and not renewed. The great depression was on, but Jelly was sure his failures were due solely to a conspiracy of publishers, booking agents, tune thieves, the American Society of Composers and Publishers—the mighty ASCAP, which had not admitted him to membership—and even to a West Indian who put a voodoo spell on him. (Morton him-self professed to be a Catholic all his life, but he had an aunt he described as a hoodoo witch who cured him of a childhood illness.)

Harrison Smith remembers him in 1932-1933. "In 1932, I produced 'Headin' For Harlem,' a musical comedy starring Lillyn Brown . . . and she engaged 'Jelly Roll' Morton as her pianist for a tour of New England. After the tour Jelly joined Laura Prampin's Orchestra at the short-lived Savoy Ballroom, Coney Island, N.Y. This was really a noisy place as it was located above a trolley car depot barn. The clang of the trolley bells and the clatter of the wheels used to give Jelly and the drummer the fits."

Perhaps at this time Morton began partly to admit that his style was not exactly the latest. According to Willie "the Lion" Smith, "Jelly Roll was a guy who always talked a lot. He used to be around the Rhythm Club every day and stand out on the corner and he used to bull and con all those fellows. He had his twenty-dollar gold piece on and he'd stand out there with a bankroll, meaning money, so every time I'd come around, almost all the guys who used to play the piano kept quiet. Sometimes I'd lay for Fats and Jimmy. Sometimes I'd even lay for Tatum. But I used to come around especially on Friday and Saturday looking for Jelly. I went around this one Friday and he was standing on the corner.

" 'Look, Mr. One Hand,' I said, 'let's go inside and let me give you your lessons in cutting.' So Jelly and I would go inside by the piano. I was the only one he would stand and listen to and then he didn't open his mouth. I must have played nearly every-thing you could name and when I got through, I said, 'Well,

Jelly, you'll keep quiet now.' And, true as I'm sitting here, Jelly would be quiet."

In 1938, in Washington, D.C., there was a small club known variously (almost from month to month) as the Blue Moon Inn, the Music Box, and the Jungle Inn in a kind of downhill billing. Business wasn't good, but a certain small avid following did build up. Pianist Billy Taylor remembers going there with some fellow music students one evening to have a sort of malicious fun listening to an old-time piano player. He came away with a respect for a man named Ferd "Jelly Roll" Morton, who could play things that young Taylor could not play, and whose spirit seemed indomitable, despite his obvious illness and age. Record collectors and jazz scholars gathered, and Morton fans from way back like Roy Carew from New Orleans, who became Morton's publisher. Through their persuasion, Alan Lomax, in charge of the folklore archives for the Library of Congress, recorded Morton's reminiscences on an inexpensive disc machine, with an undependable turntable, and a fine Steinway piano.

He had a following that gathered round to praise him in the evenings, and he had recorded his life and his music for posterity. Jelly Roll Morton, old beyond his years and not well, was again full of achievements and he decided that he was ready for a comeback.

Once again, he tried New York, that "cruel city," as he called it. And once again he swaggered and bragged in the face of its cruelty. He fired off his angry letters to *Down Beat*: he had invented jazz ("Speaking of jazz music, anytime it is mentioned musicians usually hate to give credit but they will say, 'I heard Jelly Roll play it first.'"); no one could play his style right, it was too difficult; he had transformed *Tiger Rag* from an old French quadrille into jazz; he had been the first comedy master of ceremonies; and on and on.

A story, headlined "'Robbed of Three Million Dollars,' says Jelly Roll," by George Hoefer in the October 1, 1940 *Down Beat,* is typical of the sort of pronouncements he was making, for publication or not. "Everyone today is playing my stuff," he protested, "and I don't even get credit."

"Nattily dressed in a green sport shirt and gray pants with large green spots predominating, Jelly Roll, who rides around

Harlem in a Cadillac, was savage in his attack on various publishers and musicians who, he claims, stole his original songs and ways of interpreting them.

" 'Kansas City style, Chicago style, New Orleans style—hell they are all Jelly Roll style,' he snorted as he watched Hot Lips Page rehearse a new band above a Harlem pool hall. 'I am a busy man now and I have to spend most of my time dealing with attorneys, but I am not too busy to get around and hear jazz that I myself introduced twenty-five years ago, before most of the kids was even born.'

"Jelly Roll, who says he 'invented' jazz music, recently brought suit against Melrose Music but the suit was dropped a few weeks later. That did not pacify him. His current gripe is that 'all this jazz I hear today is my own stuff and if I had been paid rightfully for my work I would now have three million dollars more than I have now.' "

There was a job at Nick's, in Greenwich Village. Once, after he had instructed the audience verbally and musically, Morton decided that perhaps it was his duty to introduce the players in his group—it included Sidney Bechet, Henry "Red" Allen, and Zutty Singleton! But it wasn't his *desire* to do so, exactly. "Ladies and Gentlemen," he said into the mike, "I want to introduce you to the members of my band. Let's see," moving his eyes around the bandstand, then turning to the mike again. "I'll start with the oldest one first." There was enough ducking and dodging behind him so that he could correct himself quickly, "Well, maybe we'll play you another number first." And he used to hold court there at Nick's in one of the back booths, but, to be sure, there were more young fans listening to him than there were musicians.

There is also a story that Morton jumped up out of the audience when one of the big swing bands of the time began playing the Fletcher Henderson version of Morton's *King Porter Stomp.* He scornfully read off the leader and the players and sat down at the piano to demonstrate how the piece should be played.

Again, there were some recording dates, often arranged with the particular help of jazz writer Charles Edward Smith. A couple of all-star sessions for Victor had more to do with a vague nostalgia for old New Orleans, however, than with Jelly Roll Morton the jazz composer, arranger, and disciplinarian.

For another label he did a very good solo album of "New Orleans Memories," based on the Library of Congress recordings. For the same label he did some more orchestral nostalgia, and some songs with fairly commercial juke-box intentions; one of them, *Sweet Substitute,* an especially beautiful blues-tinged ballad.

And still he was the Roll. He spent a great deal of time at his recording sessions arguing, perhaps bickering, with the producer in the engineering booth. On one occasion his bassist, Wellman Braud (who was from New Orleans and who had played with some of the best, including Ellington), was fed up with the stalling and bossing and the secret dealing, and complained, "Come on, let's go; let's play something." Morton grabbed a slip of music paper, wrote out a difficult bass part, and handed it to Braud, saying, "Here, practice this." And as he made his way back to his arguments in the recording booth, he muttered to the room at large, "That ought to hold him."

In 1940, Jelly Roll Morton lashed his two cars together, his Lincoln and his Cadillac, loaded in most of his worldly possessions, and set out for California. He said that his godmother was dying and his godfather was blind and needed help, but perhaps that was just an excuse. For two days a week in Los Angeles he was rehearsing a big band, with himself as a leader and occasional soloist and Buster Wilson as regular pianist, for still another comeback and the big time. The other five days of the week Morton might have to spend ill in bed with "heart trouble and asthma." In April 1941, he sent a note back to New York; it was hurriedly scrawled across an application blank for a money order in the post office; "Will write soon. Still sick," it said.

In July 1941, a Catholic High Requiem Mass was held for Ferdinand Morton.

Kid Ory and the members of Ory's band were his pallbearers.

Perhaps best personal tribute to his spirit is in his song, *The Winin' Boy.*

> I'm a poor boy, a long way from home.
> I'm a poor boy, a long, long way from home.
> Long way, I'm a poor boy from home.
> I'm gonna try to never roam alone . . .

And then the sudden recovery of his last line:

I'm the Winin' boy, don't deny my name!

There are reasons to call this man with the clown's obscene nickname important. In him, New Orleans jazz produced one of its best composers and leaders, one of its best masters of form, one of its only theorists. Most important, in him jazz produced one of its first and most durable artists.

Recordings

"The King of New Orleans Jazz," Jelly Roll Morton and his Red Hot Peppers, RCA Victor LPM 1649. (Sixteen from Morton's best Victors, but including the strange composite tape of *Dead Man Blues*.)

"Jelly Roll Morton: Stomps and Joys," RCA Victor LPV-508, and the very uneven RCA Victor LPV-524.

"Jelly Roll Morton Piano Solos," Riverside RLP 12-111.

"The Incomparable Jelly Roll Morton," Riverside RLP 12-128.

"Back O' Town," King Oliver, Riverside RLP 12-130. (The two Oliver-Morton duets are included.)

"New Orleans Memories," Jelly Roll Morton, Mainstream S/6020.

"Jelly Roll Morton: The Library of Congress Recording." Riverside 9001-9012. The Library material was reedited for commercial release (rather strangely so in a couple of spots, but the series is fascinating.) Riverside RLP 132, 133, and 140 condense the musical selections from the series, piano and vocal, into three volumes.

Note: Certain Riverside LP releases are now becoming rare in the United States, and certain European releases greatly supplement the available catalogue of early New Orleans jazz.

References

Armstrong, Lil, "About Early Chicago Days." *Down Beat,* June 1, 1951.

Barker, Danny, "Jelly Roll Morton in New York." *Jazz Panorama,* Collier, 1964.

Blesh, Rudi, and Harriett Janis, *They All Played Ragtime.* Oak, 1966.

Bontemps, Arna, and Jack Conroy, "An American Original (Jelly Roll Morton)." From *Jam Session,* edited by Ralph J. Gleason, Putnam, 1958.

Carew, Roy, "Let Jelly Roll Speak for Himself." *Record Changer,* December 1952.

————, "New Orleans Recollections." *Record Changer,* November 1943.

Collins, Mary, and John W. Miner, "From Lee Collins' Story." *Evergreen Review,* March 1965.

Davin, Tom, "Conversations with James P. Johnson." *Jazz Panorama,* Collier, and *The Jazz Review,* June and August, 1959.

Driggs, Frank, and Thornton Hagert, "Jerome Don Pasqual." *Jazz Journal,* April 1964.

Erskine, Gilbert M., "Last of the New Orleans Rhythm Kings." *Down Beat,* May 10, 1962.

————, "Little Mitch." *Down Beat,* November 7, 1963.

Gara, Larry, *The Baby Dodds Story.* Contemporary Press, 1959.

"An Interview with Lester Melrose." *Jazz Music,* nos. 16 and 17.

Jepsen, Jorgen Grunnet, *Discography of Jelly Roll Morton,* Vols. 1 and 2. Walter C. Allen, P.O. Box 501, Stanhope, New Jersey.

Kay, George W., "The Shep Allen Story." *Jazz Journal,* February 1963.

Keepnews, Orin, "Jelly Roll Morton." From *The Jazz Makers,* edited by Nat Shapiro and Nat Hentoff. Evergreen, 1958.

Lomax, Alan, *Mister Jelly Roll.* Evergreen, 1962.

Lomax, Louis E., "The American Negro's New Comedy Act." *Harper's,* June 1961.

McNarmara, Helen, "Pack My Bags and Make My Getaway: The Odyssey of Jimmy Rushing." *Down Beat,* April 8, 1965.

Morton, Jelly Roll, "A New Orleans Funeral" and "A Discourse on Jazz." From *Jam Session,* edited by Ralph J. Gleason. Putnam.

————, "I Discovered Jazz in 1902." *Frontiers of Jazz,* edited by Ralph de Toledano. Ungar.

Panassie, Hughes, "Jelly Roll Morton on Records." *Frontiers of Jazz,* edited by Ralph de Toledano. Ungar, 1963.

Russell, William, "Jelly Roll Morton and the Frog-i-more Rag." *The Art of Jazz,* edited by Martin Williams. Oxford University Press, 1959.

Shapiro, Nat, and Nat Hentoff, eds., *Hear Me Talkin' to Ya,* Rinehart, 1955, chapter 7.

Simeon, Omer, "Mostly About Morton." *The Jazz Record,* October 1945.

Smith, Charles Edward, liner notes to "Jelly Roll Morton: Stomps and Joys," RCA Victor LPV-508.

Smith, Harrison, "The 'Fablelous' Jelly Roll." *Record Research* for June/July 1957.

Smith, Willie "The Lion," and George Hoefer, *Music on My Mind: The Memoirs of an American Pianist.* Doubleday, 1964.

————, "In My Opinion." *Jazz Journal*, July 1966.
Souchon, Edmond, "Jelly Roll Morton." *The Record Changer*, February 1953.
Stearns, Marshall, *The Story of Jazz*. Signet, 1965.
Steiner, John, "Chicago." In *Jazz*, edited by Nat Hentoff and Albert J. McCarthy, Rinehart, 1959.
Thompson, Kay C., "The First Lady of Storyville, Countess Willie Piazza." *The Record Changer*, February 1951.
Williams, Martin, "Jelly Roll Morton." In *Jazz*, edited by Nat Hentoff and Albert J. McCarthy, Evergreen, 19, 1961.
————, "*Jelly Roll Morton*." Perpetua, 1963.

PAPA JOE

DURING A HOT SUMMER in the late Thirties, Louis Armstrong was playing an engagement in Savannah, Georgia, and took a stroll through the Negro section of the city. He encountered a tired but cheerful old man, standing near a drugstore tending a small vegetable stand. The man was tall, heavy-set, dark, and had a scar over one eye. Armstrong knew him immediately as his one-time mentor, his "Papa Joe"—Joseph, once "King," Oliver—the man who had brought Armstrong out of New Orleans to Chicago and subsequent fame in the mid-Twenties. The younger man broke down and cried, gave him money to buy some clothes and said he was going to send him money regularly. "King Oliver was so powerful," Armstrong was later to say of him, "he used to blow a cornet out of tune every two or three months. My! how that man could blow. . . . He was my inspiration."

By 1937, King Oliver, once billed (not without reason) as "The World's Greatest Jazz Cornetist," had fallen on his worst days. But the odds are high that at the very moment he encountered Armstrong, some trumpet player in one of the big swing bands was quoting Oliver's *Dippermouth Blues* variations note for note or that some arranger was about to interpolate the stop-time breaks from Oliver's *Snag It* into his latest score.

Jazz literature, especially the jazz literature of the Thirties and Forties has its myths; there was the Keats-like story of Bix Beiderbecke, the misunderstood artist destroyed in his youth by a hostile world. Beside it, the story of King Oliver makes a complementary tragedy. Both stories fit perfectly with the nostalgic and sentimentally defensive attitudes which some writers brought to jazz at the time. Oliver's was a medieval tragedy of the good man whom capricious fate had deprived of success and awarded only adversity and failure. And fate was commercialism and the vagaries of popular taste. Oliver could be praised because an appreciative public had flocked to hear him in Chicago in the Twenties, and Oliver could be revered because an insensitive public had abandoned him only a few years later.

The facts don't entirely fit the image of the mild, kindly and put-upon old Oliver, ekeing out his last days, earning eating money by selling vegetables and sweeping down a pool hall. When he called a rehearsal, said drummer Fred Moore, who played with him in 1931, everybody knew they had better be on time. "The King would walk in with the music on his arm and his gun in the bosom of his coat. He would throw everything down on the table and look around to see if everybody was there. Then he would pick up his gun and ask 'Is everybody here?' Everybody reported yes, we were there, then he would put his gun back on the table, and the rehearsal would go on."

Oliver "kept his place" in his younger days in New Orleans with his own little ironies. At white dances he might answer all inquiries about the names of his tunes with, "That was *Who Struck John*." He loved to "play the dozens," the sometimes scatalogical rhyming insult game that is a part of Negro American ethnic lore, with his fellow musicians. He liked to eat a lot and he weighed a lot. He was jealous of Freddy Keppard, Manuel Perez, Bunk Johnson and the others. Buster Bailey, who was clarinetist with Oliver during the Twenties, reveals that he had his reasons: "Joe was a jealous guy. He knew what some of the musicians who came to listen were after, and so he wouldn't play certain numbers. But they'd come in and sneak in and steal the riffs. They'd write down the solos, steal like mad, and then those ideas would come out on *their* records. When Joe would see them coming, he'd play something different, but they'd steal everything."

And the old man knew in his later years that he had made one bad business decision after another, while suspiciously shunning much managerial help and advice.

Without King Oliver, however, without the feeling and the form of his music, and the techniques he discovered with which to express them, jazz as we know it simply could not have been and could not be.

Joseph Oliver's mother was a cook on a plantation near the Louisiana town called Donaldsville, up the river from New Orleans but south of Baton Rouge. Oliver was born on May 11, 1885. Stella, incidentally, whom he later married in New Orleans, grew up only three miles away. One story goes that the blindness in his left eye dated from childhood when, during a kitchen accident involving a fire, some pepper was accidentally thrown in his face.

Oliver came to New Orleans when he was still a boy and worked as a "yardboy" with a Levy family, but he spent his weekends in Mandeville, just across Lake Pontchartrain, with an aunt. His own family later apparently moved to the city and lived in several places around the uptown Garden District. In 1900, Oliver's mother died, and it was then that his older half-sister Victoria Davis, who had tended him as an infant, began to look out for him in earnest—and it was to Victoria Davis that Joseph Oliver addressed his last letters in 1938.

According to Bunk Johnson, Oliver's first teacher was a man named Kenehen who formed a brass band among the children of his uptown neighborhood, with Oliver on cornet. Another story goes that he began on trombone, but blew so loud that his teacher switched him in defense of everybody's eardrums. Nearly everyone agrees he was a slow learner. But Kenehen's youngsters toured a bit nearby, and once got as far as Baton Rouge. When the young Joe Oliver returned from that trip he had a deep scar over his left eye; he would say vaguely that he had been cut in a fight, and nothing more. For the rest of his life he always wore his hat at an angle, and slightly downward over that eye.

Oliver's reputation in the city grew gradually, but he was soon skillful enough to play with the regular brass and dance bands. The details of his early career have been reported variously and the truth is that, like everyone else, he played in several bands at the same time, whenever the jobs came up for the parades and funerals and dances and picnics.

Working parades, the horn players needed strong embouchures. Red Allen has explained, "The roads were rough, and if you stepped into a hole you had to hold on to that horn to not break your notes. Maybe that was the reason King Oliver never marched with the band but always next to it, on the sidewalk, where it was smoother."

Oliver was apparently a rather stern man from his earliest days. One story says that during a dance-hall engagement, when he would stomp his foot to indicate a final chorus to a tune (a general local practice), some of his sidemen began ignoring him and playing through, saying that when they got going they didn't hear his foot. Oliver brought a brick to work the next night and slammed it to the floor when he wanted a ride-out. At other times, Oliver might play with apparent unconcern for the group, with his chair leaning against the back wall of a Storyville joint and his derby cocked over his bad eye, perhaps waiting to take one of the long intermissions he became notorious for at one period.

Like most players, Oliver continued to hold a nonmusical job. No longer a yardboy, he was now a household butler, but his employers were evidently understanding of his other career and would accept substitute help whenever Oliver wanted to fill a job.

The names of the New Orleans bands sound nostalgically elegant to us today—Onward, Magnolia, Olympia, Eagle, Melrose—but perhaps more impressive are the names of some of Oliver's fellow musicians. In the Melrose band, for example, Oliver was associated with Honoré Dutrey, later his trombonist in Chicago and on his first records. The Eagle band had Dutrey also, and it sometimes had Frankie Dusen—Bolden's trombonist and a legendary tough character. And while Oliver was playing with the Magnolia band, so, at various times were Lorenzo Tio, Sr. and George Baquet, clarinets; George "Pops" Foster, bass; and Johnny St. Cyr, guitar and banjo.

Edmond Souchon remembers having sneaked into Storyville with a young friend to hear King Oliver at the Big 25 near Basin Street in about 1907. The youngsters hunted up the oldest clothes they could find, and tore them and rubbed them in the dirt; they gathered a half-dozen copies of The Daily States or the New Orleans Item under their arms and entered Storyville as urchin newsboys.

"Except for faint red lights that shone through half-drawn shutters and the sputtering carbon lights on the corner, there was not much illumination. We could see strange figures peering out through half-open doorways. A new cop on the beat immediately tried to chase us, but the peeping female figures behind the blinds came to our rescue. They hurled invective of such vehemence—'Let them poor newsboys make a livin' you'—that he let us go. We told him we were only going as far as Joe Oliver's saloon to bring him his paper. It seemed to satisfy him."

They could now hear the music from half a block away. The place itself was twice as long as it was wide, a one-story, wooden-frame building running lengthwise along the street, with a bar at the Iberville end and an area for dancing to the rear, near Canal Street. There was a telegraph pole, just in front, across a deep and three-foot-wide gutter, and the boys sought refuge in its shadow.

"Sometimes Oliver would come outside for a breather. We wondered how we might approach him to get him to say a few words to us. Finally, I ventured, 'Mr. Oliver, here is the paper you ordered.' I'll never forget how big and tough he looked! His brown derby was tilted low over one eye, his shirt collar was open at the neck, and a bright red undershirt peeked out at the V. Wide suspenders held up an expanse of trousers of unbelievable width. He looked at us and said, 'You know damn well, white boy, I never ordered no paper.' We thought the end of the world had come. Suddenly, we realized that he had not spoken loud enough for anyone to hear but us! Then he went on, much more friendly, 'I been knowin' you kids were hanging around here to listen to my music. Do you think I'm going to chase you away for that? This is a rough neighborhood, kids, and I don't want you to get into trouble. Keep out of sight and go home at a decent time.' We were in! We had really made it!"

Not all the New Orleans players were continuously part-time musicians, for gradually more and more of them found regular jobs playing in the various bars and cabarets of Storyville; they became full-time musicians with part-time day jobs. At one point before much local fame had reached him, Oliver was playing with the quartet of pianist-composer Richard M. Jones (and including clarinetist Big Eye Louis Nelson) at the Abadie cabaret at Marais and Bienville streets, while down the street, Pete Lala's, an important tourist attraction, was featuring Freddy Keppard and getting the crowds. Jones remembered, "Joe Oliver came over to me and commanded in a nervous, harsh voice, 'Get in B-flat.' He didn't even mention a tune, just said, 'Get in B-flat.' I did, and Joe walked out on the sidewalk, lifted his horn to his lips, and blew the most beautiful stuff I have ever heard. People started pouring out of the other spots along the street to see who was blowing all that horn. Before long, our place was full and Joe came in, smiling, and said, 'Now that——won't bother me no more.'

"From then on, our place was full every night."

Oliver was developing his own plaintive trumpet style by using cups and bottles to alter his sound. Mutt Carey remembered, "Joe Oliver was very strong. He was the greatest freak trumpet player I ever knew. He did most of his playing with cups, glasses, buckets, and mutes. He was the best gut-bucket man I ever heard. I called him freak because the sounds he made were not made by the valves but through these artificial devices. In contrast, Louis played everything through the horn. . . . Some writers claimed I was the first one to use mutes and buckets but it wasn't so. I got to give Joe Oliver credit for introducing them. Joe could make his horn sound like a holy roller meeting. . . . God, what that man could do with his horn!"

Oliver worked out his effects with his cornet and his cups, water glasses, rubber suction ends of a plumber's plunger, and bottles with great care and deliberateness. Players who heard him love to tell how he could imitate a baby crying or how he would tell off a defeated rival at the end of a cutting contest by "talking" with his cornet and mute, "Get that goddam cornet out of here!" But Oliver knew how to put all of these effects to strictly musical use, and in so doing he was of course expanding the expressive range and resourcefulness of jazz. Burnett James has commented, "Oliver himself possessed great melodic sensitivity; all the same, it seems likely that he often used his mutes for purely effective purposes because he found it went down well with the contemporary audiences. I make no charge of charlatanism or insincerity; it was simply a condition under which he was accustomed to working."

In 1911, Freddy Keppard gave up his local leadership of the Olympia Band and began his tour with the Original Creole

Orchestra, and violinist A. J. Piron took over the Olympia and replaced Keppard with Joe Oliver. Piron's musical intentions were multitudinous and he had a dance group going, at the same time playing "society" jobs and featuring his own violin. Piron was undoubtedly a good teacher and it seems a reasonable conjecture that Oliver's formal knowledge of music benefited from such work. It was also at about this time that Oliver got to know Clarence Williams and made a tour around Louisiana. Williams was doing comedy and the tour was not very successful, but it established a friendship that was to mean a great deal to Oliver in later years.

By 1914, Williams was managing the Lala Café and he had booked Kid Ory's band, which had Johnny Dodds on clarinet and Ed Garland on bass. Ory hired Oliver to replace his trumpeter, and began to bill him as "King." The implication was that the crown had passed from Bolden and Keppard to Oliver; the difference, of course, was that the title was no longer awarded by an adoring public but by a band leader looking for an attractive billing. Clearly, the communal music of New Orleans was changing its character. (For the record, many illustrious players passed in and out of this Ory group—the clarinet, for example, was also handled by Sidney Bechet, Jimmy Noone, and Albert Nicholas.)

Storyville was declared out of bounds on November 10, 1917. As Louis Armstrong has put it, "Before they clamped down on Storyville there were an awful lot of killings going on. . . . Mysterious ones too. . . . Several sailors were all messed up—robbed and killed. . . . That's one of the main reasons for the closing of Storyville. . . . Those prostitutes commenced to having their pimps—hide somewheres around and either rob—or bash their brains in—anything to get that money—That's when the United States Navy commenced to getting warm. . . . And brother when they became warm—that meant trouble and more trouble. Not only for the vice displayers but for all the poor working people who made their living in Storyville such as cooks—waiters—maids—musicians—butlers—dishwashers—and lots of people whom were in different vocations. . . . I'm telling you—it was a sad sad situation for anybody to witness."

It was bassist Bill Johnson who had persuaded the first New

Orleans band to leave the city in 1911—Freddy Keppard and the Original Creole Band. And early in 1918 Johnson sent to New Orleans for cornetist Buddy Petit to join him in Chicago at the Royal Gardens Café. Petit would not come, and Johnson asked for Joe Oliver. Oliver left for Chicago.

Clarinetist Jimmy Noone left New Orleans with Oliver, and, along with drummer Paul Barbarin, the two of them did join Johnson at the Royal Gardens Café. But for a while Oliver doubled in another group at the Dreamland Café led by Lawrence Duhé and featuring such New Orleans players as trombonist Roy Palmer, clarinetist Sidney Bechet, bassist Wellman Braud, and drummer Minor Hall. Lil Hardin was on piano in Duhé's group. (Duke's name is sometimes given as Dewey.)

Oliver's reputation rose and by January of 1920 he was leading his own band at the Dreamland Café. Singer Alberta Hunter remembered, "That Dreamland was some place. It was *big* and always packed. And you had to be a singer then—there were no microphones and those bands were marvelous. King Oliver's band was there when I started (Louis wasn't with him yet), and, I'm telling you, you could sing one chorus or fifty or sixty choruses and that band would never be a beat away. And they'd always end on the same note and at the same time the singer did. . . . Singers then would go around from table to table singin' to each table, hustlin' dollars in tips. But nobody at the other tables would get mad when they couldn't hear you. I made a lot of money that way."

At the same time Oliver now doubled from one to six in the morning at a gangster hangout on State Street (it also featured boxing) called the Pekin Café, a remodeled theatre, and that latter group featured Johnny Dodds, Honoré Dutrey, Lil Hardin, Ed Garland, and Minor Hall.

Not all New Orleans jazzmen who left had headed for Chicago of course. There had been a small contingent in California since Keppard's first visit, and Kid Ory had joined them in 1919. In 1921, the manager of a San Francisco taxi dancehall called the Pergola Dance Pavillion had heard Ory and wanted his music. Ory had other contracts, and recommended that the manager send for Oliver to "play continuously, dance music as

played in so-called 'nickle dances,' . . . between 8 and 12 P.M."
Oliver accepted.

A well-known photograph of the Oliver band taken in 1921
in California shows Minor Hall, Honoré Dutrey, Oliver (playing
with a mute), Lil Hardin (dressed in gingham), saxophonist
David Jones, Johnny Dodds, Jimmy Palao on violin, and Ed
Garland.

Johnny Dodds was often called "Toilet" by his fellow New
Orleans musicians, and the nickname was a deep compliment to
his blues playing. To singer Tommy Brookins, he was "the greatest clarinetist that ever lived and I've never heard any clarinetist
play like he did in the lower register of his instrument."

Johnny and his brother Warren "Baby," twelve years his
junior, were New Orleans born, and were decidedly uptown
Negro, not downtown colored Creole. Johnny had begun playing as a child on a tin flute or pennywhistle, with Baby accompanying on tin cans with chair rounds. The household was
musical; his father and an uncle played violin, a sister played
melodeon, there were several harmonicas around the place, and
his father also constructed homemade reed instruments from
bamboo. When Johnny Dodds' toy whistle broke, his father
brought home a real clarinet.

But becoming a professional musician was perhaps another
thing, for even in a poor Negro household, musicians were apt
to be thought of as "no good." And since he was very likely to
work in Storyville, a musician was often less than no good.

Johnny Dodds' first clarinet inspiration was Sidney Bechet.
By the time he was nineteen, he was working at various odd
jobs in the day and playing clarinet when and where he could
at night, usually for pennies on the curbstone, with a little group
of his own. Already he had the biggest clarinet sound anyone
had ever heard.

It was apparently George "Pops" Foster, the bass player, who
one day heard him practicing, thought him too good to be
working for change on street corners, and recommended him
to Kid Ory. He worked for Ory in New Orleans between 1911
and 1917, as work presented itself. One of his associates with

Ory was of course King Oliver. In 1917, Johnny Dodds joined trumpeter Mutt Carey's four-piece ensemble for a vaudeville tour with a group called "Mack's Merrymakers"; when that show passed through Chicago, Carey left it to try the Windy City and Johnny rejoined Ory back home in New Orleans. But in 1920, when Oliver landed his job at the Dreamland, he had sent for Johnny Dodds. Dodds arrived with his clarinet wrapped in newspapers.

Later, when the Dodds brothers and Honoré Dutrey and the others left Oliver in 1924 (to move ahead of Oliver's story for a moment), Johnny took a group into Burt Kelly's Stable where he remained for six years. His trumpeter was either Freddy Keppard or, later, Natty Dominique.

It was Johnny Dodds' most successful period. Tommy Brookins has reported that "no one had a fixed salary but the tips were such that they used to make between a $125 and $170 a week. I ought to say that the place was frequented by gangsters and that they had easy money."

Johnny Dodds recorded under his own name for Paramount, Brunswick, Vocalion, Okeh, Victor, and, as a sideman on records, he worked for Louis Armstrong, Ida Cox, Jelly Roll Morton, Lovie Austin, Jimmy Blythe, and (quite literally) dozens of others. He was, according to George Mitchell, "a quiet and serious man . . . but how Johnny could play that clarinet! He couldn't read music, but if he played through a thing once, he had it. He kept us all going on those records. . . ."

It has been asserted that Johnny Dodds "never made a bad record." That is the sort of tribute which can probably do no good to any man's reputation. (And he did make a few records which seem deliberately corny, like *San* and *Clarinet Wobble*.) But he was a great blues player, as the South-side Negro audiences who bought his records knew, and as his moving choruses in slow sections of Louis Armstrong's Hot Five versions of *Gully Low Blues* and *S.O.L. Blues* can attest. He was also an excellent player in an older, pre-Armstrong "stomp" style, and the best recorded solo example of this driving, punching Johnny Dodds is probably Jimmy Blythe's piece called *Ape Man*, by the little trio with the marvelous name of "Blythe's Washboard Ragamuffins." Johnny Dodds was also a moving ensemble player; try him on Armstrong's *Skit-dat-de-dat* if his recorded work with Oliver's ensembles is not immediately convincing.

Johnny Dodds had been a good businessman, promoting record dates and jobs for himself and his brother, and saving his money. But by the Thirties he was no longer able to work as a musician, and he earned his living driving a taxi. It was because of the depression partly, no doubt. And partly the fact that Dodds' style belonged to the Twenties. Perhaps as a self-taught and, in a sense, rudimentary player, Johnny Dodds had played his music by 1930.

Johnny Dodds recorded in 1938 and again in June 1940, when there had begun the earnest revival of interest in New Orleans jazz which followed on the publication of *Jazzmen*. But the latter records were almost his last musical job, for he died suddenly of a stroke on August 8, 1940.

Lil Hardin, the pianist from Memphis and Fisk University, later to be Louis Armstrong's second wife, has spoken of the character of the Oliver men, "King Oliver was sober. . . . He smoked cigars, but he didn't drink. None of them drank hardly. And Dutrey, he was a very business sort of a fellow. He was always buying property or something."

In California the band played for nickel dances for six months, and then Minor Hall left, somewhat chagrined at Oliver's stern discipline. Oliver sent for Baby Dodds. Brother Johnny Dodds had been against it. "No, that guy can't play enough drums. He never will play. He drinks too much." But Davy Jones had worked with Baby on the riverboats and knew more about his recent style: "If you can get that fellow, you better get him. Don't let him get away from you or you'll be sorry." The event had a special meaning for the drummer who spoke in his autobiography of the special companionship of New Orleans groups. "The musicians of those days were remarkable men. When the leader of an orchestra would hire a man, there was no jealousy in the gang. Everybody took him in as a brother, and he was treated accordingly. If a fellow came to work with a sandwich or an orange, the new man would be offered a piece of it. That's the way they were. They believed in harmony. . . . If those men would happen to like you enough to pick you up, they would either make a musician out of you, or you wouldn't be any musician. In their way, they were rough, but in a way they weren't rough. Everything they told you they would make you do for your own benefit."

The Oliver band moved south to Los Angeles and there Oliver also appeared with a large orchestra led by Jelly Roll Morton, including three trumpets and three reeds. Oliver later went back to Oakland, but a reengagement at the Pergola fell through, and they moved into another dancehall. Soon, only the Dodds brothers, Ed Garland, and Oliver were left for a job in Oakland, and Ory briefly joined them again.

In 1922, King Oliver returned to Chicago and was booked into the Lincoln Gardens, the Royal Gardens renamed, and suddenly success and fame caught up to him. He had Honoré Dutrey on trombone, and Johnny and Baby Dodds. The music affected not only the public; musicians from all over the country, who had long been aware of the New Orleans style as such, suddenly began talking about the Oliver band, which played the style with a comparative instrumental sophistication but also had the spontaneous passion they knew in the Negro folk idiom as well. Clarinetist Garvin Bushell says that trumpeter Bubber Miley, then touring with singer Mamie Smith, came upon Oliver one evening, and he and Miley went back often. "It was the first time I'd heard New Orleans jazz to any advantage and I studied them every night for the entire week we were in town. I was very much impressed with their blues and their sound. The trumpets and clarinets in the East had a better 'legitimate' quality, but *their* sound touched you more. It was less cultivated but more impressive of how the people felt. Bubber and I sat there with our mouths open.

"We talked with the Dodds brothers. They felt very highly about what they were playing as though they knew they were doing something new that nobody else could do. I'd say they did regard themselves as artists in the sense we use the term today. . . . I'd heard a New Orleans band that played a lot where a carnival was taking place. It was the Thomas New Orleans Jug Band, and it was more primitive than Oliver's. . . . It had the same beat as Oliver's—what we called in Ohio the 'shimmy' beat. They played mostly blues and they played four beat, as did Oliver. . . . After we'd heard Oliver and Dodds, they were our criterion."

The Lincoln Gardens, the old Thirty-first Street Royal Gardens renamed, was basically an empty room which could hold about six or seven hundred people. On one side was a balcony with tables and around the dance floor below were benches. Drummer George Wettling described it this way: "There was a painted canvas sign about two-by-four feet square hanging outside the beat-looking building that housed the Lincoln Gardens Café, a sign that read "King Oliver and His Creole Jazz Band." From the looks of the place on the outside one would never guess that on the inside was the hottest band ever to sit on a bandstand. But once you got through the crowded hallway into the café proper it was a sight to behold.

"The most striking thing that hit your eye once you got into the hall was a big crystal ball that was made of small pieces of reflecting glass and hung over the center of the dance floor. A couple of spotlights shone on the big ball as it turned and threw reflected spots of light all over the room and the dancers. Usually they'd dance the Bunny Hug to a slow blues like *London Blues* or some other tune in a like slow-blues tempo, and how the dancers would grind away. The ceiling of the place was made lower than it actually was by chicken wire that was stretched out and over the wire were spread great bunches of artificial maple leaves. I'll guarantee that chicken wire was the only artificial thing in the place."

Trumpeter George Mitchell told Gilbert Erskine, "The Lincoln Gardens was a large place, but there were usually so many people in there that you could hardly turn around. The main floor was covered with tables, and at the far end was a raised platform for dancers. Beyond it was another platform for the band. Baby Dodds was on the left, the bass on the right; Lil Hardin was right in the middle, right behind the horns. . . . Joe controlled the band with his feet. Even when everyone was playing loud and fast, you could hear BUMP, BUMP, his feet stomping between the beats, signaling another chorus or break. . . . The crowds loved that band, and Joe did his best to please them."

Oliver soon decided to use a second cornet—to fulfill the role that Oliver had played in New Orleans behind Manuel Perez and that Bunk Johnson had played behind Buddy Bolden. In 1922, a young Louis Armstrong received a telegram to come to Chicago. Lil Hardin remembers that they all talked about "Little Louie" for months before he arrived, but he didn't look so little when he got there and his playing was anything but little. "King Oliver . . . said to me one night," she has reported, "that Louis could play better than he could. He said, 'But as long as I got him with me, he won't be able to get ahead of me. I'll still be king.'"

More and more, there were people coming not to dance, but to listen at the Lincoln Gardens, and of course particularly musicians. Lil Hardin continues, "A bunch of white musicians, ten, twelve, fifteen, sometimes twenty would come, and they would row up right in front of the bandstand. . . . Louis and Joe said they were some of Paul Whiteman's band and that Bix was in the bunch. . . . They used to talk to Louis and King Oliver and Johnny. . . . Several of them would sit in occasionally. But they would listen so intently."

And Wettling has said, "There were no musical papers out then to tell you what was supposed to be hot and what wasn't. You just had to know. . . ." Wettling came with a young fan named Gootch who knew, and about this time Eddie Condon, Floyd O'Brien and the other young Chicagoans were gathering nightly. If they looked old enough (like Wettling), they came inside; if they didn't, they might get away with sitting on the curbstone outside and hearing what they could from there, which was probably a lot. "If anyone ever looked good in front of a band," said Wettling, "it was Joe Oliver. He had a way of standing there in front of Louie, Johnny, and Baby Dodds and the other cats, that was too much. I think one of the greatest thrills I ever got was hearing Joe play *Dipper Mouth Blues*. He and Louie Armstrong had some breaks they played together that I've never heard played since. I don't know how they knew what was coming up next, but they would play those breaks and never miss. Joe would stand there fingering his horn with his right hand and working his mute with his left, and how he would rock the place. Unless you were lucky enough to hear that band in the flesh you can't imagine how they played and

what swing they got. After they would knock everybody out
with about forty minutes of *High Society,* Joe would look down
at me and wink and then say 'Hotter than a forty-five.'

"They always had a water pail on the stand with a big piece
of ice in it and a dipper. Anyone who got thirsty would just go
over to the bucket and help himself to a drink. Usually this
was after they had played for about an hour. The place was
informal and if the boys in the band wanted to take their coats
off and really get comfortable they did."

George Mitchell was one of those who knew how Oliver
and Armstrong would execute the spontaneous breaks together.
"Louis was marvelous, and he learned everything fast. Joe
would play a tag at the end of a chorus and use the tag later in
a cornet break. Louis would listen to the tag and play a harmony
part, right along with Joe in the break."

Saxophonist Bud Freeman was taken there by drummer Dave
Tough. He told Ira Gitler in a *Down Beat* interview, "Dave was
the first to introduce me to jazz as played by the real players,
and that was the old King Oliver Band. . . . Dave had been
going to hear them since he was about fifteen. . . . I'll never
forget how beautifully they treated us. They seemed to know
that we were there for the music."

Baby Dodds hated to quit when 3 A.M. came. "We worked
to make music, and we played music to make people like it. . . .
Sometimes the band played so softly you could hardly hear it. . . .
You could hear the people's feet dancing."

The year following Armstrong's arrival, the Lincoln Gardens
group, with some slight changes in personnel, toured a bit
through the nearby Middle West. And more important, on March
31, 1923, the band entered the studios of the Gennett Record
Company in Richmond, Indiana. With these recordings, crude
as they are technically, a legendary jazz band set down at least
glimpses of its power for posterity. Baby Dodds remembered the
Gennett first session this way: "Joe Oliver got the contract
through someone who had heard the band play at the Gardens
and Joe decided which tunes we would record. They were all
numbers which we had worked out many times on the bandstand. We journeyed from Chicago to Richmond by train and
we did all that recording in one day because none of us had

quarters to sleep in Richmond. We went in the morning and came back at night. Of course everybody was on edge. We were all working hard and perspirations as big as a thumb dropped off us. Even Joe Oliver was nervous; Joe was no different from any of the rest. The only really smooth-working person there was Lil Armstrong. She was very unconcerned and much at ease." As a testament to his own nervousness Baby Dodds also confessed that the famous shout of, "Oh, play that thing" in *Dipper Mouth Blues* came about because (as they played) he himself forgot his drum break, and an alert Bill Johnson covered for him with a holler. The effect remained in the piece.

The calmer Lil Hardin Armstrong herself remembers the first Oliver Gennett session, "We were recording in a great big horn then, you know the style then. And the band was around the horn. And Louis was there, right there, as he always was, right next to Joe. It didn't work out. You couldn't hear Joe's playing. So they moved Louis 'way over in the corner, away from the band. He was looking so sad. And I'd look at him and smile—you know. That's the only way they could get the balance. Louis was, well he was at least 12 or 15 feet from us on the whole session."

Altogether, King Oliver's Creole Jazz Band recorded some thirty-seven sides for four different labels that have so far been released, if we include alternate "takes" of the same piece made at the same session. (There are some further alternate takes from Gennett sessions in existence, but they are still unreleased.) They are among the most celebrated recordings in jazz history, and many of them have been constantly in print in the United States and abroad except for a brief period during the Thirties. Today Oliver's greatest reputation rests on them, and they are a basic reason that we are interested in his story. They do not have merely historical or documentary interest, and their emotional impact cuts across the years.

Aside from the great energy of emotion and rhythm, which does come through the crude recording, the most immediately impressive characteristic of the music of King Oliver's Creole Jazz Band is its unity, the wonderful integration of parts with which the individual players contribute to a dense, often heterophonic texture of improvised melodies. The tempos are right, the excitement of the music is projected with firmness and ease, and the peaks and climaxes come with musical excitement rather than personal frenzy, with each individual in exact control of what he is about.

It took a kind of individual and collective discipline and consistency. There is obviously less control from the band's leadership, less control due to rehearsal and prearrangement, than there was in Jelly Roll Morton's music. Morton maintained a balance between the leader-composer and his group. In the Oliver band, balance is a result of the intuitive understanding of the individual players for themselves and for each other.

Nearly everyone who has been exposed to jazz knows more or less how the style goes, for New Orleans jazz has been popularized since 1917. But Oliver's music represents artistically a peak for the style, a final brilliant flowering before a decline. The wonderfully continuous rhythmic momentum of the band establishes a 4/4 movement. Oliver's phrasing hints at rhythmic things to come, as Armstrong's phrasing already begins to carry them out. Individually, several of the other players in the group did not quite grasp this new manner of making rhythm and melody, and the ensemble cohesion of this music therefore seems all the more remarkable.

One cannot hear their records without sooner or later giving his attention to the details which make this momentum and cohesion possible: the way that Johnny Dodds' improvised countermelodies fill in between the trumpet's melodies and almost seem to lead them from one phrase to the next. Honoré Dutrey was a limited trombonist, with limited lung power, limited technique, and limited ideas. But he knew his place in the ensemble and he could fulfill it with graceful agility.

From the rhythm instruments, there is wonderful sympathetic propulsion. Hear them behind Oliver's delightful choruses on *Alligator Hop*. Or hear the spontaneously appropriate hints at New Orleans tango rhythm that occur to Lil Armstrong during *Weatherbird Rag* and *Mandy Lee Blues* and *Snake Rag*, to be picked up by Dutrey, and carried along until just the tantalizing moment-too-soon before monotony.

Then there is the marvelous interplay between Oliver and Armstrong—marvelous on first hearing, and durably marvelous.

On the Paramount version of *Riverside Blues,* on the Columbia *London Blues.* And notice the contribution of each trumpeter on the third strain of *Chattanooga Stomp.* The section opens in harmony between a muted Oliver and the clarinet. Gradually the two instruments pull further apart until they play almost polyphonically. Then Armstrong breaks through the last notes of their chorus, calling to the group that it is time now to improvise together for thirty-two bars. He is immediately joined by Oliver, who could not wait to begin the interplay, it seems.

Snake Rag preserves some of the famous unison breaks between Oliver and Armstrong that have become legend. The rhythm stops momentarily and the two cornetists rattle off together an unexpectedly suspenseful phrase until the band rejoins them. As we have seen, the cornetists would amaze the audience of dancers and musicians at the Lincoln Gardens with these breaks, coming up with different but perfectly executed phrases each time with no apparent signal or clue. But Armstrong, like George Mitchell above, later revealed that Oliver would telegraph him the break by playing it as part of his improvisation in the previous chorus.

Larry Gushee has written of the phenomenal character of the Creole Band's discipline "which chiefly finds expression as consistency and limitation. . . . Begin with a group of musicians out of the common run, who are guided by some dominant principle or personality and the resultant sound will be truly unique, pleasing to the ears because it is musical, to the soul because it is integral. . . . We have no record of how Louis sounded before he came to Chicago—we know he is full of the spirit of King Joe although their ideas of instrumental tone were divergent. Johnny Dodds' rare gift [is] . . . phrasing, his ability to use his clarinet to bridge the gap between trumpet phrases . . . and to place the final note of his phrase on the beginning of a trumpet phrase. . . . A riff produces somewhat the same kind of excitement as does Oliver's 'consistency' stemming ultimately from the irritation born of sameness and expectation of change unfulfilled . . . the excitement of riffs, however, is bought too cheap . . . most effective in the physical presence of a band. The Creole Band's way is less obvious, more complex, and, in the long run, makes a *record* that remains satisfying year after year. . . . This band . . . was one of the very best that jazz has ever known."

On Baby Dodds' contribution to these records, limited as Dodds was mainly to his wood blocks because of the crude recording technique, Bruce King has commented in detail. "On *Chimes Blues* we hear him playing subtle variations on his blocks, syncopating his beat, playing in double time, using shuffle rhythms, and playing rolls. On *Froggie Moore* he uses a different variation of his beat on each theme, developing his part with shifting accents, and Spanish rhythms. On *Canal Street Blues* his wood blocks interplay with the horns. Behind Johnny Dodds' solo his figures first follow the descending runs of the clarinet and then contrast with them during the second half of the chorus. Perhaps he is at his best on *Mandy Lee Blues* where his part is completely constructed from various beats and syncopations which follow the melody. Here we find lots of double-time figures, always implying contrasting time values above the stated beat. On *Snake Rag* we hear him phrasing in unison with the horns, then double timing the second theme, changing his beats on the later choruses, and simplifying his patterns for the ride-out. There is a progressive movement from order to excitement to order."

The group's repertory on records did not include the various popular hits it was surely required to play on the job. The band recorded its specialties, most of them the compositions of Oliver, Lil Hardin, Louis Armstrong, and old New Orleans acquaintances like A. J. Piron and Alphonse Picou. This apparently involved a limited number of selections. At any rate, the group did record several of these numbers twice, sometimes in alternate "takes" at the same session, and sometimes also in different versions for different record companies. Nothing enables us to get inside this music so well, and to grasp the manner and extent of the improvising of its players, as comparing the two versions of *Snake Rag*, of *Working Man Blues*, of *Riverside Blues*, of *Dippermouth Blues*, and, finally, the three versions of *Mabel's Dream*.

The King Oliver band recorded *Mabel's Dream* for Columbia and for Paramount, and Paramount released two different "takes" that were recorded consecutively on the same day. The three versions make a fascinating comparison. The Columbia version was done first, but in style it seems the last. It is faster, more spirited, and, as we shall see, Armstrong dominates an important part of it. The two Paramount versions are Oliver's. They are very different and they probably reveal more about Oliver's style than anything we have on records.

Mabel's Dream is a piece in three themes, like a ragtime composition and like many other pieces in Oliver's repertory. Although the piece is structured like a rag, it is not played with the clipped rhythms, simple syncopations, and simple optimism of ragtime. The Oliver band, one might say, plays this rag as if it were a blues, with more complex and varied rhythms, more complex and deeper emotion.

The first theme amounts to an introduction. The second is built on a nice little descending phrase, which is filled out in the performance by stop-time breaks played by the clarinet and the trombone. The three different recordings treat this opening material pretty much the same way, even to the clarinet-trombone breaks, but on the faster Columbia version the ensemble texture seems a little denser.

The third theme is almost a succession of chords, the melody tied very closely to the harmony—Jelly Roll Morton would have called this the "organ section."

On each of the two Paramount takes of *Mabel's Dream*, Oliver in his solo takes the same general approach to the third section. He has three choruses, and each time he makes of them a developing set of related variations. On each take, his theme statement is fairly straight, with a minimum departure from the melody as written. This accomplished, Oliver's first intention is to begin to make his improvisation swing harder. He recasts the line, rephrases it, and accentuates the rhythm by note-doublings here and there.

On the first Paramount version, he first reduces his theme to a bare minimum of notes, but in the open places in the melody, in the rests, he fills in with original blueslike melodic fragments —one could call this a distillation of the theme plus an obligatto, both played by the same instrument. And of course, along with the greater rhythmic emphasis and the melodic transformation, the feeling is changing. The final variation is the most drastic departure, the most blueslike melody, and to play it he used his wa-wa mute.

In the second Paramount *Mabel's Dream*, the general outline is the same, but Oliver's second chorus has more swing and departs further from the written melody. His third chorus is entirely original—original in itself and quite different from the one he had just improvised on the previous take. This time, it is as if Oliver had taken the little blueslike interpolations and comments he interjected into the first two choruses, and developed them until they gradually took over and dictated the content of his third chorus.

But in both versions the episode of the third theme and its variations is a whole, as if Oliver had thought out all three of his choruses at once in a classic plan.

During 1924, the King Oliver band toured through the Middle West on the Orpheum Theatre circuit, through Wisconsin, Michigan, Ohio, even to Pennsylvania. But the personnel was in a state of flux, and we discover that John Lindsey and Zue Robinson have each been in on trombone in place of Dutrey; we find that Buster Bailey and then Albert Nicholas and Rudy Jackson are on reeds and that Charlie Jackson is sometimes on bass saxophone; we find Bud Scott replacing on banjo and Clifford "Snags" Jones replacing on drums.

Oliver always wanted his men to be "band men," but Lil Armstrong's explanation indicates there was a little more to all the changes of sidemen than that. "Johnny Dodds found out that Joe had been collecting $95 for each member of the band, while he had been paying us $75. So naturally he had been making $20 a week a piece off us for I don't know how long. So Johnny Dodds and Baby Dodds, they threatened to beat Joe up. So Joe brought his pistol every night to work in his trumpet case in case anything happened. Everybody gave in the notice except Louis. Louis always was so crazy about Joe, you know he was his idol, so he wouldn't quit. If Louis didn't quit, so naturally I wouldn't quit. So Louis and I stayed with Joe. Now that is why you don't find Dutrey, Johnny Dodds, and Baby Dodds on this Eastern tour with us. He had to replace everybody except Louis and myself."

In June, Armstrong left. Lil had encouraged the move. At first he had no job but soon he was to play with Ollie Powers at the Dreamland Café for three months, and then go to New York in September to join Fletcher Henderson. Oliver sent to New Orleans for Lee Collins. Collins remembered finding George Filhe on trombone, Junie C. Cobb on clarinet and saxophone, Stomp Evans on saxophone, "Diamond Lil" Hardaway on piano, Bud Scott on guitar, Bert Cobb on bass and sousaphone, and Snags Jones on drums, at his first rehearsal with the group.

"Joe Oliver said, 'Lee, for your benefit we are going to open with *Panama Rag*,' and then he stomped off. That band really swung up a breeze and Joe told me to take some choruses. So I did, and the more I would blow with those guys the better I would get. . . . After rehearsal, Joe telephoned his wife, Mrs. Stella, to tell her that he was was bringing Lee Collins home to dinner.

"But I really felt at a disadvantage the first night I played with the Creole Jazz Band at the Lincoln Gardens because Louis had made such a great hit that no one thought he could be replaced.

"Joe called *King Porter Stomp* for the opener and then *Panama*. Everybody gathered around the stand to find out what I could do and see if I was going to be able to make it in that band. . . . Joe was all smiles after we finished playing the first set. Roy [Williams, the bouncer] kidded him, he said, 'Joe, this is the first time I seen you smile since your boy Louis left the band. . . .

" 'That's Lee Collins, my little Creole boy,' Joe laughed. . . .

"Joe Oliver was a fine man. He gave all the cornet players a chance to show what they could do and was not jealous of his musicians.

"The Lincoln Gardens caught fire on Christmas Eve of 1924." For that Christmas Eve night at the Lincoln Gardens, King Oliver had asked pianist Luis Russell to reform his band for him and Russell had sent to New Orleans for reed men Barney Bigard and Albert Nicholas and drummer Paul Barbarin.

King Oliver took a temporary job with a local Chicago orchestra at the Plantation Club called the Symphonic Syncopators and led by Dave Peyton. He received billing as "the world's greatest jazz cornetist," and a contemporary photograph shows the King sitting stoutly and proudly in the midst of Peyton's group, with his music book ostentatiously closed. Gradually Oliver brought

New Orleans players into the group, Albert Nicholas, Barney
Bigard, Paul Barbarin, Luis Russell, trumpeter Tommy Ladnier,
and others, and they soon took over the job as the Dixie Syncopators. All went well until March 1925, when someone tossed
a bomb into the Plantation Club—Chicago was a rough town in
those days—and the police closed the place down.

Oliver's music was changing. We have already noticed that
by this time he might have two, and perhaps three, reed men
in his band. The next King Oliver music that we know is from
recordings on which his group is called, variously, the "Dixie
Syncopators" or the "Savannah Syncopators." It featured a reed
section and some obviously written arrangements and these
innovations have been called Oliver's efforts to keep up with the
times, and even his efforts to go commercial. Indeed, there has
been a great deal of ink spilled in jazz commentary protesting
that saxophones were unknown in New Orleans and quite inappropriate to its music.

Saxophones were not unknown; the earliest photographs of
New Orleans bands show saxes, and apparently the earliest
groups, downtown and uptown, used them on occasion. The
riverboat bands used them. Most of the players were thereby
used to them. Perhaps they were inappropriate to the music, but
some of the earliest recorded examples of New Orleans jazz
feature them. And there is a 1919 photograph of the King Oliver
group playing at a Liberty Bond drive in Chicago that has a
saxophone section.

At any rate, we could see how a band with a reed section
playing written parts could grow out of Oliver's previous music.
There are harmonized passages in the Creole band's recordings
and these could easily be taken over by a sax section. But to
show that such changes are logical and evolutionary is not to
claim that they are necessarily improvements.

Oliver's way of enlarging his band, his gradual approach to
big-band jazz, is interesting, for what he did was substitute the
saxophones for the improvising clarinet of the Creole band. He
retained the rest of his group, but somewhat restricted its license
to improvise. In short, he made a prototype big band out of what
was already there.

In New York, Fletcher Henderson and Don Redman made a

big band by virtually scrapping everything and starting anew. That is, they took a commercial American dance band, with its trumpet, trombone and reed sections, and its general style, and transformed it into a jazz band. The going was slow for Henderson and Redman and it was not until about 1932 that the job was done.

One would expect that Oliver, who was merely modifying an already musically successful approach, would find things a bit more easy, but not so. There is great unevenness in the Dixie Syncopators' recordings, and it is hard to understand how a man whose conception was once so sure and poised could offer such indecisive music only a few years later. The Syncopators' rhythms are usually heavy, the horns and percussion are often unsure, the ensembles are sometimes sloppy. One passage will swing beautifully, the next will flounder. A solo will swing for four bars, not swing for six, then swing again for two more. We know that jazz was undergoing a rhythmic change—that Armstrong was leading the way and that Oliver had helped him find that way. But such knowledge will not fully explain the Syncopators' curious failures.

Curious indeed they are, for a slow blues like *Black Snake Blues*, which would give a folk musician no rhythmic trouble, has in Oliver's version a dull and unmoving pulse thudding away throughout.

The nadir is probably *West End Blues*, a lovely Oliver tune, especially in its second theme, and a piece which Louis Armstrong later elaborated into a revolutionary performance. With the Syncopators, Oliver opens the record with a rhythmically archaic chorus, and there is a clarinet solo, a sort of amateurish burlesque in which blues clichés alternate with corny whinneys. The confusion is completed by Oliver's ending, which is so honest, so proud, and so beautiful.

There are compensations. *Deep Henderson* offers a piano solo by Luis Russell that is shallow emotionally, archaic rhythmically, and, like several of the arrangements Russell wrote for the group, almost a series of tricks melodically. But at the end of the recording, Oliver's horn pierces through magnificently.

Jackass Blues makes the strongest and most revealing sort of case for Oliver's intuitive taste as a player. We know that his solo is a work of art when we hear it, but under scrutiny it is very simple. It is made up of several of his *Dippermouth Blues* phrases put together in a different order, yet that order proves to have its own logic and compositional character. The 1928 *Tin Roof Blues* is another otherwise undistinguished recording, but it is salvaged by a lovely Oliver solo toward the end. (Incidentally, *Tin Roof* is the subject of an error that has been compounded many times in jazz literature; it was not, as has been claimed, stolen by the New Orleans rhythm king from King Oliver's earlier piece, *Jazzin' Babies Blues.* The two pieces have nothing to do with each other, except that a fairly common trombone-bass-tuba theme occurs in both—and in some other contemporary blues pieces as well.)

Some well-known or soon-to-be illustrious men worked with the Syncopators during these years. Besides Luis Russell, there were Albert Nichols, Barney Bigard, Dannell Howard, and (on records) Johnny Dodds and Omer Simeon on reeds. There was Paul Barbarin on drums; there was Kid Ory on trombone. Perhaps, again, it was Oliver's determination that his players should be band men first. For the older style had depended on an intuitive group discipline, but now there were more soloists and therefore more individuality was called for.

There are some nearly complete successes among the Syncopators' records, however, and one man was behind at least two of them. He was an alto saxophonist named Billy Paige. He was from Detroit, and it was while working with him that Don Redman developed as an arranger. Paige recorded with the group between March and May of 1926, and he arranged *Too Bad* and *Snag It*. Paige did not employ the band for the pointless clutter of effects that we hear on the other arrangements, and he used the saxophone section quite musically. And in his pieces the players seem to know where they are going and the rhythmic momentum is exceptional.

Too Bad is fast but the tempo never takes control away from the players. Its little theme, credited to Elmer Schoebel and Billy Meyers, might be monotonous if it were not handled with some rhythmic variety. Paige began with some Charleston figures, executed in a manner that is still as irresistible as it is old-fashioned. Even Barney Bigard's slap-tongue sax solo fits the air of breezy humor Paige establishes. Again Oliver's final entrance gives the performance an emotional grounding and depth. *Too Bad* reveals unexpected resources in this middle-sized band. But perhaps equally important, the arrangement is in a sense a sketch for a later and even better piece called *Wa Wa Wa*.

Paige's score for the blues *Snag It* has the same uncluttered directness and, at the same time, a nice variety of effects. But perhaps the real point of the performance is again Oliver, both because he wrote the piece and because he plays so well on it. There was a second *Snag It* (sometimes issued as *Snag It #2*) made several months later which might prove the point, for Oliver does not play so well on it and it is not as good as the first *Snag It*.

Wa Wa Wa is a fast stomp. If it did nothing else it would preserve, in a single performance, aspects of Oliver's sense of form as a soloist which are merely hinted at elsewhere on the surviving records. It is probably Oliver's most intense playing and its variety of muted brass sounds is, as Walter Allen has remarked, the best evidence we have of New Orleans trumpeter Mutt Carey's pronouncement that "Joe could make his horn sound like a Holy Roller meeting." The effect of Oliver's own musical momentum, and that of his fellow trumpeter on the record, Bob Shoffner, is confirmed when Albert Nicholas loses his rhythmic momentum in his own break. There is also some awkwardness in the saxophone section and the clarinet trio. But the over-all power of *Wa Wa Wa*, its elemental energy and joy, are not hampered by such minor weakness.

If *Wa Wa Wa* is the most artistically durable record from this period, it was not the most successful at the time. Oliver's coupling of *Someday Sweetheart* and *Dead Man Blues* were his best sellers, reportedly to 50,000 copies, very good indeed for those days. *Dead Man Blues* was written by Jelly Roll Morton, who characteristically claimed that it was *Dead Man* that had provoked all the sales for Oliver's record. The truth is that it was probably the Spikes Brothers' *Someday Sweetheart*, which Morton also said he had a compositional hand in.

Luis Russell basted his arrangement of *Sweetheart* with plenty of schmaltz, but Oliver performs the verse with the kind of rhythmic ease that must have touched the young Armstrong deeply. After a rather shallow theme statement from Bert Cobb's tuba, Barney Bigard offers an effective (and entirely corny) sixteen bars of theme. He is answered by thirty-two bars of Johnny Dodds' low register clarinet over stop time chords—a humorous and honest response to the situation. Oliver rehired Dodds just for this recording, knowing full well what he wanted of him, and Dodds' slight parody of the implicit sentimentality of *Someday Swetheart* is very effective.

In its composer's version, *Dead Man Blues* is probably Jelly Roll Morton's recorded masterpiece. Oliver obviously began with the same Melrose stock arrangement of the piece, but his sections do not play with the unity or swing of Morton's studio group and his tempo is a bit fast, so that the mood of his performance becomes coy or affected. A listener is left with a grudging appreciation for Bob Shoffner's behind-the-beat solo.

Almost as big a hit, and the most durable of all of Oliver's pieces, was *Sugar Foot Stomp*, which of course was a new title for Oliver's *Dippermouth Blues*. It is an interesting performance, even if it is not as successful as either of the versions Oliver had done previously with the Creole Jazz Band. Albert Nicholas begins his clarinet solo with a version of Johnny Dodds' original choruses, but almost immediately Nicholas converts his style to that of his real master, Jimmy Noone. Kid Ory's solo shows how trombonists at the time were searching for a solo style and trying to convert their horns from "bass" instruments to brass solo horns. Ory plays some blues ideas that several trumpeters had been using at the time, particularly Louis Armstrong in his *Gut Bucket Blues* solo. Toward the end, Ory plays some ascending figures which call forth riff patterns from the group, and thereby he outlines the kind of thing arrangers were writing for trombone sections the next fifteen years. Oliver finishes the record with his three traditional muted trumpet choruses—that superb episode that somehow resolves anguish and joy—but here his execution seems a bit shaky compared to earlier versions of the piece.

After the Plantation Club was closed in March of 1927, Oliver was able to play dances and short engagements in Milwaukee and Detroit. In St. Louis the group was stranded for a while, but St. Louis was merely a stop on the way, for King Oliver was really en route to New York, where the center of jazz was moving, and where Oliver's ambition dictated he should go.

In May 1927, the Chicago Negro newspaper *Defender* boasted of a favorite adopted son, "King Oliver Made Good at the Savoy," and in another edition, "King Oliver Takes New York by Storm." Oliver did have an engagement at the Savoy, and by 1927 an engagement at the Savoy Ballroom in Harlem was already a test which any ambitious Negro band needed to pass. Oliver's men arrived for the job by the cheapest and slowest trains, and they climbed onto the bandstand still tired and dirty from their trip. They were there for two weeks, which means that they did not fail the test. But neither did they take New York by storm. Oliver had come to New York too late. In another sense, he had been there for years for, as Louis Armstrong has put it, "all this time the cats were coming out from New York with those big shows and picking up on what he was playing. . . . When he got there everybody was playing him. Even I had been there long before him."

Why had Oliver not undertaken the big city before? Simply because the Lincoln Gardens was controlled behind the scenes by the Chicago gangster syndicate, and no booker would have dared incur their wrath by making him an offer.

For the next three years Joseph "King" Oliver had no permanent band and only a few play dates—as one musician put it, he carried his office in his hat. At first he had played one-night jobs in New York and New Jersey, then Philadelphia, Baltimore, and Washington. His musicians had drifted away from him, seeking steadier work, and he had to assemble virtually a new band for each one-night stand. All musicians respected him and his contribution to jazz, but, as we have seen, Oliver's imitators and legitimate followers had preceded him to New York. Most important, Louis Armstrong's reinterpretation of jazz had already captured a generation.

At this time, Oliver missed what was very probably the opportunity of a lifetime. A new club, the Cotton Club, located in Harlem but largely designed for white "slummers," was to open and Oliver was offered the chance to form a band to play for dancing, floor shows, and, as it developed, radio broadcasts which carried the music across the country. According to jazz historian George Hoefer, "Oliver was offered the job by a group of New York hoodlums, who were actually behind the Cotton Club, as a courtesy to the Chicago Capone mob."

Oliver, however, proud and still acting as his own agent, was sure his name and his music were being exploited at the price the club was offering ("somebody brainwashed him about the money," says Red Allen), so the job went to another—a young leader from Washington named Edward Kennedy "Duke" Ellington. Ironically it was at about this time that the young Ellington first began to find himself as a composer chiefly and admittedly through the presence in his orchestra of a young wa-wa trumpeter, Bubber Miley. And Miley's inspiration was of course King Oliver.

Recordings kept King Oliver going during this period. He still had his contract with Vocalion-Brunswick, but the orchestra billed as Oliver's might actually be Elmer Snowden's, or the group Luis Russell had formed out of Oliver's old band, or simply the best men he could get hold of. At the same time, Oliver's old friend Clarence Williams used the trumpeter on instrumental recording dates and as accompanist to several blues singers.

Clarence Williams, according to almost everyone who meets him, was a kind, soft-spoken, and unassuming man. According to the Columbia Records 1927 "race" catalog, he was a composer, player, singer, and accompanist to many of the best blues singers of the day, including Bessie Smith.

Actually, he was a poor singer and only a fair pianist. He was apparently good as a composer. He was also good at revising, refining, and publishing pieces brought to him by other composers. And he was a superb promoter of the songs he published; around that talent all his other talents centered. The Clarence Williams catalog includes *Michigan Water Blues, Baby Won't You Please Come Home, My Bucket's Got a Hole in It, Gulf Coast Blues, Everybody Loves My Baby, I Wish I Could Shimmy Like My Sister Kate, I Found a New Baby, Sugar Blues,* and *You're Some Pretty Doll.*

Clarence Williams was born in Plaquemine, Louisiana, and raised by people who owned the local hotel. As a child, he cooked, mixed drinks, and entertained the guests with songs. With a small group of youngsters he would serenade in the streets and pass the hat. He could play a little piano then—very little, by his own admission.

When he was fourteen, Buddy Bolden came through town. "His trumpet playing excited me so that I said, 'I'm goin' to New Orleans.' I had never heard anything like that before in my whole life."

Almost from its beginning, Clarence Williams's story sounds like Horatio Alger, except that he didn't gain the business by marrying the boss's daughter, and except that the Storyville *milieu* in which Williams operated would probably have upset young Horatio into a willing disbelief. Williams worked hard and took advantage of his opportunities. He made enough money from shining shoes to get a home and some furniture. He went to the hotels and cabarets where Negro musicians worked and said, "Want to get your suits cleaned? Just give 'em to me and pay me on payday." This saved the men the trouble of going to the tailor, and Clarence Williams profited. In his own words, he kept figuring ways to get some money, ways that didn't take a lot of time.

Meanwhile, he played a little piano, sometimes working all night just for drinks or whatever he could get. He listened and he imitated. He got a job at a spaghetti place. He could only play a few pieces—perhaps six—and if someone wanted a waltz, he'd play one of the six in ¾ time. Or he'd say he didn't have the music for a requested piece with him but he'd bring it in the next night. Then he'd go out and learn it. He listened to the lady pianist who demonstrated songs in a music store and pick up the new pieces by ear. Or he'd follow around a truck promoting the local appearance of a big national star like Sophie Tucker, and learn her new hits by ear.

Soon, in order to get the lady in the music store to play a new piece over and over until he learned it, Clarence Williams had had to buy a copy. He decided it would be cheaper if he took piano lessons from her, so he did. After eight lessons, he figured he knew all there was to know about playing the piano. He was also the first local performer to write away to New York for copies of the new sheet music hits.

So, Clarence Williams learned *Some of These Days, Alexander's Ragtime Band, Chinatown, My Chinatown, That's a Plenty.*

Not long after the spaghetti house job, Clarence Williams followed Tony Jackson into Countess Willie Piazza's brothel.

Violinist A. J. Piron was one of the most successful Creole orchestra leaders in that city, working the fine hotels, country clubs, and society dances. Piron played any and all kinds of music, but, as some of his records testify, his groups could play very good New Orleans jazz on occasion. Clarence Williams and Piron formed the first Negro music publishing company in New Orleans, and Williams worked hard to promote their pieces. He would even go from house to house demonstrating his new songs and selling sheet music copies to families and the neighbors who came in to hear. (A very poor household might have a piano in those days, even if no one played it.) At the same time, Williams continued with his other promotions.

It was perhaps inevitable that two strong personalities like those of Williams and Piron would clash sooner or later. In 1916, Williams was forming a group to go on the Orpheum Theatre circuit with Johnny St. Cyr, Jimmy Noone, Oscar (later Papa) Celestine, and Piron, but Piron succeeded in breaking up the band before the contract was signed.

Meanwhile, however, the publishing venture had been doing very well. Young Louis Armstrong had written a tune, *I Wish I Could Shimmy Like My Sister Kate,* and the Piron-Williams company agreed to publish it, buying it for $50. Armstrong, unaware of what was involved, had sold his piece outright, relinquishing all claim to it.

There had been a trickle of royalties from up North into Clarence Williams' office, but in 1916, someone slipped a long envelope under his door which contained a royalty of $1600 from Columbia Records for *Brown Skin, Who You For?* Again, Clarence Williams saw his chance. He headed out, briefly to Chicago but then to New York.

He opened a song publishing office near Times Square, and one day a woman named Lucy Fletcher, who needed money to support her five children, came in with some words she wanted him to set to music. The two of them worked up *Sugar Blues.* In September of 1922, it was recorded by singer Sarah Martin with Williams at the piano. Once again, Clarence Williams was on his way.

In the same year, he married a popular singer, Eva Taylor (she was in the highly successful Negro revue *Shuffle Along*), and he began to record with her.

Williams had seen the boom in blues recordings, made for the Negro market, and was taking advantage of it; he had also seen that the best way to promote his own publications was no longer throught sheet-music sales, but on records. He would promote the record dates himself, pick the singer, the musicians, and sometimes function as leader. He worked with Bessie Smith. He used Sarah Martin and Eva Taylor. And Williams was not only promoting his vocal pieces, using singers, but was making many small group instrumental recordings. He used young Louis Armstrong, who was then with Fletcher Henderson, Sidney Bechet, and Buster Bailey. He used a St. Louis trumpeter named Ed Allen, whose style was comparable to King Oliver's.

Clarence Williams' career frequently crossed that of another New Orleans composer who had the same last name but who was no kin to him, Spencer Williams. Clarence published many of Spencer Williams's best pieces and is sometimes given co-composer credit with him. (In those days, as Sidney Bechet once put it, a publisher sometimes was rated as high as a composer.)

Spencer Williams considered Tony Jackson an old friend, and Lulu White, who ran the illustrious Mahogany Hall on Basin Street where Jackson worked, was Spencer Williams' aunt. When his mother died, he went to live with Lulu White who adopted him. "I'd go to sleep to the sound of the mechanical piano playing ragtime tunes, and when I woke up in the morning it would still be playing. The saloons in those days never had the doors closed, and the hinges were all rusty and dusty. Little boys and grownups would walk along the avenues, swaying and whistling jazz tunes."

In 1907, Spencer Williams had moved to Chicago, and 1913 to New York, where he became an established composer. He was a life-long friend of Fats Waller, and they collaborated on *Squeeze Me* in 1919. He wrote *I Ain't Got Nobody* for the great Negro minstrel comedian Bert Williams. He wrote for Sophie

Tucker. He either wrote or co-wrote *Basin Street Blues, I Ain't Got Nobody, Mahogany Hall Stomp, Royal Garden Blues* (some oldtimers say the real credit for this one should be King Oliver's), *I Found a New Baby, I Ain't Gonna Give Nobody None of My Jelly Roll, Everybody Loves My Baby,* and *Shim-Me-Sha-Wabble.* Clarence Williams published most of them.

By 1925, Spencer Williams was on the first of several trips to Europe, on this occasion to compose material for Josephine Baker at the *Folies Bergère*. By 1932, he had settled permanently in London with his wife, an English dancer, Agnes Bage. He did very little subsequent composing but lived a quiet life off his royalties. From 1951 to 1957 Spencer Williams lived in Stockholm. Then he returned to New York, in rather poor health, and he died at seventy-five in July 1965.

Clarence Williams had also been largely inactive in music after the early Thirties. He kept up publication of his "standards," of course, but largely he ran a hobby shop on 125th Street in Manhattan and lived quietly in his own comfortable house on Madison Street in Brooklyn. As a member of the American Society of Composers and Performers, he had a high rating and a good income. (ASCAP pays royalties according to rating, rating being based on an estimate of the over-all popularity and frequency of performance of a composer's pieces.) Incidentally, when his old friend Jelly Roll Morton was finally admitted to ASCAP in 1940, Clarence Williams felt that his rating was too low and tried to get it increased. Williams had similarly intervened at ASCAP for his friend and sometime rival A. J. Piron many years before.

In 1966, speaking to Sinclair Traill, pianist Willie the Lion Smith gave tribute to Clarence Williams in these words: "I knew Clarence from the first time he came to New York. He was a help to everybody was Clarence. Helped Jack Palmer, the white fellow who wrote the lyrics to *Found a New Baby,* and he helped everybody who wrote any jazz tunes in those days. Clarence had a publishing house, and he was the only one that would give us writers a break to get in—no one on Broadway would. But Clarence started James P. Johnson, Fats Waller, and Willie the Lion Smith. Every single writer you name, Clarence did something for them. . . . Clarence wasn't a great pianist, but he was a great

organizer and had a pretty good disposition. . . . He sold his catalogue to Decca Records, who sold it to Leeds Music Publishing
Company. I think he got something like $40,000 for that cata-
logue!"

King Oliver and his Dixie Syncopators made a last recording
date for Brunswick on November 14, 1928. Oliver used the Luis
Russell band, including Russell, J. C. Higgenbotham on trombone, Charlie Holmes on reeds, and Paul Barbarin on drums.
Only one side was issued from the date, *Slow and Easy*. But by
January of the following year, Oliver was in the Victor studios,
under a new contract.

Victor Records was a powerful company even in those days,
and Oliver learned to his regret it could be rather dictatorial
toward its contract artists. For Jimmy O'Keefe at Brunswick,
Oliver had recorded his own music. At Victor, he often found
himself recording what Victor decided he should record. At
least, that is the way jazz history has told the story for twenty
years, and when one encounters an Oliver Victor performance
like *Everybody Does It in Hawaii*, with effects from Roy Smeck's
steel guitar, he may be led to believe it. But it happens that a
majority of the numbers recorded by Victor were scored by
Oliver's nephew and protégé, trumpeter Dave Nelson, and were
written by Nelson or Luis Russell or Paul Barbarin or Oliver.

The general standard of professionalism on these records is
very high, but the soloists frequently do not meet the standards
of emotion of Oliver's earlier sidemen. There are some of the
same problems with swing among the soloists that one hears with
the Syncopators, although there is less rhythmic tripping and
faltering. On the Victors, either a player swings or he doesn't,
but he usually keeps fairly steady time. More important, there
is a change in the style and conception of the music. Oliver had
apparently abandoned his idea of an expanded and modified
New Orleans style, and adopted the New York conception of a
transformed dance orchestra style. Performances like *I Can't
Stop Loving You* and *I Want You Just Myself* sound almost like
a mélange of devices, borrowed from various dance bands,
unassimilated.

Oliver's own playing at this time is a series of contradictions.

On one record date, he might play no solos at all, or, according to some of the players present, might spoil an entire session by playing so badly that the records could not be released. A few days later Oliver would play the simple, quiet solos of a trumpeter whose embrochure was weakened by age and perhaps misuse, but who had faced the facts about his future and, within his limitations, made lovely music. But on the next date, a bravura soloist suddenly tears through, say, on *Too Late* or *New Orleans Shout,* and it *is* Joseph "King" Oliver, not Dave Nelson nor another substitute trumpeter.

One of the most celebrated of the Victor recordings is a piece called *Sweet Like This,* combining twelve- and sixteen-bar blues themes of a touching, nostalgic lyricism. The improvisation is not startling but it is good, and only the writing for the reeds seems really dated. (Incidentally, most commentators assign the first trumpet solo, on open horn, to Dave Nelson, and the muted variation on *Sweet Like This* to Oliver. One would expect it, but the slightly weak embrochure audible on the first solo and the firmer lip behind the second solo lead me to believe that the usual roles of who played muted horn and who played open were reversed.) *Too Late,* a better arrangement with exciting Oliver, is from the same record date. So is *What Do You Want Me to Do,* one of Oliver's best later pieces, with (as usual for any jazz orchestra at the time) rather shaky writing for the reeds but with a lovely obligato by the leader to the tuba's opening theme-statement.

A ballad called *I'm Lonesome Sweetheart* provokes the kind of frustration one feels all too often with Oliver's Victors. One endures some plodding, Lombardo-like saxophone playing and a vocal chorus, and then he encounters Oliver's horn offering— unless the master was imitating the pupil—the kind of ideas which so obviously inspired Armstrong and in turn all of jazz.

Oliver's bravura horn can be heard also on *Rhythm Club Stomp* and *Edna* and *Struggle Buggy* and *Nelson Stomp,* the latter featuring one of the more cohesive and sustained arrangements of the series.

On the other hand, *Freakish Light Blues, Call of the Freaks,* and *Trumpet's Prayer* belong to Luis Russell as leader and composer-arranger and to Louis Metcalfe as soloist. *West End Blues* presents Metcalfe in a direct imitation of Louis Armstrong's version of Oliver's piece. Similarly, the really good trumpet solos on *Mule Face Blues* and on *Stingaree Blues* are Red Allen's.

Oliver made thirty-eight titles for Victor. At least ten of them are successful for almost their whole length, and several others have fine moments. When we remember that by this time Oliver was working with a conception of orchestral jazz which was new not only to him but to almost everyone, and which was not perfected for several years afterward, we cannot really call the Victor series a failure.

The records which King Oliver was making at the same time, as a sideman with Clarence Williams and others and as a blues accompanist, are very revealing of his playing style. For example, Oliver has the solo at the end of Williams' *Bimbo* (*I'm Gonna Take My Bimbo Back to Bamboo Isle*), which has some delightfully unexpected accents. And Oliver plays with a more tellingly plaintive feeling on Williams' *What You Want Me to Do* than on his own version of that piece.

The most frequently reissued Oliver accompaniments from the period are those done with Sara Martin—her arresting *Death Sting Me,* and the rest. On these Oliver fills in sympathetic but cautious responses between the singers' lines. Oliver's great accompaniment on Sippie Wallace's *Morning Dove Blues* has never been reissued. Here he builds gradually and beautifully, beginning with simple fragments of melody, direct responses to the singer, and gradually developing them into a beautifully complementing, interplaying part of the performance—a nearly perfect balance of voice and instrument.

On February 18, 1931, King Oliver did his last record date for Victor. The contract was up and not renewed. There was one subsequent pickup recording with a male trio and Oliver as a sideman, present to do some wa-wa "talking" effects on one number. That was it. And with the end of his recording career, the end of King Oliver's life in New York had to come. The next year he had a new band, one of his own, composed of younger men, and he set off on a tour of the South and Southwest. In the beginning things went well, but soon salaries had to be cut and the players began to leave him.

One might say that Oliver spent the rest of his life making

this tour. He was an old man, not because he was fifty-one; he seems to have been one of those people who are simply born old. He would sit sullenly in front of the band on the stand, often speaking shortly and gruffly to his men—if he spoke at all—standing only for his own solos. He had frequent colds and he felt he had heart trouble, which he probably did. He had the pyorrhea and gum troubles which had plagued him for years and he continued to lose his teeth. Could he still play? One hears stories that he could still play, on occasion and when he chose to, as late as 1936.

He was still a band man, even if he did not always know who would be left in his band two days hence. Drummer Fred Moore has said of those days, "We went on a tour by bus, jumped from New York to Wichita, Kansas, where we played the Eltorian Ballroom. Oliver had a contract for three months, but when we got there he didn't want to play his recording arrangements; the manager didn't go for that, so we were only there three weeks. From there we went to Ft. Worth, Texas, following Louis Armstrong on the same tour. Louis was getting $1.25 admission ahead of us, and Oliver was getting $1. We toured St. Louis, Kansas City, and smaller places, playing ballrooms, both white and colored. But business was poor and the band started to break up. We finally got stranded in Kansas City when there were no more bookings."

Oliver's pride still stood in his way: "They wanted to send us to New Orleans for a date that Louis Armstrong had got and couldn't fill; the King wanted more money than Louis, so no date."

And his pride showed in other ways, "When we went to eat, the King would order his, double portions. He wouldn't drink a glass of milk, but a quart bottle. A small steak, King would order double. Not three slices of bread, but a whole loaf. He was crazy about Boston baked beans and hot dogs."

And yet if he had not had that pride, would he have been able to hang on at all?

For seven depression years, Oliver continued the "tour." Men continued to leave him, cars and buses continued to break down, engagements were broken, bookers used his name without using his band or collected an advance and skipped out. Jobs were played without payment, and fire—that phenomenon which seems to have plagued Joseph Oliver ever since he was blinded as a child—several times destroyed buses and equipment.

Once, in the West Virginia mountains, as a freezing winter wind streaked by. Oliver's bus broke down, and in desperation to keep warm, the musicians burned the tires. But the King kept up a front—the uniforms were neat and clean and he constantly admonished his men to be on time. In Vicksburg, there was a radio wire, one of several chances the band got to broadcast briefly, but their singer, Rudy McDonnel, was not allowed to use it—such are the strange ways of Jim Crow.

Some entries from the notebooks that saxophonist Paul Barnes kept of his tour with Oliver during 1934-1935 tell the story. Barnes used "W" to indicate white audiences, "N" for Negroes; he entered each man's wages, or a (c) if the date was cancelled.

1934
May 9—Williamson, W.Va.	N.	1.50
May 10—Norton, Va.		(c)
May 11—Bristol, Tenn./Va.	W.	.50
August 2—Fulton, Ky.	N.	.00
August 4—Clarksville, Tenn.	W.	1.00
August 12—Danville, Ky.	N.	.75
August 13—Crab Orchard, Ky.	W.	.75
October 28—Greenville, S.C.	N.	.15
October 31—Danville, Va.	N.	(c)
November 21—Huntington, W.Va.	W.	.00

and this was Christmas:
December 18—Ashland, Ky.	W.	2.71
December 24—Charleston, W.Va.	N.	.00
December 25—Ashland, Ky.	W.	5.00
December 26—Welch, W.Va.	W.	4.00
December 27—Williamson, W.Va.	N.	4.00

In 1936 Oliver was living in Savannah, Georgia. He had not enough clothes and he was frequently ill. He could no longer play, but if a musical job came, he would fulfill it. If it did not he ran a fruit stand, or swept out a poolhall.

He rehearsed a band for a while in a local hall for a "Battle of Music" with his old friend Papa Celestin; Oliver was sure he would come from New Orleans for him. When a regional booker auditioned Oliver's group he just walked out, it was so bad. Oliver assessed his mistakes too. He felt he had once made money he should have saved and didn't, and that he had had the best business advice and management on occasion and didn't know how to use it. And he had now fallen onto days when every manager and booker cheated him. "I am in terrible shape now. . . . Doctors advised me long ago to give up and quit but I can't. I don't have any money and I can't do anything else, so here I am." There was also more personal reflection, "Well, the only wrong I do is chase women and that I'm not the only man doing. . . . But I always had the greatest esteem for my home."

His letters from this period written to his half-sister in Harlem and preserved in Frederick Ramsey, Jr.'s, chapter on Oliver in *Jazzmen* are surely among the most moving documents in the jazz literature.

> I receive your card, you don't know how much I appreciate your thinking about the old man. . . . Thank God I only need one thing and that is clothes. I am not making enough money to buy clothes as I can't play any more. . . .
> Soon as the weather can fit my clothes I known I can do better in New York. . . .
> We are still having nice weather here. The Lord is sure good to me here without an overcoat. . . .
> My heart don't bother me just a little at times. But my breath is still short, and I'm not at all fat. . . . Don't think I will ever raise enough money to buy a ticket to New York. I am not one to give up quick. If I was I don't know where I would be today. I always feel like I've got a chance. I still feel I'm going to snap out of the rut I've been in for several years. What makes me feel optimistic at times. Looks like every time one door close on me another door opens . . . I am going to try and save myself a ticket to New York. . . .
> I open the pool rooms at 9 A.M. and close at 12 midnite. If the money was only a quarter as much as the hours I'd be all set. But at least I can thank God for what I am getting.

On the 8th of April 1938, Joseph Oliver, aged fifty-three, died of a cerebral hemorrhage. The half-sister who had watched over him during his youth, and to whom he had addressed his last letters, spent the money she had saved for rent having his body brought to New York. On the twelfth of April he was buried at the Woodlawn Cemetery in the Bronx. Louis Armstrong, Clarence Williams, and a loyal group of friends and relations attended. "Most of the musicians turned out," Armstrong has said. "The people who really knew him didn't forget him. . . . I didn't like the sermon that preacher gave. . . . [King Oliver] was a great man. I'll always remember him but I don't care to remember him in Savannah, or the funeral. . . ." No headstone was placed on his grave.

Recordings

"King Oliver and His Creole Jazzmen": Riverside 12-122, Epic 16003, and three selections on Riverside 12-101.

Riverside 12-130 includes two duets by Oliver and Jelly Roll Morton, Oliver's accompaniments to Sarah Martin, plus some Clarence Williams recordings which do not have solos by King Oliver despite the intimation of the back-liner of the record.

One title by Oliver's Creole Jazz Band is included in Columbia's "Jazz Odyssey, Volume I: The Sound of New Orleans" (C3L 30), and two titles in "Jazz Odyssey, Volume II: The Sound of Chicago" (C3L 32).

A collection of Oliver's Syncopator recordings, including *Deep Henderson, Jackass Blues, Wa-Wa-Wa, Farewell Blues, Every Tub, Show Boat Shuffle, New Wang Wang Blues, Sobbin' Blues, Tack Annie, Willie the Weeper, Someday Sweetheart,* and *Dead Man Blues* is available in Great Britain and on the continent on Ace of Hearts AH 34. A second Syncopators' collection is now on Ace of Hearts AH 91.

A selection from Oliver's Victor recordings, "King in New York," appears on RCA Victor LPV-529, edited and annotated by this writer.

Oliver's beautifully structured choruses on the "Blind Willie Dunn" *Jet Black Blues* are in Columbia's Joe Venuti-Eddy Lang album, Columbia C2L 24.

"In the Alley: Johnny Dodds," Riverside RLP 12-135, included the most recent appearance of the Blythe-Dodds *Ape Man.*

"Louis Armstrong and His Hot Five," Columbia CL 851; "Louis Armstrong and His Hot Seven," Columbia CL 852.

Johnny Dodds-Kid Ory, Epic 16004.

The recently issued British Riverside RLP 8805 collects all the Creole Jazz Band pieces released on Gennett and Paramount, except that it repeats the same take of *Southern Stomps* instead of the alternate version. The first three selections on Milestone 2002, "The Immortal Johnny Dodds," are not by Dodds, but the remainder of the LP offers a cross section of his work.

References

Allen, Walter C., and Brian Rust, *King Joe Oliver*. Sidgwick and Jackson.

Armstrong, Lil, "About Early Chicago Days." *Down Beat*, June 1, 1951.

———, *Satchmo and Me*. Recorded reminiscences, Riverside RLP 12-120.

Armstrong, Louis, "Joe Oliver Is Still King." *Record Changer*, July 1950.

Barker, Danny, "Jelly Roll Morton in New York." *Jazz Panorama*, edited by Martin Williams. Collier, 1964.

Bechet, Sidney, *Treat It Gentle, an Autobiography*. Hill & Wang, 1960.

Charters, Samuel B., and Leonard Kunstadt, *Jazz: A History of the New York Scene*. Doubleday, 1962.

Charters, Samuel B., *Jazz: New Orleans*. Oak Publications, 1965.

Collins, Mary, and John W. Miner, "From Lee Collins' Story." *Evergreen Review* #35, March 1965. (An excerpt from the trumpeter's autobiography.)

Erskine, Gilbert M., "Little Mitch." *Down Beat*, November 7, 1963.

Gara, Larry, *The Baby Dodds Story*. Contemporary Press.

Gitler, Ira, "Saga of a Saxophone Sage." *Down Beat*, May 24, 1962.

Gushee, Larry, "King Oliver." *Jazz Panorama*, edited by Martin Williams. Collier.

Hentoff, Nat, "Jazz in the Twenties: Garvin Bushell." *Jazz Panorama*, edited by Martin Williams. Collier, 1964.

Hentoff, Nat, "Warren 'Baby' Dodds." *The Jazz Makers*. Rinehart, 1964.

Hentoff, Nat, and Nat Shapiro, eds., *Hear Me Talkin to Ya*. Rinehart, 1955.

Hoefer, George, "Luis Russell." *Down Beat*, November 8, 1962.

Jackson, Preston, "King Oliver." From *Frontiers of Jazz*, edited by Ralph de Toledano, Ungar, 9.

James, Burnett, "King Oliver as Father-Figure." From *Essays on Jazz*, Sidgwick and Jackson, 19.

King, Bruce, "The Gigantic Baby Dodds." *The Jazz Review*, August 1960.

Kunstadt, Len, and Bob Colton, "Pioneer—Clarence Williams." *Record Research*, November/December, 1956.

Moore, Fred, "King Oliver's Last Tour." *The Jazz Record*, April 1945.

Ostransky, Leroy, "New Orleans Style." From *The Anatomy of Jazz*, University of Washington Press, 1960, chapter 8.

Ramsey, Frederick, Jr., "King Oliver." From *Jazzmen*, Harvest.

———, "King Oliver in Savannah." *Saturday Review*, March 17, 1956.

Shain, Cy, "New Orleans Trumpeters." *The Jazz Record*, November 1946.

Wettling, George, "A Tribute to Baby Dodds." *Down Beat*, March 29, 1962.

———, "Lincoln Gardens." *HRS Rag*, December 1939.

Williams, Eugene, "King Oliver," liner notes to Brunswick album B-1022.

———, "Johnny Dodds," liner notes to Brunswick Records set B-1020.

Williams, Martin, *King Oliver*. Perpetua, 1962.

N. O. R. K.

SAXOPHONIST BUD FREEMAN, in discussing the origins of so-
called "Chicago Style," names King Oliver, Louis Armstrong,
Bix Beiderbecke, Jimmy Noone, and Bessie Smith as prime influences, but, he says, it was "the New Orleans Rhythm Kings who
planted the seed."

It may come as something of a surprise for some people to find
the N.O.R.K. mentioned in such illustrious company; there are
few commentators or sympathetic listeners who could exclude
the likes of Armstrong or Beiderbecke or Bessie Smith from the
canon. But, while granting the Rhythm Kings their position in
history, some might hesitate to grant their music itself an equally
durable place.

Perhaps the subsequent careers of the group's members have
something to do with its artistic reputation. Cornetist Paul Mares
(pronounced Mare-es) spent relatively few years as a really successful musician and spent his later years largely sitting on the
sidelines, feeding musicians in the small restaurant he ran or
doing factory work. Clarinetist Leon Rappolo, whose life has
been romanticized in a way that makes him seem a minor Bix
Beiderbecke entered a mental home while still in his early twenties, and spent the rest of his life there. George Brunis (née
Brunies)—his relentless activities as a bandstand cut-up have
sometimes obscured his rare abilities as an ensemble trombonist.
Drummer Ben Pollack (actually from Chicago) weathered the
pressures of the late Twenties and early Thirties with some fairly
commercial music. So did saxophonist Jack Pettis. And the
group's early mentor and pianist, Elmer Schoebel, later spent

more time in commercial dance bands and as a compiler of "stock" orchestrations than as a jazzman; similarly, his replacement, Mel Stitzel, is better remembered for his stock arrangements than his jazz piano playing.

Listening to the New Orleans Rhythm Kings records today, it is perhaps difficult for us to put things in proper perspective. We have heard Oliver's and Morton's recordings. But when the first N.O.R.K. records appeared in 1922, there were no Oliver or Morton discs. However, there were Original Dixieland Jazz Band records. The quality which the Kings did have, and which surely attracted so many people to them, was rhythmic. Not that the group was rhythmically original or particularly imaginative, but it did reflect the changes taking place in New Orleans jazz, as it moved from the clipped, staccato accents of Freddie Keppard, and apparently Buddy Bolden (which the O.D.J.B. reflected), to the smoother and more flexible rhythm of, say, the King Oliver groups. There was also in the N.O.R.K.'s music, again as in Oliver's and Morton's, some use of harmonized passages. And there was a repertory that included *Farewell Blues, Nobody's Sweetheart, Bugle Call Rag, Tin Roof Blues, Milenberg Joys,* etc. The approach of the N.O.R.K., then, was cooler; and anyone who has heard Bud Freeman play, at any stage of his career, will understand his youthful feelings for the Kings, and particularly for the group's sometime saxophonist, Jack Pettis.

The New Orleans Rhythm Kings came together almost by accident, and the ensemble was first known by another name, the Friar's Society Orchestra. It did not live long as a group and therefore its members had their separate lives both before and after there was any N.O.R.K.

Paul Mares was born in New Orleans the same year as Louis Armstrong. He has described himself and his early associates as "a bunch of kids in knee pants playing around the corner from a red light." When he was out of knee pants, but still in his teens, Mares was playing nightly excursion jobs on the riverboat S.S. Capitol. He was already a big husky, likeable young man, playing with drive but unable to read music and self-taught simply because he had fallen in love with New Orleans music and felt a call to play it himself.

As we have seen, the first white New Orleans group to play in

Chicago had been that of trombonist Tom Brown. And the Original Dixieland Jazz Band had ben very popular in that city even before it moved on to New York and to national fame. From that time on, there was some demand for New Orleans music in Chicago—or perhaps even from 1911, when Freddy Keppard and the Original Creole Orchestra had played the Grand Theatre.

Early in 1920, cornetist Albert "Abbie" Brunies, George's brother, received an offer to come up. It had been dispatched by a New Orleans drummer called "Ragbaby" Stevens who had vainly tried to instruct Chicago musicians in the down-home style. Brunies however decided to stay in New Orleans, where he could stick with his taxi business while taking musical jobs on the side, and he passed the request on to Paul Mares, who headed for Chicago.

For about a year Mares held various musical jobs, the principal one being to join Stevens at a place called Campbell's Gardens. Encouraged by word of Mares' comparative success, George Brunis also headed north. These two, however, did encounter several Chicagoans with talents for jazz, particularly a group with a job at the Blatz Beer Garden which included saxophonist Jack Pettis, drummer Frank Snyder, and pianist Elmer Schoebel, from Champaign—these plus such frequent sitters-in as young cornetist Muggsy Spanier. In the summer of 1920 Mares, Brunis, Schoebel, and Black were key men in a group which managed to get a riverboat job. In Davenport, Iowa, they ran into a then nineteen-year-old clarinetist from New Orleans named Leon Rappolo who was playing with the band of Carlisle Evans, and who, incidentally, introduced them to a local cornetist named Bix Beiderbecke.

The group returned to Chicago and found a couple of jobs in the fall and early winter. Then, early in 1921, there was an offer from a place called Friar's Inn. Mares organized the band for that job: he sent for Rappolo, now back in New Orleans; he had Arnold Loyocano on bass; he had Brunis, Pettis, and banjoist Louis Black, drummer Frank Snyder, and Schoebel. Musically, however, Schoebel was unquestionably the leader. He could read and arrange and teach the others. They auditioned, legend has it, with *Wabash Blues* and got the job.

The Friar's Inn was a basement on the Chicago Loop with tables and a dance floor. The manager was a man named Mike Fritzel, who tried to give the place a high-toned atmosphere, hence the "Society" orchestra. But before long it had become a hangout for big-time, high-spending gangsters, and even Al Capone and Dion O'Bannion started to come in. But the band, once it had been misnamed as a Society group, was apparently left alone. The musicians were nearly all under age and didn't drink in the club, but they clowned around on the bandstand, playing boyish pranks, including putting oil of mustard in each other's chairs and on each other's horns.

During the day the group would call rehearsals for itself but nobody showed up. In the easy atmosphere of the Friar's Inn, it was apparently simple enough for them to rehearse on the bandstand. But part of their fun was to pretend to misunderstand Elmer Schoebel's musical instructions and make deliberate mistakes. The pianist, however, wrote *Nobody's Sweetheart* and introduced it with the group, and it was through his encouragement, and a consequent interest in harmony, that Rappolo composed *Farewell Blues*. Adapting more traditional ideas to their own uses, the Kings played *Bugle Call Rag* (they called it *Bugle Call Blues* at first) and *Tin Roof Blues,* which featured Brunis in his version of an apparently traditional tuba-bass blues solo. It seems the Rhythm Kings all had good ears because they picked up current pop tunes after one keyboard run-through from Schoebel, a business which used to amaze song pluggers and composers who had dropped by with their latest would-be hits.

Bassist Loyacano has said that he was forced into the Friar's job because the group needed a bass man and he was the only one around. The Kings, he feels, renewed the interests of both audiences and musicians. "In my estimation, this was the starting of a new jazz era, because jazz had died down, and this band had what the previous bands didn't have. They had more men, more drive, and had more harmony.

"*Farewell Blues* was originated because these guys were fishing for harmony, and the notes sounded like a train whistle. I was a good reader and so was Elmer, and we sort of helped the others when they needed it. But the hours were just too long; from eight at night until six or eight in the morning. We were at the Friar's Inn, and we played as long as the customers were there. We used to have fellows throw us hundred dollar bills to keep us playing, in Chicago!"

The young men were anxious to record and apparently rushed into the first situation that presented itself. An offer came from Gennett Records, based on their local success in the Chicago Friar's Club and encouraged by their manager, Husk O'Hare. The Friar's Society Orchestra went down to Richmond, Indiana, studios in late August of 1922, and in March and July of the following year. Each trip involved two sessions on the two separate days, and thus there were six in all.

The August 29th and 30th dates included Mares, Brunis, Rappolo, Pettis, Schoebel, Lew Black on banjo, Arnold Loyacano on bass, and Frank Snyder on drums. In numbers like *Eccentric* (featuring Rappolo), *Tiger Rag,* and *Livery Stable Blues,* the repertory obviously was drawn from that of the Original Dixieland Jazz Band. But the group also did *Farewell Blues* and *Bugle Call Blues* at the August sessions.

By the March 12th and 13th dates, issued as by the "New Orleans Rhythm Kings" (a change of managers, after a falling out with Husk O'Hare, meant the change in the group's name), Schoebel had turned over his chair to Mel Stitzel to take a dance-hall job, and Ben Pollack was the drummer. Stitzel and Pollack were the only members of the rhythm section, and there were no saxophones among the horns but only Mares, Brunis, and Rappolo. This time the titles included *That's a Plenty, Weary Blues, Wolverine Blues, Tin Roof Blues,* and, as the label spelled it, *Shimmesshawabble.*

The last N.O.R.K.–Gennett session was by a much-expanded group, including a saxophone section of three and, on certain titles, Jelly Roll Morton on piano, thus marking it the first racially mixed jazz record date. This time the titles included *Clarinet Marmalade* (from the O.D.J.B. repertory again, and featuring Rappolo), Morton's *Mr. Jelly Lord, London Blues,* and *Milenberg Joys,* credited to Rappolo, Mares, and Morton jointly. The latter, particularly, was a quite successful piece.

Recording the Rhythm Kings in 1922 put Gennett Records in the business of recording jazz, and during the next few years the company took down and preserved music by King Oliver, Jelly

Roll Morton, Bix Beiderbecke and the Wolverines, Louis Armstrong and Sidney Bechet with Clarence Williams, even by the young Duke Ellington and Fletcher Henderson. Gennett Records' history is interesting. The label began in 1916 as a branch of the Starr Piano Company, which was owned by the Gennett family. In a corner of the piano factory there was a little recording studio which used acoustical equipment, with the large, conical recording horns. The factory was near a railroad spur, and sessions frequently had to be interrupted because of the engine noises. Through patent litigation started by Victor Records, Gennett won a fight which put the recording stylus apparatus in the public domain.

The general policy at Gennett was catholic to say the least, and alongside the Creole Jazz Band, the catalog might list a speech by William Jennings Bryan, a dance tune by Guy Lombardo, a song by Ukulele Ike, and a ranting oration by a leader of the Ku Klux Klan!

The other midwestern company which followed Gennett in making invaluable jazz recordings during the period was of course Paramount Records, beginning the following year. Paramount also recorded Oliver and Morton; Paramount recorded Freddie Keppard and Johnny Dodds and Tommy Ladnier. But the company's specialty became the vocal blues, with Papa Charlie Jackson, Blind Lemon Jefferson, Ma Rainey, and others. Paramount was owned by a furniture company, the Wisconsin Chair Company of Grafton. In 1917, the factory had started producing phonographs and by the early Twenties had discovered that its phonographs would sell better if it produced records to go with them. Then the management further discovered that records alone, particularly records produced for the Negro market, would sell very well indeed. The company also acquired rights in 1924 to a New York-based, Negro-managed label called Black Swan.

Most of Paramount's recording was done in Chicago at the Loop "laboratories" of a man named Orlando Marsh. The supervisor-producer in Chicago was a young Negro booking agent named J. Mayo Williams, but Paramount's treatment of its Negro performers who went over to its Port Washington, Wisconsin, studios to record was just about contemptuous.

Paramount's general operation was cheap and shoddy in all aspects of production, and the quality of its recordings show it. It is said that when the use of microphones came in, Paramount slapped its claim of a new electrical process on its labels on the rationale that, after all, there was a light bulb in the studio.

Today, the rights to Gennett Records have passed to the Riverside label. Paramount is owned by the Chicago chemist and long-time jazz enthusiast, John Steiner, who has often leased the material to other companies, currently to Milestone.

Chicago cornetist Jimmy MacPartland has described the first encounter of himself, Bud Freeman, Jim Lannigan, and Frank Teschmacher, the "Austin High School Gang," with the music of the N.O.R.K. in a local record shop: "I believe the first tune we played was *Farewell Blues.* Boy, when we heard that—I'll tell you we went out of our minds. Everybody flipped. It was wonderful. So we put the others on—*Tiger Rag, Discontented, Tin Roof Blues, Bugle Call,* and such titles.

"We stayed there from about three in the afternoon until eight at night, just listening to those records one after another, over and over again. Right then and there we decided we would get a band and try to play like these guys."

Actually, the Gennett sides are the only recordings by the Friar's Society Orchestra–New Orleans Rhythm Kings, and they just about encompass the career of the group as such. In late January of 1925, Mares was back in the recording studios for Okeh, but this time in New Orleans with only himself and Rappolo from the original Rhythm Kings. He used Santo Pecora on trombone (Brunis had stayed in Chicago) and a local rhythm section. By late March of the same year, in a session for Victor, only Mares himself was left of the original group.

Mares' return to New Orleans was not permanent, but, back in Chicago, he became a rather isolated figure. When he worked, he used few of his former associates and few of the younger local men whom his work had once inspired. There was a recording session in 1935 for which Mares revived the "Friar's Society Orchestra" name. The date was set by the Mills Music Publishing Company, which had kept tabs of the earlier N.O.R.K. tunes that had become successful standards by then.

This time Mares was offering a blues which he called *Reincarnation* and a variant of *Basin Street Blues* which he called *Land of Dreams*. However, when the date was made, Okeh Records was about to disappear, one more music business victim of the great depression. The pianist on these sides, incidentally, is Jess Stacy, and it is said that it was on the basis of these performances that Benny Goodman hired him for his band.

During the late Thirties there was a small restaurant on the north side of Chicago, called the P & M New Orleans Barbecue, operated by Paul Mares. Monday nights there were special ones and featured music, most often with the sidemen of the Bob Crosby Orchestra like Eddie Miller, Mattie Matlock, Nappy Lamara, Irving Fazola, and Ray Bauduc—all of them from Louisiana—plus Chicagoans who were still in town like Jimmy MacPartland and Boyce Brown. But once the Crosby band success dictated a move to New York, Monday-night business at the P & M Barbecue declined.

During the Second World War, Mares did factory work in war plants. Shortly before he died, on August 18, 1949, he had been putting in appearances at Chicago jam sessions and hoping to organize a dixieland group of his own.

Mares, according to commentator George Avakian, was basically inspired by King Oliver, but also knew his early Armstrong. Indeed, it is said that he told Oliver that if he brought the younger man up from New Orleans, that the King would thereby soon uncrown himself.

Mares himself once candidly summed up his music and his brief moment in the sun this way: "Actually, the band was playing good music. We had only two tempos, slow drag and the two-four one-step. We did our best to copy the colored music we'd heard at home. We did the best we could, but naturally we couldn't play real colored style." As Bud Freeman has said, "We were taken with the Kings when we first heard them. But after we heard King Oliver, we knew the difference."

When Leon Rappolo left Chicago to return to New Orleans, he was barely of legal age. Apparently neither he nor no other members of the band had taken to drink while working in the Friar's Inn. But Rappolo had taken to marijuana, probably before the Friar's job. Clarinetist Don Murray remembered him at the Inn, "riding high on his clarinet, with one foot braced high up on a pillar alongside the stand and so full of marijuana he could scarcely move out of his chair at the finish of a set."

Rappolo's return south was largely for the sake of his health, and he was in terrible shape physically and mentally. It was partly a matter of the hours he had been keeping, partly a matter of the state of his psyche which was made evident by an increasingly eccentric behavior. In early 1925, before Leon Rappolo was twenty-five, he was in a mental institution; he remained there until he died in 1943.

Rappolo had apparently lived out the better part of his destiny, personally and artistically, in his first twenty-five years. His was obviously a sad and misfortunate life. But it was also, I think, a tragic one in the sense that those closest to him, including his somewhat strict but understanding parents, saw the coming self-destruction, but no one could keep him from it, least of all Rappolo himself. There seemed no salvation for him, but only a necessary destiny in music.

Joseph Leon Rappolo's family was Sicilian, and its traditions were musical. His grandfather had been a celebrated clarinetist in the old country and his father had kept up music, both as a player and a teacher, in the new one. Leon was born in Lutcher, about thirty-five miles up the river from New Orleans, on March 16, 1902.

His parents were apparently of two minds about a musical career for the youngster. Unless a man was a celebrated concert player, the profession of music in southern Louisiana included performances in a popular idiom which was no longer "old world," but was increasingly influenced by American Negro music, and which was most often played in pretty disreputable places. Therefore, the elder Rappolo was not exactly pleased when Leon fashioned a cigar box instrument as a child. However, when the youngster was about to enter a school called Rugby Academy, his father gave him a violin, and took him to his first teacher, a man named Carrie, who was a Negro.

However, Leon had already become enamored of the brass band and dance music he heard around him, and he realized that if he wanted to play in such groups, he wouldn't get very far with a violin. Possibly that is what his father had in mind in presenting him with the instrument, but Leon soon lost interest in his musical studies altogether.

According to family memory, the young Rappolo's musical impulses next began to attach themselves to his father's clarinet, while he meanwhile overtly took up the snare drum. He was not supposed to touch his father's instrument, but inevitably he did, and his mother kept the knowledge from her husband as long as she could. When his father did find out, he sent him to a teacher, a man named Sonta Guriffre.

Others have remembered his first encounter with the instrument another way. Rappolo's father ran a saloon catering to Negroes, and saxophonist Jack Weber has said that the first time Rappolo picked up a clarinet was in his father's saloon. From time to time, a colored band would drop in to ballyhoo a coming dance. "Late at night they'd serenade the saloon for free drinks. And once in a while these musicians would stop off and shoot a game or two of pool. Rappolo's kid would tease the clarinet players in these bands to teach him some licks. And they did. Later on, playing with Eddie Shields at Toro's Cabaret, he'd learn from Eddie the things Eddie's brother, Larry, had shown him."

Perhaps both these stories tell a part of the truth. But Leon Rappolo was soon putting in time in the New Orleans District, and there are stories of nights when the teen-age clarinetist visited Storyville specifically to find Louis Armstrong and hear him play. The trumpeter knew him, and would greet him with a circled thumb and index finger from the bandstand.

Trombonist Preston Jackson later remembered that Rappolo constantly jotted down ideas on his cuff as he listened to King Oliver at the Lincoln Gardens. But Rappolo apparently never learned to read very well except for what Elmer Schoebel taught him. However, he did play the clarinet with a certain learned clarity and precision, no doubt because of the musical background of his family and childhood, and his early studies with Guriffre. Schoebel says, "He was a handsome kid for one thing, and his clarinet sounded like a symphony man. He played from his soul you might say. Many nights when he was playing something particularly nice, I have seen tears in his eyes."

Rappolo played with the band at Toro's, with Eddie Shields

at the piano and Santo Pecora on trombone, with his father's approval; it was apparently one way of keeping an eye on him. At fourteen he had tried to run away from home with a pit band touring the Orpheum Theatre cricuits, and his father had the police pick him up in Hattiesburg, Mississippi.

Inevitably, young Leon Rappolo had been drawn to the Brunies family. The Brunies father was musical and so was the mother. All five sons were too, and all were involved with the jazz music of New Orleans. Henry was a trombonist, Richard played trumpet. The better-known brother, Merritt, played alto horn and trumpet. The still better-known Albert ("Abbie") played trumpet, bass, and drums. And the best-known, George, played alto horn, drums, and, of course, trombone.

When Mares had sent for Rappolo to join him in Chicago, the young clarinetist had been appearing with Abbie at the Halfway House. When he returned to New Orleans, he went back to the Halfway House with Abbie Brunies, and he made his very last records with Abbie's group. He could still play, but otherwise he usually sat numbly on the bandstand. One of his milder eccentricities was to show up for work wearing white socks with his tuxedo; one of his major ones was to throw his best clarinet into Lake Ponchartrain.

Rappolo was deeply responsive to sounds; there are legends, like those about Bix, of his listening by the hour to the wind blowing through telephone wires in open country, and he used to lean against a favorite post in the Friar's Inn because the spot gave his playing a resonance he admired. That quality comes through on his records. Perhaps his memorable recorded performance is his touching playing on *She's Crying for Me Blues,* made with Mares in New Orleans in January 1925. The ideas do not seem particularly striking or particularly original, but the sound and the emotion are his own.

When George Brunis played his first New Orleans job (in a Storyville joint) he was still a schoolboy, small and a little overweight. The manager of the place was appalled; they had sent him a boy. But the bartender, a man named Albert Callahan— possibly the toughest and toughest-looking man in the district— listened to his playing and declared that he was "a musician! "

When Brunis's records with the New Orleans Rhythm Kings began to appear, his playing attracted a number of young trombonists. Brunis knew the New Orleans ensemble style and played it well. And he also obviously knew his instrument well—better, perhaps, than any trombonist these men had heard in the style up to then. Thus Brunis on records attracted players like Jack Teagarden, players who were soon to convert their horns from accompanying bass instruments into solo brass instruments.

Brunis was born in New Orleans in 1902, and he was playing professionally by the time he was sixteen. There is a favorite story about an early job at a picnic on Lake Ponchartrain which illustrates the kind of gusto he had and which he retained over forty years in music: he blew and pumped so hard that the slide flew off his horn, out of his hands, and into the mire along the lakeshore. He spent the rest of the number wading through the ooze in his bare feet retrieving it. Perhaps he did it deliberately; he was, according to Schoebel, "Iron Head" and always a clown.

After the Friar's Inn group broke up, and while Mares returned briefly to New Orleans, Brunis remained to take a group into a nearby place called Valentino Inn. There he was heard by Ted Lewis who liked him, auditioned him, and hired him. Brunis remained with Lewis for seventeen years. He was joined by cornetist Muggsy Spanier, and the two provided Lewis, "the high-hatted tragedian of jazz," with just about the only worthwhile jazz he had. Lewis's hokey act, on the other hand, provided Brunis with material for his own later mimicry and burlesque.

Brunis left Lewis in 1935, and for a while he was, along with clarinetist Pee Wee Russell, in Louis Prima's group on Fifty-second Street. This was a Louis Prima of Armstrong-derived trumpet and vocals who held forth at the Famous Door to considerable success. At this same period, incidentally, Brunis, with Muggsy Spanier, revived the New Orleans Rhythm Kings name in a recording session for Decca.

Since his days with the Rhythm Kings, drummer Ben Pollack had been leading fairly successful and relatively commercial bands, which, however, harbored jazz players like Jimmy Mac-Partland, Benny Goodman, and Jack Teagarden—and perhaps allowed them a half-chorus solo toward the end of a number. In 1936 Muggsy Spanier left Ted Lewis and joined Pollack, but by early 1938 he suffered a complete physical collapse for which drinking was partly to blame.

Spanier made a miraculous recovery at the Touro Infirmary in New Orleans, and returned to music the following year in Chicago. He was on his own this time, and he put together a seven-piece group he called his Ragtime Band, with a clarinetist named Rod Cless, and with George Brunis on trombone. The ensemble did not last long, but while it did insiders praised it highly. And through its recordings, its reputation grew steadily, long after it had disbanded. It made sixteen titles between July and December 1939 which are still in print. And on them one can hear why Spanier was rediscovered, and why Brunis was too. Indeed, the music of this group probably had as much to do as any other one thing with the rediscovery of New Orleans music by writers and the public, a rediscovery which began about this time and lasted well into the mid-Fifties.

When the group broke up, Brunis briefly went back with Ted Lewis, but he soon realized that the sales of those Spanier recordings had been steady, and that because of his work on them—vocal as well as instrumental, by the way—he was once again very much in demand as a traditional jazzman. Indeed, the Brunis trombone, with its harmonic precision, percussive enthusiasm, and constant ensemble sympathy, on Spanier recordings like *Sister Kate* or *At the Jazz Band Ball* or *Riverboat Shuffle*, is basic to their considerable success.

Brunis returned to New York, to Nick's in Greenwich Village, to Eddie Condon's new place (once the guitarist had become an entrepreneur in the nightclub business), to Jimmy Ryan's on Fifty-second Street.

Brunis made a successful recording, a burlesque of an old piece called *You're Some Pretty Doll* which he retitled *(You're Some) Ugly Child*. Brunis, on the advice of a numerologist, respelled his name (for a while he wanted it to be Gorg Brunis).

Brunis never stopped clowning. His antics brought in the customers to Condon's but soon he was doing so much joking and effeminate camping around on the bandstand (the place had once been a "drag" joint featuring female impersonators, "The Howdy Club") that he soon found himself *persona non grata*. On Fifty-second Street he turned the inevitable nightly requests for *When the Saints Go Marching In* into a parade which toured the club and sometimes ended up in the ladies room and other times in a club across the street where perhaps some bebop was being played. And Brunis appeared at a Town Hall concert, manipulated his trombone slide with his foot, and technically outplayed the two other trombonists on the program.

In 1951, he was back in Chicago periodically announcing "when this job is up, I'm going to quit music and open up a delicatessen." He said that for seven and a half years running during one job at the 1111 (Eleven-Eleven Club.)

In 1962, Brunis went back with Ted Lewis for a few jobs and received featured billing. Soon he was thinking about retiring altogether. He had kept up his Social Security, he said, and he was just about eligible. He thought he'd go back to New Orleans. By 1965, he had gone down South and was across the Mississippi border in Biloxi. He had rejoined his brothers Abbie and Merritt, and the talk was not so much about opening restaurants or going into retirement or taking out Social Security as it was about getting back to playing again.

Recordings

"N.O.R.K." (Riverside 12-102) is a collection of the Gennett recordings of the New Orleans Rhythm Kings, including *Shimmesshawabble*,

Weary Blues, Clarinet Marmalade, Wolverine Blues, and the titles with Jelly Roll Morton. A later Riverside issue (146) has *Tin Roof Blues, Bugle Call Blues, Farewell Blues*, etc.

In the "Riverside History of Classic Jazz" (album SPD 11) there is the N.O.R.K. version of *Livery Stable Blues*. (Incidentally the title by the Original Memphis Melody Boys included in the same album does not feature Mares and Rappolo, as was long believed by record collectors. This pick-up ensemble features the N.O.R.K. rhythm section, but not its hornmen.)

In Columbia's "Jazz Odyssey Volume I, The Sound of New Orleans (1917-1947)," (C3L 30) there are titles recorded by Mares and Rappolo in New Orleans, *I Never Knew What a Gal Could Do, Golden Leaf Strut* (actually a retitled *Milenberg Joys*), and *She's Crying for Me Blues*. The set also includes *Barbarita* by the Halfway House Dance Orchestra of Abbie Brunies and featuring Rappolo.

George Brunis sat in with Bix Beiderbecke and the Wolverines for a couple of titles, last available on Riverside RLP 12-123.

The sides by the Muggsy Spanier Ragtimers with Brunis are collected on "The Great Sixteen," RCA Victor LPM 1295. The many titles than Brunis recorded for the Commodore label are out of print but may be found in some specialty shops, and may be reissued on Mainstream.

References

Avakian, George, "Paul Mares, New Orleans Rhythm Kings." *The Record Changer,* November 1949.

Beall, George, "The New Orleans Rhythm Kings." From *Frontiers of Jazz,* edited by Ralph de Toledano, Ungar, 1962.

Hoefer, George, liner notes for "George Brunis: King of the Tailgate Trombone," Commodore FL 30,015.

Miller, Paul Eduard, "Musicians' Bio-Discographies." *Esquire's 1945 Jazz Book,* A. S. Barnes, 1945.

Rust, Brian, *Jazz Records, A–Z, 1897–1931,* second edition. Published by the author at 38 Grimsdyle Road, Hatch End, Middlesex, England.

Shapiro, Nat, and Nat Hentoff, eds., *Hear Me Talkin' to Ya.* Rinehart, 1955.

Smith, Charles Edward, "White New Orleans." From *Jazzmen,* edited by Frederick Ramsey, Jr. and Charles Edward Smith, Harcourt, Brace and Co., 1939.

Steiner, John, "Chicago." From *Jazz,* edited by Nat Hentoff and Albert J. McCarthy, Rinehart, 1959.

SIDNEY

CLARINETIST AND SOPRANO SAXOPHONIST SIDNEY BECHET was
praised in the first jazz critique, an appreciation written by the
Swiss conductor Ernest Ansermet who heard Bechet in London
in 1919. Ansermet called him an "artist of genius," and described
his blues as "admirable equally for their richness of invention,
their force of accent, and their daring novelty and unexpected
turns." He continued, "These solos already show the germ of a
new style. Their form is gripping, abrupt, harsh, with a brusque
and pitiless ending like that of Bach's Second Brandenburg
Concerto." And he concluded that perhaps Bechet's "own way"
would be "the highway along which the whole world will move
tomorrow."

In his autobiography, *Treat It Gentle,* Sidney Bechet showed
that he had thought about his music as deeply as he played it,
that he was a rare esthetician and theorist, and a wise man.
Indeed, for much of its length *Treat It Gentle* is probably as
perceptive and eloquent a book as has ever been written by any
American artist. And it is therefore something of a frustration
to anyone else who undertakes to write about Bechet. It is an
exceptional book in so many ways: Bechet's second chapter, the
story of his grandfather Omar, is as vivid a narrative as exists
in Southern literature.

What Bechet does not say in *Treat It Gentle,* and of course
could not say, is that he was probably the greatest instrumenta-
list to come out of New Orleans after Louis Armstrong. There
seems to me no question that he was the greatest New Orleans
reed man. Late in his life, in 1957, Bechet undertook a program
of standards with the most advanced and celebrated "modern-

ist" French jazzman, pianist Martial Solal, and played pieces like *Embraceable You, All the Things You Are, These Foolish Things*, such pieces as would be beyond most New Orleans clarinetists to play correctly—probably including Jimmy Noone. In 1932, he recorded *Shag*, an early original on the chord sequence that became the second most common in jazz after the blues, that of Gershwin's *I Got Rhythm*. By the late Thirties and early Forties, Bechet was wending his way, for nonthematic solos, through chord structures like those to *Sweet Sue, Limehouse Blues, I'm Coming Virginia, I Know That You Know, Just One of Those Things*, and *Sleepytime Down South* without stumbling or faking. Yet his blues had been and remained as basic, as forceful, as earthy, and as personally eloquent as those of any man in American music.

Bechet was always careful to emphasize what he considered the basis of music, and these included emotion, rhythm, and spontaneous melody. Richard Hadlock has written of the saxophone lessons he took from Bechet:

"Sidney would run off a complex series of phrases and leave me alone in his room for a couple of hours to wrestle with what he had played. One lesson could easily take up an entire afternoon, and Sidney favored giving a lesson every day.

"'Look, when you emphasize a note, you throw your whole body into it,' he would say, cutting a wide arc with his horn as he slashed into a phrase.

"'I'm going to give you one note today,' he once told me. 'See how many ways you can play that note—growl it, smear it, flat it, sharp it, do anything you want to it. That's how you express your feelings in this music. It's like talking.

"'Always try to complete your phrases and your ideas,' he repeated over and over. 'There are lots of otherwise good musicians who sound terrible because they start a new idea without finishing the last one.'"

For myself, I wrote soon after his death in 1959, "I believe that it was one night many years ago, watching Bechet play, and realizing that everything—the man, the instrument, the melodies, the emotion—had, by some secret process, become an artistic whole, integrated and indivisible, that I first came to know what music really is."

Bechet was always aware of the New Orleans tradition and at several times in his career he formed and recorded with New Orleans-style bands. But at the same time, he had little patience with musicians who did not contribute to the music and help it to grow, and in his way he kept exploring his own talent all his life. In the late Thirties and early Forties, Sidney Bechet was working and recording with swing-era players like Rex Stewart, Frankie Newton, Red Allen, Charlie Shavers, trombonists like J. C. Higginbotham, Sandy Williams, and Vic Dickenson, pianists like Earl Hines, Sonny White, and drummers like Sidney Catlett, J. C. Heard, and Kenny Clarke. He named Art Tatum as his favorite pianist. And Sidney Bechet was improvising on tunes like *Indian Summer, What Is This Thing Called Love,* and *Laura.* Bechet, along with Louis Armstrong, was a musician who had the musical respect of the young modernists, and particularly their artistic leader, Charlie Parker.

One important aspect of his style is that rhythmically Bechet could hold his own with jazzmen of later styles and schools. It was not only a matter of his having steady time or his being able to swing. He could swing virtually in the manner of late New Orleans style. (And, once again, as we shall see, the rhythmic consideration will lead us back to Bunk Johnson and King Oliver.) On Louis Armstrong's 1924–1925 New York recordings, made with pick-up ensembles led by Perry Bradford or Clarence Williams, say, hardly anyone else matters *except* on those records when Bechet is also present, and on those records Bechet matters. Indeed, on a title like *Cakewalking Babies,* with superb breaks by both players, it would be hard to say which man comes off best.

Bechet's work refuses to fit neatly into preconceived categories about New Orleans music. He left the city relatively early for a man his age and he was already a recognized and influential musician by the teens of the century. Quite early, apparently, he had a developed, forceful, declamatory solo style. He had served an apprenticeship on clarinet and, like most New Orleans youngsters, he had greatly admired the local cornet players. When he discovered his real instrument, the soprano saxophone, he developed a style that was a combination of a trumpetlike lead, plus elements from a clarinetlike obligato, fused together in a single melodic part. Although he was always aware of the cooperative necessities of ensemble improvising, he was not always an ideal ensemble player in the older style and in the sense that Dodds and Noone and Simeon were—he had simply burst out of a secondary role. Memorable ensemble improvising on Bechet records often comes when there is interplay (technical and emotional) between Bechet and a trumpeter like Tommy Ladnier, where the two agree to stand on almost equal footing. Or it comes on recordings where Bechet frankly has the lead with no trumpeter and with perhaps another reed like Albert Nicholas's clarinet or Ernie Caceres' baritone.

There is also an excellent example of collective improvising in the opening ensemble to the *Society Blues* which Bechet did toward the end of his life at the Brussels World's Fair in 1958. There, Bechet's soprano frankly has the ensemble lead; Buck Clayton's relatively intricate swing style trumpet improvises a secondary part; Vic Dickenson's trombone, a third. The two choruses that result leave one wishing for at least two more. And the most uniquely integrated ensemble in recorded jazz is on Bechet's 1941 Victor recordings of *Blues of Bechet* and *Sheik of Araby*, an early example of multiple recording on which he plays, variously, soprano sax, clarinet, tenor sax, piano, bass, and drums.

Bechet spoke of music this way:

"But, you know, no music is my music. It's everybody's who can feel it. You're here . . . well, if there's music, you feel it— then it's yours too. You got to be in the sun to feel the sun. It's that way with music too.

"My race, their music . . . it's their way of giving you something, of showing you how to be happy. It's what they've got to make *them* happy. The spiritual, that's sad; but there's a way in it that's happy too. We can be told: 'Maybe you don't belong in Heaven, and you haven't got a place on this earth; you're not in our class, our race.' But somewhere, all God's children wear a crown, and someday we're going to wear ours too.

"A way of saying something from inside himself, as far back as time, as far back as Africa, in the jungle, and the way the drums talked across the jungle, the way they filled the whole air with a sound like the blood beating inside himself. . . .

"Oh, I can be mean—I know that. But not to the music. That's a thing you gotta trust. You gotta mean it, and you gotta treat it gentle. The music, it's that road. There's good things alongside it, and there's miseries. You stop by the way and you can't ever be sure what you're going to find waiting. But the music itself, the road itself—there's no stopping that. It goes on all the time. It's the thing that brings you to everything else. You have to trust that. There's no one ever came back who can't tell you that."

In the life of such a man, whose inner being is musical and who is directly in touch with that inner being, one would expect to find early evidence of the prodigy, and so one does with Bechet. When he was only six years old, in 1903, there was a birthday party for one of his brothers at which Freddy Keppard's band played. In another part of the house, where he thought he could not be heard, little Sidney played along with the musicians on his brother Leonard's clarinet. So able and so carried away was the youngster that he was heard. And Creole clarinetist George Baquet was so impressed that he determined to instruct him.

The Bechet household was musical and so was the family heritage. The grandfather, Omar, a slave, was a great natural musician, a drummer, singer, and dancer in the Congo Square. "Everyone loved him," Sidney wrote. "They waited for him to start things: dances, shouts, moods even . . . he was a musician . . . it was all there inside of him, something he was always sure of all the things that was happening to him outside, they had to get there to be measured—there inside him where the music was." Omar was killed by a slave owner, who, in repentance, freed Bechet's grandmother, kept her as a member of his household and almost as a member of the family, asked her to take his name, Bechet, and gave her an inheritance when he died. With that inheritance, Bechet's father went to an integrated private school, and helped establish his household.

Bechet's father was a shoemaker but he was a friend to musicians; he felt and appreciated music deeply; he sang and was an excellent dancer and played a little trumpet. There were always instruments around the house, and most of his five sons and two daughters played them. "Everyone in our house liked music.

The only known photograph of Charles "Buddy" Bolden was supplied to the editors of *Jazzmen* by trombonist Willy Cornish. It shows (standing) Jimmy Johnson on bass; Bolden; Cornish; Willy Warner on clarinet; (seated) Brock Mumford on guitar and Frank Lewis also with a clarinet.

One version of Jelly Roll Morton's Red Hot Peppers assembled in Chicago for his Victor recordings featured Andrew Hilaire on drums, Kid Ory on trombone, George Mitchell on trumpet, Johnny Lindsay on bass, Morton on piano, Johnny St. Cyr on banjo, and Omer Simeon on clarinet.

from the Duncan Schiedt collection

A formal 1923 grouping of King Oliver's Creole Jazz Band with Johnny Dodds, clarinet; Baby Dodds, drums; Honore Dutrey, trombone; Louis Armstrong, cornet; Joe Oliver, cornet; Lil Armstrong, piano; and Bill Johnson, banjo.

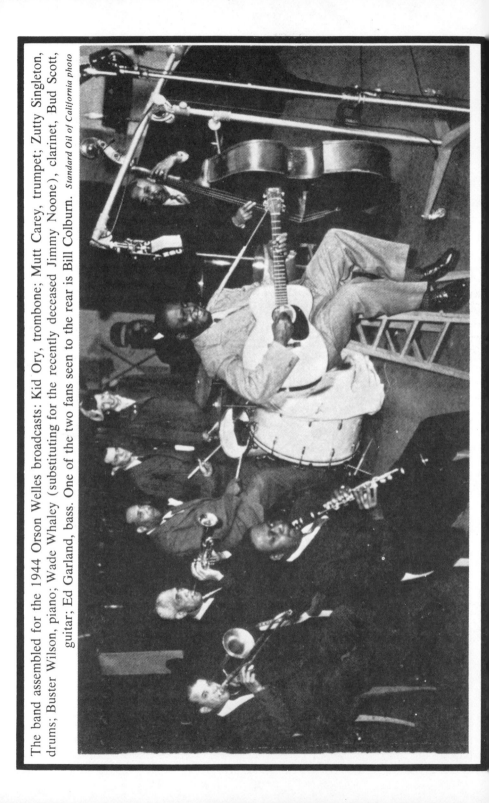

The band assembled for the 1944 Orson Welles broadcasts: Kid Ory, trombone; Mutt Carey, trumpet; Zutty Singleton, drums; Buster Wilson, piano; Wade Whaley (substituting for the recently deceased Jimmy Noone), clarinet, Bud Scott, guitar; Ed Garland, bass. One of the two fans seen to the rear is Bill Colburn. *Standard Oil of California photo*

from the Duncan Schiedt collection

A more sober mood for the young New Orleans Rhythm Kings than was evident at the Friars' Inn. George Brunis, Paul Mares, Frank Snyder, Leon Rappolo, Elmer Schoebel, Jack Pettis, Lew Black, and Arnold Loyocano.

Henry "Red" Allen, Jr., in an early publicity shot. On the second trip to New York, he stayed.

Sidney Bechet in a publicity pose that is less intense than if he were actually playing the soprano sax he holds.

An elegant Bunk Johnson during the years of celebrity and controversy.

from the Duncan Schiedt collection

Zutty Singleton — Face, and his drum set.

When they heard it played right, they answered to it from way down inside themselves."

"When we were still very young," he reported to Kay C. Thompson, "my mother used to take us to the opera. In those days, it was the best classical music available, and my mother wanted us to become acquainted with it."

Music obviously was primary for Bechet when he was in short pants. He told Dick Hadlock, "my mother would punish me by taking my clarinet away for a while. It was more important than anything."

Young Sidney second-lined the parades (and he notes that sometimes people would get together in New Orleans and pool the money for a parade just for the fun of having one). He was especially fond of trumpeter Manuel Perez's band. He notes that the Creole players in that band would play more complicated pieces like *Black Smoke, Pineapple Rag, Canadian Capers,* and that whatever they played they could play better from what they learned from playing pieces like those. He admired Henry Allen, Sr.'s brass band. And he loved the Grand Marshals in the parade, the "best strutters" in the various social clubs who would prance with batons in front of the bands as they paraded down the streets. (One wonders just how some of the proud white American parents of high-school "drum majorettes" would respond if they knew the real origin in Negro-American culture of their daughters' gyrations.)

Bechet's brother Leonard, who subsequently became a dentist, played guitar in a group called the Silver Bells Band. "The first band I played in was a family group, composed of my brothers and myself. Joseph played guitar; Albert, violin; Homer, bass; Leonard, trombone; and of course, I played clarinet." And for a while young Sidney played with the group too. But, he says, "I could see there were other bands who were doing more to advance ragtime, playing it with better feeling." Baquet, the youngster realized, played too legitimately for him. Big Eye Louis Nelson played with more feeling, and the interpretive moans, groans, and happy sounds that Sidney wanted to get. He took some lessons from Nelson and some from Lorenzo Tio, but "I guess you come right down to it, a musicianer just has to learn for himself, just by playing and listening." The family encouraged him to take up another trade, of course (bricklaying, cooking), but "My mind was on other things."

By 1908, Bechet was well acquainted with Buddy Petit and started playing regularly with Bunk Johnson in the Eagle Band, Buddy Bolden's old group. Wearing borrowed long pants, he was soon being led down to the district by an older brother to play in bands with grown men; he wondered what all those scantily dressed women were doing standing in doorways. The Creole players Bechet felt, could play ragtime, but you couldn't beat Bunk Johnson for the blues.

It was Bunk Johnson who introduced Bechet to Louis Armstrong. In later years Armstrong recalled how a trio composed only of Bechet, a drummer, and himself would roll through the New Orleans streets playing from the back of a furniture wagon to advertize Saturday night boxing. Bechet later felt that he had helped introduce little Louis around, and helped him get to know the other musicians in his early days. It is important to remember, certainly, that the young Bechet was then not just a talented kid in the opinion of New Orleans players. While still in his early teens, he was acknowledged as one of the best clarinetists in the city—to many *the* best. Other local clarinetists would go to great pains to procure two horns for themselves, one tuned in B-flat and one in A, and this made certain keys much easier for them to play. But Bechet used only a B-flat instrument, no matter what the key, no matter what the piece, and this with the old and more difficult "Albert system" of clarinet fingering.

By about 1912, Sidney Bechet was becoming restless and beginning to experience a wanderlust that stayed with him the rest of his life. Clarence Williams, impressed with the local success of his publishing and sheet-music venture, had decided to branch out. He persuaded a group of musicians to tour with him and help demonstrate his wares elsewhere. The men apparently thought they were going north, but they ended up plugging Williams' numbers in one ten-cent store after another across Texas. Bechet and pianist Louis Wade quit in Galveston, and Bechet tried to work his way home. He received no help from one particular white man who had apparently befriended him, and who was the sort of man who had convinced himself he was friendly with Negroes, but who turned out to be a bully.

Back in New Orleans, Bechet landed a job at Pete Lala's Big 25 and of course renewed his associations with the best musicians in town. But by the summer of 1917, Bechet was on tour, again with his friend pianist Louis Wade, this time as a part of the Bruce Stock Company which journeyed through Alabama, Georgia, Ohio, Indiana, and, by fall, Chicago. There, Bechet joined Freddy Keppard, Lawrence Duhé, and drummer Minor Hall at the Deluxe Café. When Bechet and Duhé moved to the nearby Dreamland, they sent a call back home to King Oliver to come and join them, and Bechet meanwhile doubled with the band of Eddie Venson at an after-hours place called the Royal Gardens, the place that later was renamed the Lincoln Gardens.

Bechet briefly rejoined Keppard, after a dispute over money, and when the Royal Gardens closed in 1919, he found another late-hours gig at the Pekin with Tony Jackson.

It was at the latter club that Bechet was heard by Will Marion Cook, who had brought his successful Southern Syncopated Orchestra to Chicago for a concert. Cook was a violinist who had been taught the instrument since childhood and raised with the promise and the strict training of a virtuoso. In young manhood, however, he was abruptly and cruelly told that there was no chance for a Negro classical violinist to succeed. Thus, Cook's Southern Syncopated Orchestra.

Cook was so impressed with Bechet that he asked him to join him, and thus it was that Bechet went East to New York and thence on his first trip to Europe in 1919, where there were concerts at Royal Philharmonic Hall in London.

Bechet was a highly paid featured player in an ensemble of thirty-six pieces. The number is of course impressive, but twenty of the thirty-six were usually playing banjos and there was a great deal of group singing, particularly on spirituals. Bechet performed *Characteristic Blues* and *Song of Songs* as his featured numbers.

By this time Sidney had begun to play soprano saxophone regularly. He had first been attracted to the instrument while with Tony Jackson in Chicago. He heard a recording of a piece called *Bull Frog Blues* by a saxophone sextet called the Six Brown Brothers that featured the horn. Passing a pawn shop soon afterward, he noticed a curved model soprano sax in the window and bought it. It was a defective horn and Bechet could do nothing with it and finally took it back. In London, he saw a straight soprano in an instrument-maker's window, tried it (playing *Whispering*), and was delighted with the result— here was an instrument with the volume, the full sound, and the power in both registers that his talent called for.

Cook disbanded in London, and the drummer from the orchestra, Benny Peyton, formed a small group that included Bechet to play at the Embassy Club. There they were heard by Edward, Prince of Wales, and often by the admiring Ernest Ansermet. And while there also, Bechet made his first recordings, versions of *High Society* and *Tiger Rag*, for the English Columbia label, recorded the 11th of November 1921—records that were never released nor subsequently discovered.

The Peyton ensemble visited Paris in the fall of 1921, but by early November Sidney Bechet arrived back in New York. His next most important job involved him with a touring show in which he played both clarinet and soprano saxophone and did a little character acting (probably low comic), playing a Chinese. But in that show was a singer named Bessie Smith with whom Bechet was impressed, artistically and personally. Upon this impression, there followed once again a very important event, which was, however, utterly frustrated for posterity. Bechet took the great young singer to Okeh Rekords in New York and recorded a test of her doing *Sister Kate*. The decision of the Okeh executives was that the label already had enough blues singers, and they did not sign her. Thus, a recording by Bessie Smith, with Bubber Miley, Bechet, Charlie Irvis, Buddy Christian on banjo, and Clarence Williams on piano was never issued and was subsequently destroyed.

However, Clarence Williams took Bessie Smith over to Columbia Records, recorded her with a different accompaniment, and gained her a contract that ultimately lasted through 1931 and that resulted in recordings, many of which have been in print ever since.

Williams' various promotions, however, did include the Okeh Company, where he recorded his "Blue Five" or his "Harlem Trio," and the Gennett label with his "Red Onion Jazz Babies."

He often used Bechet and, on occasion, he used both Bechet and Louis Armstrong.

Beginning with *Wildcat Blues* and *Kansas City Man* recorded on July 30, 1923, these are the first recordings with Sidney Bechet that have survived. Most of the tunes belonged to Williams's publishing house, of course. Often the young ensembles accompanied singers, one of them, Eva Taylor, Williams's wife. Classic early Bechet, like *Wildcat Blues,* or with Armstrong, *Texas Moaner Blues, Mandy Make Up Your Mind,* and *Cake Walking Babies,* come from these sessions.

Clarence Williams consistently billed himself and his singers on the record label, but never the members of his group. After much insisting, Williams finally gave in and listed Bechet's name on a record—one on which he did not play.

In 1923, Sidney worked briefly with the Duke Ellington orchestra at the Kentucky Club. Sonny Greer, Ellington's drummer of many years, remembered, "Sidney Bechet came in one night and pulled out his soprano. Right away, he, Bubber, and Charlie Irvis got to jamming against each other. It was wonderful. So then we hired him and he played with The Washingtonians, clarinet and soprano. He fitted our band like a glove. . . . Bechet always played *Dear Old Southland* on stage, and he was Johnny Hodges' inspiration. He liked Johnny, and Johnny studied him. But Bechet was always a rover who wanted to see over the other side of the hill."

And Duke Ellington has said "that was when Bechet was with us too, and played in our band. Bubber Miley and Bechet used to sit side by side, and Bechet would blow ten choruses and then Bubber would get up, with his plunger and blow another ten choruses. And so every time one would get through the other would take over while the other was resting. Then he would go back and have a *taste* and then come back fresh and full of new ideas. Oh what a pity some of those things weren't recorded! The invention, the soul invention, the musical emotion ran high."

Soon, Bechet had opened up a little spot, a restaurant basically, on Lenox Avenue which he called the Club Basha (friends often call him "Bash" or pronounce his name as if it were Bash followed by a long *a*) but the enterprise lasted only until 1925.

Sidney Bechet next joined a Paris-bound show called the *Revue Nègre* which starred Josephine Baker. Ultimately, as a result of her presence in this show, Miss Baker became, and long remained, the toast of Paris. The *Revue* itself broke up in Berlin the following year and Bechet, again with Benny Peyton, took a group on a tour of Russia, with Bechet billed as "The Talking Saxophone," for appearances in Moscow, Kiev, and Odessa.

In the Russian capital, the touring Peyton group encountered another American orchestra, that of Sam Wooding, and Sidney Bechet encountered a fellow New Orleans musician who was his own age but whom he had never met, trumpeter Tommy Ladnier, who was later to become one of the most effective musical companions of his career.

Returning to Berlin, Bechet led an international and "mixed" fourteen-piece band for the *Black and White Revue* of Louis Douglas for a European tour. He was also made American representative to a World's Fair of Music in Frankfort, held at the Beethoven Hall.

In Paris in 1928, Sidney Bechet was arrested, jailed for eleven months, and ultimately deported because of his involvement in a shooting scrape in Montmartre at a nightclub called Joe Zelli's Royal Box. In the fight, Bechet had been verbally goaded and was shot at before he defended himself. He acknowledged, "And all the time, I don't like it. There's a kind of disgust to it. I'm not for covering up any part of what's true: I can be mean. It takes an awful lot; someone's got to do a lot to me. But when I do get mean, I can be powerful mean. That's the way I was right then on the street outside that cabaret."

Bechet had at that time begun an association with bandleader Noble Sissle as a featured soloist, an alliance which lasted off and on for the next ten years. Immediately after the Paris incident, however, Bechet had returned to Berlin. Soon Sissle got him back to New York briefly, but then took him and Tommy Ladnier to Europe again, where Bechet and Ladnier once again stayed in Berlin for a while.

The off-again on-again association with Sissle continued, for Bechet returned to New York in the winter of 1930-1931 to rejoin him. On occasion, incidentally, Bechet played baritone sax in the section in addition to being Sissle's featured soloist on soprano and clarinet. One story connected with the Bechet-Ladnier-Sissle association is more revealing of Jelly Roll Morton than of Bechet, but it is certainly worth relating. Sissle was appearing in the Rockland Palace in Harlem and promoter-manager Harrison Smith had arranged for a young singer to audition with the orchestra. Smith told Albert McCarthy, "I was at the entrance of the hall and who do you suppose walked in? None other than Professor Ferd (Jelly Roll) Morton with his consort Fussy Mabel, 'Queen of the Dips' (Pickpockets). Though I greeted them most cordially they resented my presence. Jelly's prime purpose in coming to the hall was to raid Sissle of Bechet and Ladnier. Assuming that I was connected with the affair Jelly got angry and came back with two detectives, who stated that he had pressed charges against me and they would have to escort me to court. We all piled into Jelly's Lincoln car which I had helped to get and rolled on to Magistrates Court. We woke up 'His Honour' at 2 o'clock in the morning and he was plenty sore and cussed us all out for waking him up. Jelly and Mabel accused me of everything possible even to poisoning Jelly's grandpappy's mule. Jelly apologized to the detectives and offered to drive them back to the hall, but they came back with me."

Bechet left Sissle again toward the end of 1931 in an argument over salary, and it was at about this time that he spent a few weeks instructing Johnny Hodges on soprano saxophone while the Ellington orchestra played an engagement in Philadelphia.

In 1932, Bechet formed, with Tommy Ladnier, a New Orleans-style group he called the Feetwarmers. This later-to-be-celebrated ensemble played only a few jobs around New York and in September recorded six titles for Victor. Most of the recordings have been in print ever since. These records offer a youthful Bechet, a player of daring passion and musical flight—particularly on titles like *I Found a New Baby, Lay Your Racket,* or a revived *Maple Leaf Rag.*

One interesting aspect of the date was, as we have mentioned, the presence of a tune called *Shag* which was actually the first nonthematic use by jazz musicians of the harmonic structure which soon became a standard in jazz, the chordal outline to Gershwin's *I Got Rhythm*. Saxophonist Bob Wilber comments, "that bridge, the D 7/G 7/C 7/F 7, had not been used by jazz musicians as a pattern for improvisation before. Sidney had complete mastery of that pattern on that record. He did some fantastic things with it."

More important, perhaps, is the style of the ensemble. Bechet said that he wanted to form a New Orleans-style group, but; with the presence of Bechet's own assertive melodic voice, with Ladnier's pungent but somewhat subdued variant of King Oliver's style, and with Teddy Nixon's trombone, the result is a kind of transitional style. The horns play on almost equal footing in the improvised ensembles, so that the heterophonic approach of an earlier day, with one horn leading and the others following, moves toward a polyphonic texture, with all players participating equally.

These first Feetwarmers records, however, had little immediate effect on Sidney Bechet's career, and by end of 1933 he was the proprietor of a small tailor shop at 128th Street and St. Nicholas Avenue. Sidney pressed pants. Tommy Ladnier shined shoes. But there was a lot of music made in the backroom by both the proprietors and visiting friends.

A year later, an alliance with Noble Sissle again put Bechet to work as a professional musician, and from this period come the Bechet-Sissle recordings like *Dear Old Southland, Characteristic Blues, Blackstick,* and *When the Sun Sets Down.*
Bob Wilber commented in *The Jazz Review:*

> *Blackstick* and *When the Sun Sets Down South* are musts for any collection. They are two of Sidney's best originals, the arrangements are well-constructed around his clarinet and soprano and his playing is superb. *Sweet Patootie* contains some unimpressive blues-singing by O'Neil Spencer but the short clarinet and soprano choruses are marvelous. I would call this Bechet's "middle period." His playing is refined and disciplined, his solos carefully constructed. I get the same feeling of purity listening to Armstrong's playing in the late 'thirties.

However, neither Bechet nor Sissle were exactly national celebrities, and the great player was hardly having the career that his talent deserved in playing featured sideman to Noble Sissle. What ultimately gave Bechet the opportunity for a re-

newed career on his own was the national popularity of the
"swing" style. During the late Thirties, there had developed an
audience which had been made aware of jazz by the popularity
of the big swing bands, and was ready to appreciate both the
improvising soloist and something of the heritage of the music.

By October 1938, Sidney Bechet had opened at Nick's in
Greenwich Village. He had recorded with an ensemble that
drew its personnel from the two groups then appearing at Nick's,
his own and Bobby Hackett's, the records on which Bechet often
has the lead voice with Ernie Caceres weaving in and out behind
him on tenor and baritone saxophones, and with Zutty Singleton on drums. Bechet had also recorded by this time with
Tommy Ladnier in a group put together by the visiting French
jazz writer Hughes Panassie. He had appeared, again with Ladnier, at the first of John Hammond's historically oriented Carnegie Hall concerts "Spirituals to Swing." None of this insured
Bechet either steady work or steady income, but all of it gave
him stature with both the "inside" fans and the journalists of the
jazz world.

Wilfred Mellers, in his history of American music, *Music in
a New Found Land,* has built his appreciative comments on
Bechet largely around the 1939 version of *Really the Blues,* done
with Ladnier, and a blues Bechet did several years later called
Out of the Gallion. (The gallion is an urban black ghetto.)

> In his art there is the profound melancholy of the blues, and there
> is often exuberance in plenty. Tension and angularity are, however,
> less evident than in Armstrong's playing; far from being "tight, like
> this," Bechet's music is relatively supple and flexible. . . . He changed
> from clarinet to soprano saxophone. . . . because its liquid, voluptu-
> ous sonority could impart greater richness to the flowing cantilena
> that makes him the supreme lyricist of jazz. So the flexibility of his
> lines does not promote screwed-up cross-rhythms, as it does in
> Armstrong; it rather enhances the "speaking" poignancy of the
> melody. It is here that Bechet's distinctively Negroid character is
> evident; no jazz player uses more extravagant portamenti and a
> wider vibrato, and while this does not destroy the line's lyricism, it
> gives it an almost hysterical edge. In the marvelous *Out of the
> Gallion* the blues line is always winging and singing; yet the song
> becomes a sob, protected from self-indulgence because it does not
> break into fragments but remains suspended, airborne. In *Really the
> Blues* we find a comparable technique used not merely in monologue.

but also in duologue with Tommy Ladnier's trumpet—a most sensitive player who, preserving Armstrong's ferocity, could yet adapt his trumpet sonority to the sensual contours of Bechet's sax. Frequent passages in parallel thirds emphasize the voluptuousness. In fast tempi Bechet does not relinquish his lyricism, so that the frenzy he generates remains untortured.

Gradually—all too gradually to be sure—Bechet's established historical reputation among jazz fans began to help his current career. In mid-1939 he made a record for Blue Note which sold very well (despite the fact that he was having reed trouble when it was done) and the piece became a standard nightly feature for Bechet—variations on Gershwin's *Summertime*. From February 1940, and continuing through October 1941, Bechet began the new series of "Feetwarmers" recordings for Victor with varying personnel. During the same period he worked for the HRS label (the Bechet-Muggsy Spanier "Big Four"), and on occasion for Blue Note, on recordings which most commentators feel, caught him at the height of his powers and constitute his best recorded work.

Bob Wilber remembers his first acquaintance with Bechet's Victor recordings, an experience which was shared by hundreds of jazz fans of his generation. "I was thirteen or fourteen. I had been listening for four or five years by then to the big bands and the popular music of that era, but this was the first time I had heard Sidney. It was on the Victor record of *Rose Room* and *Lady Be Good*. That was my first real exposure to small band improvisation, and I was fascinated. I remember on that record I was as fascinated by Charlie Shavers as I was by Sidney the way these two horns would interweave. Then I began to get more of those Victor records as they came out.

"I love Sidney's chorus on *Sleepy Time Down South*. I think it's a masterpiece. And I love his playing on a thing called *Swing Parade;* the way he weaves in and out of the ensemble is really masterful. Also the things he did on HRS at about the same time with Muggsy Spanier and the quartet. It would be hard to say which of those I like best, *China Boy, Sweet Lorraine, Sweet Sue, That's a Plenty, Lazy River, Four or Five Times, Squeeze Me, If I Could Be with You. . . .* I feel this was Sidney's great period in this playing."

One Victor session which Wilber mentions is the one which produced *Blues of Bechet,* the early example of multiple recordings by Bechet's one-man band, with himself on various reeds plus piano bass and drums. "The way he plays counterpoint against himself is really something."

Among the Victors there are several others which might be singled out. The session which produced *Shake It and Break It, Old Man Blues,* and *Nobody Knows the Way I Feel This Morning* was exceptional, individually (Sidney De Paris was on trumpet, Sandy Williams on trombone, and Sidney Catlett on drums) and collectively. During a brief Chicago trip, Bechet did a lovely reading of Earl Hines's *Blues in Thirds* with the composer on piano. *Texas Moaner,* a remake of one of Bechet's early titles with Clarence Williams, has the leader's style contrasted with the then "advanced" trumpet of young Charlie Shavers. There is also Bechet's lovely reading of the Cole Porter theme *What Is This Thing Called Love,* a performance long unissued in the United States.

At about this time, Bechet was pursued by the American Communist Party. It is perhaps almost an accident that he was, since the party line on jazz had wavered a great deal: with the popularity of the swing bands at its peak, jazz was briefly declared to be a decadent bourgeois art. "Folk music," however, was not, and folk performers were actively pursued—indeed, a couple were captured and encouraged to sing such incongruous and uncharacteristic airs as the *Bourgeois Blues.* Similarly, and particularly during the alliances of the Second World War, the party went after important figures in "traditional" jazz. They went after Bechet and had him playing at the Log Cabin at a camp at Fonda, New York. Bechet played the job, accepted the salary (a good one), and commented "I can't see anything to that stuff."

By this time Sidney Bechet could keep going with nightclub engagements, record dates, and concerts and make a fairly steady living as a musician. With the dixieland revival that followed on the Second World War, he was able to keep it up. In December 1944, following the end of the ban on recordings that had been declared by the American Federation of Musicians, Bechet resumed making records, first (and most frequently) for

Blue Note on a session which produced the beautifully paced and structured solo *Blue Horizon*. There were also some 1945 sessions for Mezz Mezzrow's King Jazz label. British critic Max Harrison is particularly fond of these sessions and, when they were reissued in a limited edition, wrote in *Jazz Monthly*:

> The recognized masterpieces such as *Gone Away Blues* and *Out of the Gallion* are here . . . it can only be said that the best titles in the King Jazz catalogue represent Bechet's personal evaluation of the New Orleans past strictly in terms of his own art. . . . The appeal of Bechet's work, especially on these sessions, is due at once to its sensuality and its violence, a combination found elsewhere in jazz but rarely mixed in such strong proportions. While it was never perfectly captured by any recording, the violence is obvious in the intensity of his performance, in its sheer naked force, and in the athleticism of some of his phrases. Yet the virtuoso technique always gives the impression that there is still more power in reserve, and so the violence does not swamp the sensuality implicit in the wide vibrato and warm, full tone. In all this he is aided by the character of the soprano saxophone and the vehicle of his expression is a highly personal and almost inexhaustible melodic invention. In his finest moments here Bechet plays with a passion—almost ecstasy—that is only equalled by Armstrong, Beiderbecke, and Parker in *their* best moments. . . .

With the recordings and the club dates, Bechet was still not exactly affluent. He was also concerned, as always, with the preservation of the jazz heritage and with the development of its future. And for such reasons, Bechet undertook teaching.

During the postwar dixieland revival there appeared a goodly number of young musicians—almost all of them white, it should be noted—who were determined to learn the traditional styles. These facts brought together Sidney Bechet and a young man named Bob Wilber:

"I was about sixteen. I was living in Scarsdale in Westchester. There was quite a bunch of young guys in Scarsdale who were very interested in jazz and were avid record collectors. By the time I was fifteen or sixteen I heard all the Louis's and Beiderbecke's and all the great things.

"I guess I first picked up the soprano when I was about fifteen because of Sidney's work. I had no particular interest in the instrument other than that I was fascinated by the way he played it.

"The first time I heard Sidney in person I believe was at a session held at the Pied Piper in the Village, the place which later became the Cafe Bohemia. At that time Wilbur De Paris was running what were called "swing soirés" once a week down there. I remember Bechet had Bill Coleman on trumpet, Wilbur on trombone of course, Mary Lou Williams on piano. It was a good session—a good band. And that's the first time I met him.

"The idea of studying with him really came about through getting to know Mezz Mezzrow, who at that time had King Jazz records and was doing a series of concerts at high schools around the New York area. I first met Mezzrow when he was playing at Ryan's. We had a 'hot jazz club' at high school and in my junior year, which would be 1944, we held a jazz concert and got a band out from New York including Mezzrow, Rod Cless, and Sterling Bose on trumpet, Wilbur De Paris, Pops Foster, Danny Alvin, Art Hodes—I guess that was it. By that time we had our own little band out in Scarsdale. We played on the concert too.

"So I got to know Mezzrow and I used to go up to the King Jazz Record Company office. One day I was up there and he said, 'You know, Sidney's opening up a school of music. He's going to teach.' And I said, 'Gee, I sure would like to study with him.' Mezz said, 'Okay, I'll set it up for you.' Then he told me the date and told me how to get out to this house in Brooklyn on Quincy Street where Sidney lived. This was the Spring of 1946.

"I took the subway out there and finally found the house. It was a kind of an old ramshackle three- or four-story wooden house in Brooklyn, with a sign out front: 'Sidney Bechet School of Music.' I went in and there was Sidney.

"I was apparently the first pupil that had showed up for instruction. The lessons would be for an hour; I've forgotten how much he charged. Soon, I think there was one or two other guys who were studying too, but it was no big deal or anything.

"Still, he was very interested in teaching, and he was thinking about the book he wanted to write on jazz improvisation and how it was done, because he felt that so many younger players didn't really understand what it was all about.

"When he taught, he would sit down on the piano stool (he had an old upright piano) with his horn and I'd get my horn out, and he'd demonstrate things on his horn. I'd try to play them the way he demonstrated.

"One thing he was very interested in was the concept of interpreting a song. You start out with an exposition of the melody in which you want to bring out the beauty of it. And then you start your variations, but at first they are closely related to the melody. Then, as you go on to another chorus, you get further away—you do something a little less based on the melody but more on the harmony. Sidney was much more harmonically oriented than most of the players of his generation—he would sit at the piano and voice chords. Then at the end, you would come back to the melody and there would be some kind of coda which would bring the thing to a conclusion. He was very concerned about telling a story to the audience. In other words, the start, the theme, the development, the variations, and coming to a definite conclusion. The idea of the form was very important to him.

"At the time, I was the only one who was studying with him with the definite idea of becoming a professional player. I was playing engagements around New York and we had a little band of—composed of guys from around Westchester County. Some from Scarsdale, some from Larchmont, a couple from Greenwich, Connecticut. We called ourselves the Wildcats, and we were playing at Jimmy Ryan's occasionally on the Sunday sessions and we made some records.

"My parents were a little dubious about the idea of my being a jazz musician, as you can imagine. But they liked Sidney very much; he made a very good impression on them; they thought he was a marvelous person. Sidney had a wonderfully gracious manner about him. He could be a very charming person when he wanted to be—and with people from all walks of life and all strata of society who had maybe never had that much contact with either a Negro or a jazz musician. He had a way of making contact with people—all kinds of people. He did it in his music, obviously, and he could do it in his personal contacts.

"Sidney was constantly composing. He loved to write tunes and melodies and he worked at the piano practically every day. He had one of the early tape machines that came out right after the war, a big heavy monster of a thing. And he used to use it to tape things that he was working on at the piano or tape things with his horn too. This kind of practice with a tape machine is commonplace today.

"At that time he was working on an extended piece which, as far as I could figure out, Sidney had been working on all his life; it was sort of his one big work. It was the piece which was later put on in Paris as a combination of a ballet and Bechet score, *La nuit est une sorcière*. At the time that I was studying with him (he had an extra room in the house and I moved in and lived there with him), he was working on these themes. He was really trying to combine the blues and the spirituals with his conception of the classical idiom, which was pretty much Nineteenth Century. The idiom that he felt comfortable in was, you would say, a pre-impressionist type of harmony, which was true, I suppose, of other people in his era of jazz.

"I think Sidney had a very strong feeling that there was *a* way to play jazz, and I do think he would tend to romanticize the players of the early days in New Orleans—I don't think they maybe were quite as good as he remembered them. But he had a definite idea about the idea of theme and variation in jazz and respecting the melody and the parts that the various instruments should play. It wasn't a doctrinaire or hide-bound thing in which he wouldn't allow the players any freedom. But in a sense you might say he was like Jelly Roll in that he wanted a certain discipline in the music. He wasn't just for complete freedom of expression in jamming, without any consideration of how your part fitted with the other musicians. True, he played a lead himself when he was the lead instrument, or when he felt a soprano should have the lead. Even when there was a trumpet he'd play lead sometimes. But this was done intentionally, and because he wanted that sound. But he could also play a marvelous counterpoint to a lead—he was masterful at it. He had a fantastic ear for finding the note that nobody else was playing in an ensemble. Say at a session where there might be half a dozen or even ten horns on the stand, Sidney would find that unplayed note, or find that little hole there where he had a chance to put something in that was meaningful.

"A lot of musicians have the idea—those who have worked with Sidney or listened to him—that he just sort of played and disregarded everything around him, that it was a matter strictly of self expression. But that wasn't true of his playing. He was very conscious of what everybody else was doing and he wanted everything to be related.

"At the same time, he didn't have any idea of keeping jazz the way it was played in New Orleans. His idea of jazz was a form, and within that form you could develop new players expressing new ideas.

"One interesting thing is the way that Sidney used to work out choruses on tunes. Over a period of years he would use these choruses as the finale or climax to his interpretation. When I heard the solo that Johnny Hodges plays on *The Shiek of Araby* with Duke Ellington, I said, why, there's the same chorus that Sidney taught me to play in 1946 when I was studying with him. And I bet Johnny learned it from Sidney when *he* was studying with him. The only time Sidney ever recorded it himself was for Victor on the one-man-band record where he played it on tenor.

"His variations on *China Boy* which he always played as a climax whenever he played the tune—I'll bet he had those things since the Twenties. His chorus on *I Know That You Know*. He always played that chorus. These things were set things that he would lead up to, but he would always lead up to them with improvised choruses. When he really had to fly, when he really had to have something to top what he'd already done—this was again his sense of form—he'd have these choruses. A lot of musicians get to that climax and they don't know where to go, they have nothing left to go on to. He taught me all these set choruses that he had on tunes: *I Know That You Know, China Boy, The Sheik of Araby*.

"At that time when I started studying with him he was working on a very involved set of variations on *Intermezzo*, that melody from the Ingrid Bergman-Leslie Howard movie. It's a melody with a lot of nonchord notes that he would harmonize with passing chords and everything. He had a series of variations in double-time supposed to be played against the melody in the long meter. He used the same idea on *Laura*. He even had the verse in there. He never actually played *Intermezzo* in a club, but it was going to be something when he got finished with it.

"He felt his featured showpieces were a very important part

of his repertoire, and he never got tired of playing *Summertime* or his version of *Dear Old Southland,* in which he interpolated *Sometimes I Feel Like a Motherless Child* and then go into the double-time, and then the long ending with a cadenza—a real interpretation.

"Generally when he played the blues, however, he was extemporaneous. At the same time, he would stretch out in terms of form, with a definite development from one chorus to the next. A classic example is *Blue Horizon,* which was improvised but which is still a composition in its effect.

"I think some of the best things he recorded were the things that he did for Victor in the late Thirties and early Forties, when his professional career was at a low ebb. And, incidentally, Sidney Catlett and Kenny Clarke, his two favorite drummers, are on several of those records.

"I am thinking about *Shake It and Break It.* The way he plays on that. The way he plays a melody like *Indian Summer.* It seems at this period everything was together in his playing—his complete control of the instrument. He still had the exuberance of youth you can hear on the early 1932 Feetwarmers records, but it was a little more tempered by a knowledge of what the horn could and couldn't do.

"At that point also he had his right vibrato, one which was essentially right for the instrument. A lot of mucisians said 'he's great, but gee, that terrible vibrato'—nanny goat vibrato or something. The point is, the higher you go on an instrument, the faster vibrato you have to have. That is also true of singers. A slow vibrato just doesn't sound good. So Sidney was using the vibrato which was appropriate for a soprano, which is fairly fast, and sometimes he didn't have it under control as well as other times. But at this period he had the control down beautifully.

"It's interesting that by the time I was hearing Sidney in person and studying with him and playing with him on the job at Ryan's, his tone on the instrument had changed. It had a different texture. It was grayer, I might say, with less purity and brilliance and more rough edges. Listen to the King Jazz records he did with Mezzrow. They are great things for Sidney but his playing is heavy and almost coarse compared to the way he was playing just a few years earlier. His instrument, the soprano saxophone, is very hard to play in tune. But it is also very flexible, so that you can move the pitch of a note around by the use of your embouchure. If you hear the correct pitch in your head—if you've got a good ear for pitch—you can play it in tune, although even then it's difficult, especially in the touchy upper register.

"Bechet had a thing he'd do—he'd take a standard facing, a mouthpiece, and take a file and open up the tip himself. He got the results he wanted. Usually such things are done on a machine and they're supposed to be to the thousandth of an inch, very carefully measured with a caliphter. He'd just take this file, or some sandpaper, and open up the thing until he blew it and it sounded good to him. And of course the more open the tip on the mouthpiece the more intonation problems you have, too, the more difficult it makes it to control.

"Sidney didn't mind working out of town—going to Philadelphia for a couple of weeks, say. He was happy for any work that came along, but there just wasn't that much happening for him. It's an amazing thing about a man with his talent and his ability to communicate. Apparently nobody in music management or recording had the slightest idea what to do with him or how to bring his talent to the public. And of course, later he went to France and made a fortune for himself—and for a lot of other people involved in his career. He didn't sing or tell jokes or mug but he had marvelous showmanship. He was a showman from the minute he put his horn in his mouth. However, that wasn't what the music business people understood by showmanship, of course."

Bechet's decision to move permanently to Paris came gradually. The first step came in 1949 when he went over for the Paris Jazz Festival, a catholic and comprehensive event which (as some privately made recordings of a performance at the Salle Pleyel attest) brought Bechet and Charlie Parker playing blues together on the same stage. He returned to the states in 1950, on which occasion he appeared at a memorial concert to the singer Leadbelly, playing with Count Basie, and he came back again in 1953.

But Sidney Bechet came to realize that he felt at home in France—or at least more at home than he had ever felt anywhere else. It was, he often said, close to Africa. At the same time, the culture was closer to the culture he had grown up with in New Orleans. And France was receptive to Bechet as his own country was not.

New Orleans revivalism was a popular success and Bechet recorded and appeared with a succession of young French players, chiefly the groups of Claude Luter and André Rewèliotty. Bechet became a celebrity and his appearances in French music halls were as avidly attended as those of Maurice Chevalier, his appearances in clubs as fashionable as those of Edith Piaf. He became much sought after by the upper-crust in Paris and on the Riviera. His marriage at Antibes (his third, by the way) was an international event, given a spread of several pages in *Life*. (His wife was Elizabeth Ziegler whom he had known in the Twenties as a dresser with a German show and who had meanwhile married and divorced a Frenchman; the marriage with Bechet was short-lived.)

Perhaps the most singular event during Bechet's years in France, however, was the alliance made in a recording studio at Bechet's own insistence. It came about in March 1957, with a second date in June. Bechet performed a series of standards with the most able and articulate of French modern jazzmen, pianist Martial Solal. He had heard Solal in an adjoining studio during one of his own record dates and determined to record with him. The most interesting selections, incidentally, were those made at the second date which also featured Bechet's old associate, drummer Kenny Clarke, including *All the Things You Are* and *It Don't Mean a Thing (If It Ain't Got That Swing)*. Solal has commented that, for his part, he "wanted to prove that any style of jazz could be played with any other. It was very exciting to make this album. The sessions went so fast and easy for us, one tune after another." Bechet did not ask Solal to simplify his playing in any way, nor simplify his accompaniments harmonically. "I can't even when I try," Solal says.

Sidney Bechet had had a troublesome stomach during the 1950's and on one occasion, during a return to the United States, he was set to have some X-rays. He felt so much better after taking a liquid which was supposed to line his stomach in preparation for the pictures that he never showed up to have them taken. He always distrusted doctors and medical procedures, despite his personal respect for his dentist brother Leonard.

Sidney Bechet died in Paris in 1959, the same year in which jazz lost Baby Dodds and Omer Simeon, and two great players from a generation later than Bechet's, Billie Holiday and Lester Young. But when Sidney Bechet died, he was still at the height of his fame and (as the records he made at the 1958 Brussels World's Fair attest) still in touch with his highest creative powers.

"You tell it to the music, and the music tells it to you," he said in *Treat It Gentle*. "That's the life there is to a musicianer."

Recordings

RCA Victor's Vintage series promises to reissue its Bechet recordings. So far there has appeared "Bechet of New Orleans" (LPV 510) which includes three of the 1932 Feetwarmers selections, along with *Shake It and Break It, Texas Moaner, Sleepy Time Down South,* and *I Ain't Gonna Give Nobody None of My Jelly Roll.* (The "take" of *Shiek of Araby* included in this album is not quite as good as the original version.) Victor LPV-535 includes *Shag, Indian Summer, Blues in Thirds, Limehouse Blues,* and *Nobody Knows the Way I Feel This Morning.* Several overseas releases supplement the Bechet-Victor collection, including French RCA 430.216 and 430.639.

Bechet on Blue Note includes BLP 1201 with *Blue Horizon, Summertime, Dear Old Southland,* and an interesting alliance between Bechet and clarinetist Albert Nicholas (but with an inferior rhythm section) on *Blame It on the Blues* and *Weary Way Blues.* The series also includes Blue Note 1202, 1203, and 1204.

The Bechet-Spanier "Big Four" selections last appeared on Riverside RLP 138.

Earlier Bechet with Noble Sissle was on Brunswick BL 54048, along with some later Bechet done in France in the mid-Fifties.

Bechet's appearance with Tommy Ladnier at the "Spirituals to Swing" concert at Carnegie Hall in 1938 is a part of a Vanguard album (8523/4) that documents that event and the second "Spirituals to Swing" concert of the following year.

A Columbia album (CL 836) collected the 1938 titles by Bechet with Ernie Caceres and Zutty Singleton (*Jungle Drums, Chant in the Night,* and *What a Dream*), plus some quartet readings (including

Laura and *Love for Sale*) and three selections which include Bechet with Bob Wilber and his group.

The Sidney Bechet-Martial Solal recordings appeared in the United States on Pacific Jazz 1236.

And the Brussels World's Fair performances, including *Society Blues* were on Columbia CL 1410.

Texas Moaner Blues by the Clarence Williams Blue Five, with Bechet and Armstrong is included in Columbia's "The Sound of New Orleans" (C3L 30).

References

Ansermet, Ernest, "Sidney Bechet in 1919." From *The Art of Jazz,* edited by Martin T. Williams, Oxford, 1959.

Bechet, Sidney, *Treat It Gentle,* Hill & Wang, 1960.

Ellington, Duke, "The Most Essential Instrument," *Jazz Journal,* December 1965.

Greer, Sonny, "In Those Days," as told to Stanley Dance. From booklet accompanying "The Ellington Era, 1927–1940," vol. 2, Columbia album C3L 39.

Hadlock, Richard, "Sidney Bechet: How to Live Music." From *San Francisco Examiner,* January 17, 1965.

Harrison, Max, "Review of the Sidney Bechet-Mezz Mezzrow 1945–1947 Recordings." *Jazz Monthly,* February 1966.

Hillman, J. C., "Tommy Ladnier." *Jazz Journal,* August 1965.

Hoefer, George, "Sid Bechet Has Led Long, Colorful Life as Jazzman." *Down Beat,* December 14, 1951.

Jepsen, Grunnet, "Discographie de Sidney Bechet," in two parts. *Les Cahiers du Jazz,* nos. 10 and 11.

McCarthy, Albert J., "The Story of Tommy Ladnier." *The Record Changer,* July 1946.

Mellers, Wilfred, *Music in a New Found Land.* Knopf, 1965.

Thompson, Kay C., "An Interview with Sidney Bechet." *The Record Changer,* July 1949.

Wilber, Bob, "Review of 'The Sidney Bechet Story,' " Brunswick BL 54048. *The Jazz Review,* January 1960.

Williams, Martin, "A Conversation with Martial Solal." *Saturday Review,* July 13, 1963.

LITTLE LOUIE

I remember once when Louis came out to Lincoln Park in New Orleans to listen to the Kid Ory Band. . . . I let Louis sit in my chair. Now at that time I was the "Blues King" of New Orleans, and when Louis played that day he played more blues than I ever heard in my life. It never did strike my mind that blues could be interpreted so many different ways. Every time he played a chorus it was different and you knew it was the blues . . . yes, it was all blues what I mean.
        —MUTT CAREY

AFTER "KING" BOLDEN came "King" Keppard. And then (even if it was at first a matter of billing rather than public acclaim) there was King Oliver. After Oliver? Well, there was Buddy Petit, whom all New Orleans musicians remember. It is ironic that so highly praised a musician as Buddy Petit should be relegated almost to a note in this book. But Petit achieved little renown outside his own city during his lifetime and he made no recordings (although there are rumors of a vocal accompaniment done in California), so that he survives only in the memories of those who heard him and in those he influenced. He was idolized by youngsters the way an outstanding sports figure is idolized, and he was looked up to by musicians as so outstanding a player and bandleader that when he played something, everyone wanted to play it.

Petit was born in the middle 1890s. According to J. Lee Anderson, his real name was Crawford, but he was raised by the family of Joseph Petit who played valve trombone and who, according to Sidney Bechet, restlessly founded and briefly led a number of New Orleans brass bands in succession—the Eagle, Olympia, Imperial, Superior.

When Buddy Petit began to play horn as a sideline during his employment in the Empire Rice Mills, Bunk Johnson was his musical idol. In conduct, Petit apparently resembled both Bolden and Johnson. He was so much in demand that dancehall proprietors and promoters would sign him up months in advance, and Petit never agreed to a booking without a deposit. He would frequently end up with several engagements for the same evening. Petit eventually responded by forming several bands under his own name and farming out the work, and perhaps putting in token appearances at several halls during the evening. On one occasion a promoter managed to have him arrested, and delivered by the police in time to play a dance.

Petit drank, but Sidney Bechet, who as a youngster founded the Young Olympia Band with him, has attested to Petit's seriousness as a musician: "We used to get together and just play along, learning how to put ourselves together, finding so many things in the music, so many ways of coming to the music."

Petit's visit to southern California in 1917 to join Jelly Roll Morton has been noted above, and it was apparently the jeering he took for down-home ways (unfashionable clothes, cooking in the dressing room, and eating on the bandstand) that brought about his decision to return to New Orleans. There is a mention of his later touring during the early Twenties into Texas, particularly Galveston, with a band in which Bunk Johnson eventually replaced him. Clarinetist George Lewis says that Petit played enough like Bunk Johnson that one could not tell them apart. And there is a story among New Orleans old-timers that not only did Armstrong respect him but that Petit once "carved Louis Armstrong down to the bricks" in a musical cutting contest. He died in July 1931, and Armstrong was one of his pallbearers.

Louis Daniel Armstrong was never crowned "King" by the populace or for publicity but he is the crowning glory of New Orleans jazz, and on the basis of his influence, he was the real King of Swing. The influence did not stop there, for his style has touched that of every popular artist in America (but to limit that influence to the United States is to draw a geographical line that obviously may not be drawn). His trumpeting has also affected the brass technique of almost every horn player in the Western world (where else do our symphonists get that vibrato they're not supposed to have?). And no composer of any category writes for brass the way his predecessors did, simply because Louis Armstrong played things on the trumpet that no one had played before him. It could be said that this man changed the world; he did, at the very least, change Western music—all of it—and the more that music spreads, the closer it comes to being true that he changed all the world's music.

Armstrong's musical talent was innate; it expressed itself even before it found its natural outlet in the trumpet, and many local musicians knew it. Zutty Singleton, then still in his teens and probably recently arrived in town, has said, "the first time I ever saw Louis was when he was about twelve, thirteen years old. He was singing with three other kids in an amateur show at Bill and Mary Mack's tent show in New Orleans. Louis was singing tenor then, and they broke it up that night." And Sidney Bechet has noted, "It was Bunk Johnson who was the first to make me acquainted with Louis Armstrong. Bunk told me about this quartet Louis was singing in. 'Sidney,' he said, 'I want you to go hear a little quartet, how they sing and harmonize.' He knew I was crazy about singing harmony."

As is indicated by the surname his people took, Louis Armstrong was not a downtown colored Creole. He was not uptown Negro either. Louis Armstrong was born in the poorest, blackest, most crowded section of New Orleans, the section called "back o' town," July 4, 1900. His mother and father lived with his grandmother in a little house on James Alley. The couple quarreled a lot and they split up when Armstrong was still an infant and both moved out. Little Louis' grandmother, an ex-slave, supported herself by taking in washing, and he sometimes earned a nickel by helping her with the deliveries.

After the youngster had lived with his grandmother a few years, a friend of his mother's arrived to say that his mother had become ill and asked if Louis could come stay with her and help care for her. So little Louis went off to live with his mother. En route, incidentally, he had his first abrupt experience with Jim Crow on the segregated street car that carried him to his new home.

His mother had moved to a place at Liberty and Perdido Streets, a row of rented rooms called "Brick Row" in a neighbor-

hood that had its cheap prostitutes and cheap bars that sometimes featured pianists.

Armstrong called his mother by her nickname "Mayanne" most
of his life. She had been born in Butte, Louisiana, and, like his
father, was an ex-slave. Armstrong has said in his autobiography
that all of the neighborhood—churchgoer, policeman, and rough-
neck—treated his mother with respect. She envied no one, he
says, and had a natural respect for the feelings of others. These
were qualities he admired and emulated.

At the corner of the street where his mother lived was the
Masonic Hall, nicknamed "Funky Butt Hall," and the youngster,
then only five, heard Buddy Bolden playing inside. Already there
was something about the cornet that attracted his ear—in church,
in "second lining" following parades, and overhearing what went
on in nearby bars and dancehalls.

Gradually, he began to be aware of distinctions among the
leading players. Bolden was powerful, loud, and, for the youngster, finally too rough; he did not move him. Bunk Johnson had
"the most beautiful tone, the best imagination, and the softest
sense of phrasing." King Oliver had a tone that he liked as well
as Johnson's; Oliver had range, and he had ideas that were good
in themselves and that led to still more ideas. And to Armstrong,
Freddy Keppard apparently did not seem so much a follower
of Bolden but "had a style of his own," with a beautiful tone,
marvelous endurance, and little traits that interested and amazed
him.

Louis (already nicknamed "Dipper" for Dippermouth, but not
yet Satchelmouth), doing well in school and helping out his
mother by selling papers—while duly respectful to a succession of
stepfathers—was well liked in the neighborhood. He had formed
the singing quartet of which we had heard. Almost from the
beginning, Little Louis, usually taking tenor parts, wanted to
sing bass. He carried a homemade cigar-box guitar. If anyone
was worried because these youngsters were going down into the
Storyville district and singing for roughnecks, pimps, and whores,
he would guilelessly explain that the tips were better down there,
and that people loved their singing, especially their version of
My Brazilian Beauty, and therefore wouldn't harm them.

In New Orleans, celebration of the Christmas season continued well into the new year, and usually involved as much noise as one could make, including not only fireworks but also firing guns into the air. When Louis Armstrong was twelve years old he went off to that district to sing, carrying an old pistol which one of his stepfathers had left behind. Before long he had shot it into the air, had been arrested, and was taken to juvenile court. "I was frightened . . . what were they going to do to me? Where were they going to send me? I had no idea what a Waifs' Home was. How long would I have to stay there? How serious was it to fire off a pistol in the street? Oh, I had a million minds, and I could not pacify any of them."

Armstrong, like a million other youngsters, had been attracted to the drums, but there is evidence that he had played some cornet before he was sent to the Waifs' Home. Sidney Bechet notes, "Of course, Louis was playing the cornet a bit before he went into that Jones school, but it was, you know, how kids play." And Bunk Johnson remembered responding to Louis' questions about the horn—how to place it to his mouth properly and how to finger it—about the blues and various standard tunes, as early as 1911. While he was in the Waif's Home he was allowed to choose a vocation that interested him and get some training in it. He chose music. He was taught by a man named Peter Davis, and that was very possibly the most important and fortunate experience of his life.

The Waifs' Home was run, and apparently well run, by Joseph Jones, Captain Jones ("Pops" or sometimes "Cap" to the youngsters). Not wanting a jail-like atmosphere, he set up a military one, with a bugler signaling the day's activities and a band chosen from among his charges. Both Jones and Davis were relative musical amateurs, but they got guidance and training from Joe Howard of the Allen Brass Band, and soon the Waifs' band was well known in the city.

It took Davis a while to warm up to Armstrong and longer for him to let him try the tambourine, snare drum, the bugle, and later the cornet. But when he finally let him in the school band, Davis showed the youngster elements of music, and evidently helped him to play the cornet correctly, with good embouchure, and he taught him the importance of tone. These matters of elementary technique are more important than they may seem. Many players (Armstrong included) firmly believe that Buddy Bolden's mind deteriorated because he overblew the cornet. And from the recorded evidence it seems very likely that in the playing of Freddy Keppard and King Oliver, basic flaws in fingering or in embouchure or breath control may eventually have caught up with both men. But Armstrong, like Bunk Johnson, apparently put the horn to his mouth correctly and fingered correctly from the beginning, important basic facts for a man who, all else aside, was to become and remain a superb brass player as well as superb jazzman.

At the time Louis Armstrong left the Waif's Home at fourteen, he had finished all the formal schooling he was to have. He had also affirmed within himself a self-reliance and personal dignity, partly from the way he was treated at the home and partly because of what he had brought with him. He has looked back with pride on the fact that he was taught good habits of health and cleanliness, that he learned how to scrub floors, wash, iron, cook and make beds, play baseball, swim, and play music.

Little Louie also had the proud pleasure of marching down his own street in front of his mother's house as a member of the school band. Preston Jackson remembers, "I had heard Louis play before in 1915 at a playground dedication when the Jones Waif Band featured Louis and Henry Rena. Louis was terrific even then. I was going to the school where the playground was. That's how I happened to hear him."

Louis was discharged only on condition that he was to be put in the care of his father. He did live briefly with his father and stepmother, but soon went back to living with Mayanne Armstrong again.

He went back also to selling papers, and to the job that became his favorite after music, selling coal through the streets with the peddler's cry:

> My mule is white, my face is black,
> I sells my coal two bits a sack!

But now of course he had another means of livelihood, the cornet—always a rented horn at first. Through a friend, Armstrong got a job playing in a honky-tonk of Henry Ponce. "All you have to do," his friend advised, "is put on your long pants and play the blues for the whores that hustle all night. They come in with a big stack of money in their stockings for their pimps. When you play the blues they will call you sweet names and buy you drinks and give you tips." It was Henry Ponce who remarked to Armstrong's father a few years later, with startling insight, "that an older musician did not have what this youngster had—sincerity and a kind of creative power which the world would eventually recognize."

The hours were long, and on Saturdays longer, for then Armstrong did not get away from Ponce's place until ten or eleven A.M. On weekdays he would get home at 4 A.M., sleep for a couple of hours, and report for work hauling coal from 7 in the morning till 5 in the evening. He made seventy-five cents during the day and $1.25 plus tips a night. He was fifteen years old.

The job at Ponce's did not last long; Ponce was closed down during a brief local clean-up campaign. Once again Armstrong the musician fell back on occasional parades, dances, and funerals, and Armstrong the support of his family fell back on various unskilled jobs, particularly the coal wagon.

Louis Armstrong's autobiographical *Satchmo: My Life In New Orleans,* which first appeared in 1954, is a somewhat editorially bowdlerized and "corrected" document to anyone acquainted with the natural eloquence of his highly personal writing style. But it is a valuable book because it gives us so much of the personal life of the young musician in New Orleans. And Armstrong sees the bawdiness, the humor, the strength, the delusion, and the degradation of Storyville and its environs—its pimps, gamblers, tough characters, whores, madams, barkeeps, and bouncers—with a perspective that is seldom negative but is at once as lively and more sober than any we have.

Of course his special perspective on New Orleans comes about partly through his own insight and partly because—unlike, say, Jelly Roll Morton, who has also told us much about Storyville—he was not looking back on a period of relative affluence and success but on a period of hard work and apprenticeship when he learned to put love, respect, good will, and self-reliance above other things, and a period when (again unlike Morton) his conscious devotion to his music was primary.

Armstrong is aware of facts about New Orleans life that some other men have glossed over. Once in an interview he remarked that there was "so much good music that was played in Storyville" and the music had been so much discussed, even in colleges and large universities. But he wondered if many youngsters realized that Storyville, after all, was primarily an area of prostitutes "standing in their doorways nightly in their fine and beautiful negligees—faintly calling to the boys as they passed their cribs. . . . The fleet of sailors and the crews from those big ships that come in the Mississippi River from all over the world—kept them very, very busy."

Since Armstrong has told us so much about his personal life until his early twenties, one is tempted to repeat much, even when one's focus is on his musical life. One story in particular that Armstrong has included in his book is worth noting because it is revealing of his own outlook and the environment in which it was formed. A cousin, Flora Miles, began running with some rather wild teen-age girls who lived in the heart of the honkytonk quarter, and she got pregnant and had a child. The father? An old white man who used to take the group of young girls up to his ramshackle house in the afternoons. When the child was born—a boy who was named Clarence—Flora Miles' father was told to have the old man arrested. But he was a white man and if they had tried, as Armstrong said, "the judge would have had us all thrown out in the street, including baby Clarence."

The next best thing was to take care of Clarence—Flora Miles died soon after he was born—and the job fell largely to Armstrong, who adopted the child as his son.

When things got very tough, little Louis would go over to "front o' town," and hang around the produce houses. He would go through the barrels of spoiled food—potatoes, vegetables, chickens, ducks, turkeys—and pick out the best he could find. At home, the family would cut away the spoiled parts, boil the good parts thoroughly, dress them, and put them up in baskets as attractively as possible. Then they would take them to local restaurants and sell them for whatever the proprietor wanted to pay.

After 1917 Louis Armstrong came more and more under the influence of King Oliver, musically and personally. He could not afford to hang around dances or cabarets or picnics as some youngsters did; he had to help support his family. But he did get to hold Oliver's horn on occasion during parades. And when delivering coal in Storyville, he could hear Oliver playing at Pete Lala's in "the hottest jazz band ever in New Orleans"— Oliver, Buddy Christian on guitar and banjo, Zue Robinson on trombone, Jimmy Noone on clarinet, Bob Lyons on string bass, and Henry Zeno on drums.

"I'd stand there listening to King Oliver beat out one of those good ol good-ones like *Panama* or *High Society*. . . . My, whatta punch that man had. . . . And could he shout a tune. . . . Ump. . . . All of a sudden it would dawn on the lady that I was still in her crib very silent while she hustle those tricks—and she'd say—'What's the matter with you, boy? . . . Why are you still there standing so quiet?' And there I'd have to explain to her that I was being inspired by *the* King Oliver and his orchestra. . . . And then she handed me a cute one by saying—'Well, this is no place to daydream. . . . I've got my work to do.' So I'd go home very pleased and happy that I did at least hear my idol blow at least a couple of numbers that really *gassed* me no end. . . ."

Soon Armstrong had formed a little orchestra with his friend, drummer Joe Lindsey, and the group modeled itself on the Kid Ory band with Joe Oliver. Oliver had also befriended the youngster, and when Louis did errands for Stella Oliver, Joe's wife, he was paid off in trumpet lessons from the master—"I could not have asked for anything I wanted more." Finally, the King gave Little Louis a cast-off cornet to replace the battered secondhand one the youngster had managed to buy.

However, one should never underestimate how much the young musician was learning on his own. On one occasion Sidney Bechet was astonished to hear Armstrong executing the Alphonse Picou clarinet variations on *High Society* (which he had taken from a piccolo part) on his cornet!

There is an exaggerated notion that, during the First World War when the U.S. Navy declared its own war on vice in New Orleans, there was a mass shutdown of Storyville, and a mass exodus of entertainers, barkeeps, and prostitutes. Work did

gradually get scarcer of course, so there was an exodus, but it
was not a mass movement. And as for the vice, well, much as
the earlier effort to restrict it entirely to the Storyville section
had been a partial failure, so the effort to stamp it out was
only an apparent success. Whoring and drinking simply went
underground or moved out of the district and became a little
less brassy and overt. The big, obvious houses like Lulu White's
Mahogany Hall probably suffered most.

In mid-1918, King Oliver got his offer from Chicago, and
Armstrong was among those who saw Oliver and Jimmy Noone
off on the Illinois Central train north. As the train departed and
the young cornetist climbed back on his coal wagon, Kid Ory
called out, "You still blowing that cornet?" And then he told
him everyone said to be sure to get Little Louis to take Oliver's
place in Ory's group.

Little Louis knew the Ory-Oliver repertory by heart and after
his first job with the band he knew he was in. Ory got good jobs
and Armstrong kept busy, but he held onto his coal wagon. One
occasion with Ory is typical of the musical friction that went
on in New Orleans, a friction that had a fundamental influence
on the city's jazz. One day the "reading" musicians in Joseph
Robechaux's band had a funeral to play in the daytime when
many of the sidemen had to work at their regular jobs. The
Robechaux men generally looked down on jazzmen like Ory
and Armstrong and thought they could play well only together
and in their own style, but, no one else being available, they
pieced out the group with several players from Ory's band.
When the ensemble gathered, the Robechaux men were cold,
but it soon turned out that the Ory men played all the music
put in front of them. And on the march back to town, when time
came for the group to strike the note of joy that traditionally
followed the burial in New Orleans funerals, they struck up
Panama. The Ory men took over, began to ad lib, and made
the music swing joyously. Then, in the final chorus, Armstrong
remembered how his idol Oliver used to jump to the upper
register.

"After that incident those stuck up guys wouldn't let us alone.
They patted us on the back . . . they hired us several times

afterwards. After all, we'd proved to them that any learned musician can read music, but they can't all swing. It was a good lesson for them."

Ory got good jobs, including high-paying ones at white dances and country clubs, and he began to promote dances of his own on the "off" Monday nights, downtown at "Economy Hall." If Ory didn't have a job on a Saturday night, Armstrong would play across the river in Gretna, near Algiers, in a very tough honky-tonk called the Brick House, frequented by levee workers who "would drink and fight one another like circle saws."

There Armstrong noticed that one of the girls kept giving him the eye; he found out that she was named Daisy Parker. Soon they had had several meetings, fell in love and, she at twenty-one and he at eighteen, they were married.

When Armstrong's neighbors got wind of things, several lady gossips immediately went to Mayanne Armstrong, their tongues wagging and clucking all at once. And once again, his mother treated her son's feelings with respect, telling the gossips that Little Louis had his own life to lead and that if he loved the woman enough to marry her, that was his business.

The attachment was strong, but Daisy Parker Armstrong was a suspicious and jealous wife and the relationship was turbulent.

The cornetist continued to play with Ory or, perhaps, to make a parade with Oscar Celestine's Tuxedo Brass Band, but he still had to supplement his income and often it meant picking up charcoal scraps down around the docks when the big charcoal pieces were unloaded and selling them through the streets.

Then when he was nineteen came a break, a permanent well-paying musical job, and valuable musical experience. Armstrong was invited by Fate Marable to come up to St. Louis and play on the Streckfus Riverboats, particularly the *Sydney*, in a band that included Baby Dodds, Pops Foster, and Johnny St. Cyr. Marable, a hard teacher but an excellent one, with the help of melophonist Davey Jones, taught Armstrong to read music far better and depend less on his ear, and the young cornetist played all sorts of music in all sorts of arrangements. Reedman Jerome Don Pasqual remembered Armstrong as an excellent musician but a man so personally modest and full of praise for others that he seemed "the sort of person you'd figure would go back home, settle down, and raise a big family." But still he was the best trumpeter the other players had ever heard.

Paul Whiteman's orchestra became a favorite with Captain Joe Streckfus and he wanted Marable's group to imitate them, which meant that Armstrong would take the part of Whiteman's trumpeter Henry Busse. At that point, as Pasqual remembers it, Armstrong and Baby Dodds began to lose interest. So in the early summer of 1921, Captain Joe discharged them both. Armstrong, however, remembers a close and warm personal feeling for the Streckfus family.

Back in New Orleans in late 1921, Armstrong went into Tom Anderson's The Real Thing, on Rampart Street, a favorite spot among rich, fast-spending horsemen. The leader was Paul Dominguez, a violinist, and among the sidemen was pianist Luis Russell.

Next Armstrong joined the trio of his friend Zutty Singleton at Butchy Fernandez's place, making it a quartet. After hours, sitting in by musicians was common at Fernandez's, and one particular evening Baby Dodds was rough enough on Singleton's drums to break a hole in one of them. The relationship between the two drummers was never the same afterward.

During this period, Fletcher Henderson, touring as pianist with a group that accompanied singer Ethel Waters, remembered hearing the young cornetist playing in a little dancehall. He recognized that the young man was remarkably talented and asked him to join the group. Armstrong thought it over for a day and then told Henderson he couldn't leave unless he could take Singleton with him, and Henderson, unwilling to leave his own drummer stranded, had to say no. But he later felt that this was just the young Louie's way of covering up a reluctance to leave home.

Toward the end of the year, Armstrong became a proud permanent member of the Oscar Celestine Tuxedo Brass Band, and on occasion heard the leader's encouraging, "Son, are you all right? Can you manage that?" when given an unfamiliar musical part to read.

Then, in the summer of 1922, after Little Louis had played a parade with the Tuxedo band, he acknowledged a telegram from King Oliver asking him to come and join the Creole Jazz Band at the Lincoln Gardens in Chicago.

Armstrong remembers his arrival vividly. "I'll never forget the night I joined the Oliver band. They were playing at the Lincoln Gardens, at Thirty-first near Cottage Grove. . . . I didn't come in on the train that Joe was supposed to meet. So that makes me come in all by myself. I looked all around and I didn't see anybody. I said: 'Lord, what's going to happen now?' and I wondered if I should go right back on the next train. I was just a youngster from New Orleans, and I felt real lost in Chicago. But a redcap told me: 'Why don't you get a cab and go out to the Lincoln Gardens.'

"When I got there and got out of the cab, I heard this *band*. They were really jumping then, and I commenced to worry all over again. I wondered if I could ever fit into that band. Oh, those cats were glowing!"

Lillian Hardin, Oliver's classically trained pianist (she studied for a concert career at Fisk University), remembers hearing a great deal about "Little Louie" before he arrived. When he did arrive she was quite surprised to see this decidedly pudgy young man, who seemed anything but little. She didn't pay much attention to his playing at first, but one evening Oliver confessed to her frankly that the young cornetist could outplay him, but that he would remain King as long as he could keep Louis in his band. Then Lil Hardin began to listen.

Everyone else had been listening all along. Tommy Brookins has said, "I still remember the arrival of Louis Armstrong in Chicago. The news spread like wildfire among the musicians who hurried that same evening to Lincoln Gardens. It wasn't that Louis' name was then known, but the musicians were aware of the fact that a young trumpet player had just arrived from New Orleans and was playing with Oliver." He added that one rarely heard Armstrong in solo, but on evenings when Joe Oliver wasn't feeling well he would let Louis cut loose.

However, on Oliver's recordings from this period, made between March and December 1923, there are Armstrong's solos from the very beginning. The young cornetist has a double-chorus on *Chimes Blues* from the first date, and a solo on

Froggy Moore from the second. The blues choruses, some New
Orleans musicians say, come from Bunk Johnson. The *Froggy
Moore* solo is a fairly direct paraphrase of the third theme of
the piece. But both solos have the momentous, buoyant rhythm
that was Armstrong's particular gift to jazz. One can hear Bunk
Johnson in him and one can hear Oliver in him—indeed one can
hear the whole New Orleans brass tradition in him, at least that
part of it that we know from records. But he also expressed
something that the others seemed to have been reaching for,
and this something has a fresh rhythmic impetus and energy.
The thing that delighted him about Lil Hardin's piano when
he first heard it was that she played all four beats. And thus she
filled in a rhythm that New Orleans jazz had been using or
implying almost from the beginning, and that Armstrong's ideas
fully affirmed.

There are of course other striking moments by Little Louis
on the Oliver records. We have noted examples of the interplay
of the two cornets in the Oliver chapter above. There is Arm-
strong's intro on *Krooked Blues,* and solo on the Okeh *River-
side Blues.* There is also Armstrong's strong lead just before
Oliver's celebrated solo on the Okeh version of *Dippermouth
Blues* and in the final chorus of the Okeh of *Mabel's Dream* and
Chattanooga Stomp. There are Armstrong breaks on *I Ain't
Gonna Tell Nobody,* on the Paramount version of *Riverside
Blues,* and on *Tears.*

Lil Hardin began to take personal as well as musical interest
in Armstrong, and he in her. He was still wearing second-hand
clothes and she encouraged him to buy new ones. From her
classical background, she began to rehearse with him and teach
him, and from her own insight and determination she began
to encourage him to go off on his own. When the Dodds brothers
and Dutrey left in the dispute over money, Louis and Lil of
course stayed. Oliver was keeping Armstrong's money for him,
and she encouraged Louis Armstrong to end the arrangement.

He was a masterful whistler, she says; she heard him whistle
all sorts of phrases and runs and riffs that he never used with
Oliver. Armstrong's comments on his attitudes as a sideman are
revealing. "I never did try to overblow Joe at any time when I
played with him. It wasn't any show-off thing like a youngster

probably would do today. He still played whatever part he had played, and I always played 'pretty' under him. Until I left Joe, I never did tear out. Finally, I thought it was about time to move along, and he thought so, too. He couldn't keep me any longer. But things were always very good between us—that *never* did cease."

Before long Louis and Lil had decided to marry, and Armstrong divorced Daisy Parker. Finally, when Lillian Armstrong told her husband that he should give Oliver notice, he wondered what he was supposed to do. Hang around musicians and see who needed a first, not a second, trumpet player—Lil told him. After much hesitation, and with great reluctance, Armstrong gave Papa Joe his notice, and after a couple of rebuffs, Louis Armstrong found a job with Ollie Powers' orchestra at the Dreamland.

A few months later, he got his second offer from Fletcher Henderson, and by now of course Henderson was the leader of a successful orchestra in New York.

"Louis, his style and his feeling," said Henderson's chief arranger, Don Redman, "changed our whole idea about the band musically." Before long he had changed everyone's ideas about music.

Recordings

Armstrong with King Oliver's Creole Jazz Band can be heard on Riverside 12-122 and on Epic 16003.

Columbia's "The Sound of New Orleans" (C3L 30) has Oliver's *Jazzin' Babies Blues* and two of Oscar Celestine's early recordings. The same label's "The Sound of Chicago" (C3L 32) has three Oliver titles, *New Orleans Stomp, Where Did You Stay Last Night,* and *Tears.*

References

Note: Armstrong's subsequent career and stylistic development are covered in two other volumes in this series, *Jazz Masters of the 20's,* by Richard Hadlock, and the forthcoming, *Jazz Masters of the 30's,* by Hsio Wen Shih.

Armstrong, Lil, "Satchmo and Me," Riverside LP 12-120.

Armstrong, Louis, *Satchmo: My Life in New Orleans*. Signet, 1955.

———, *Swing That Music*. Longmans, Green, 1936.

Bechet, Sidney, *Treat It Gentle, An Autobiography*. Hill & Wang, 1960.

Carey, Mutt, "New Orleans Trumpet Players." *Jazz Music*, vol. 3, no. 4, 1946.

Driggs, Frank, and Thornton Hagart, "Jerome Don Pasqual." *Jazz Journal*, April 1964.

Jackson, Preston, "King Oliver." From *Frontiers of Jazz*, edited by Ralph de Toledano. Oliver Durrell, 1947.

Meryman, Richard, "An Interview with Louis Armstrong." *Life*, April 15, 1966.

Russell, William, "Louis Armstrong." From *Jazzmen*, edited by Frederick Ramsey, Jr. and Charles Edward Smith. Harcourt, Brace and Co., 1939.

Shapiro, Nat, and Nat Hentoff, eds. *Hear Me Talkin' to Ya*. Rinehart, 1955.

ZUTTY

By the mid-1920's, drummer Zutty Singleton was already a major figure in jazz, and was associated with such major New Orleans musicians as Louis Armstrong and Jimmy Noone. However, for most people the archetypal drummer is Warren "Baby" Dodds.

Perhaps that is a correct estimate, for Baby Dodds's busy style does belong with the classic period of Crescent City music —with the style, the phrasing, the melodic rhythm of instrumentalists like Jelly Roll Morton, like his clarinetist brother Johnny Dodds, like King Oliver. Baby Dodds is perhaps a summary of jazz drums up to the era of Louis Armstrong. But Zutty Singleton sounded better playing with Armstrong.

Zutty Singleton did not summarize the past of jazz drums so much as he evoked their future, providing seminal ideas of rhythm and phrasing, along with the techniques to execute them. It is therefore particularly unfortunate that his reputation has had to live in Dodds' shadow. And he became Louis Armstrong's drummer, much as Earl Hines became Louis Armstrong's pianist. He also became, as an influence, Dave Tough's drummer, George Wettling's drummer, and—perhaps most important of all—Sidney Catlett's drummer. Thereby his ideas permeated the drumming of the swing period and in a sense evoked later periods. It is entirely appropriate that Singleton should first have attracted major attention by recording with Armstrong, that he should have affirmed his reputation while working with Roy Eldridge in the mid-Thirties, and that he should have been one of the first drummers to record with Dizzy Gillespie and Charlie Parker in the mid-Forties.

Singleton's style was not formed under the influence of Dodds or of Dodds' general school of drums, but under the influence of more sophisticated and, if you will, more "legitimate" players. "No, I didn't play like the older style drummers," he says, "I listened to Louis Cottrell—Louis senior, who played the Orpheum Theatre—to Paul Detroit, and Henry Zeno. They all knew how to phrase, and they always stayed under the band—never loud or overbearing. And they never played with too much cymbal. I liked Cottrell's roll and the tones he got. I liked the way Detroit played with the theatre acts. He helped me get to play the Lyric Theatre in New Orleans where I worked with Ethel Waters, Bessie Smith, and many other well-known singers."

"The warmth and drive and pleasure that flow out of Singleton," Whitney Balliett has written, "are irresistible. He is the sun." He continues, "Emotions chase and flicker through him, appearing when he drops his eyelids and hoists his eyebrows, when, abruptly lunging at a cymbal, his stick a truncheon, he clamps his lips shut, and when delivering a mighty roll he shakes his head from side to side with a fury that only compounds his rhythms. But just his arms and head really move; his trunk is a rigid, stately pivot."

For Singleton, the recordings he made in 1928 with Louis Armstrong and Earl Hines, in a revamped version of the Armstrong Hot Five, are the best he ever made. They begin with *Fireworks, Skip the Gutter, Don't Jive Me;* go through the revolutionary *West End Blues* and the superb *Muggles;* and they end with the salacious classic *Tight Like That.* "Hines had it too—like Louis. He has always been my favorite pianist, him and Fats Waller. Those records are my idea of jazz. We didn't call that music Dixieland or anything like that, it was just plain 'jazz' to us."

Indeed there is little on the record that one would justly have to call Dixieland—a few loosely Dixielandish ensembles perhaps. The music is largely the work of a group of soloists, in Hines and Armstrong, brilliant soloists, and in Singleton an understanding accompanist. And the musical ideas they articulated were brilliant in themselves and quickly became the first-hand inspiration for a generation of players on all instruments,

and for composers and arrangers as well. Once and twice removed, their influence can still be felt on a second and a third
generation.

"Of course," Singleton reminds us, "I had worked with Louis
before, in New Orleans. You might say he worked for me. He
had just come back from the riverboats and I got together a
little four-piece group to work at The Orchard, a place owned
by Butchy Fernandez. I had Johnny St. Cyr on banjo and guitar,
Eudell Wilson on piano, Louis, and myself. Guitar, piano, and
drums was the rhythm—it was so smooth with those three." In
view of this alliance, it is particularly interesting to note critic
André Hodeir saying about Johnny St. Cyr that he did seem
in touch with Armstrong's new musical ideas, that his "accompaniments are generally excellent," and that it is likely that he
"paved the way for modern guitarists."

Singleton, who came to New Orleans while still a school-age
youngster, clearly remembers the very first time he ever saw
Armstrong, when Louis, then twelve years old, was singing tenor
in a quartet of amateurs at Bill and Mary Mack's tent show.
Subsequently, news of Armstrong's acquired prowess on cornet
at the Waif's Home drifted back to Singleton, and, after Louis's
release, almost all the musically inclined youngsters in town
took a close look to see if he was playing as well as the stories
said.

Arthur James Singleton was born on May 14, 1898, in Bunkie,
Louisiana, in the south-central area of the state. He acquired
the name Zutty when he was still an infant; it is Creole patois
for cute and was given him by an aunt while he was still in
the cradle. He has kept it, as a professional name (although
it has been spelled various ways by various nightclub owners,
sign painters, and journalists) and once even used it singly, in
his mid-Thirties billing—Zutty and His Band.

Singleton speaks of his fascination for drums that goes back
almost as long as he can remember. His mother worked for a
McBride family in Opelousas, somewhat south of Bunkie. The
father of the household ran a local drugstore and played drums
in a town band. "I used to play with his son, Raymond, and
one afternoon we found the drum set in the basement. There
were no sticks, but I pulled the stays out of the back of a

kitchen chair and started to play. That was the first time I actually had my hands on any drums."

Zutty's first inspiration came from an uncle, Willy Bontemps, who played bass and guitar with Jack Carey, the New Orleans trombonist who used to feature *Tiger Rag* before it was called *Tiger Rag*, but was called "Jack Carey." Singleton did his first public playing with a pianist named Steve Lewis at house parties. Lewis was technically good enough later to play with A. J. Piron, but even as youngsters he and Singleton worked for white "society" dances at the New Orleans Country Club, the Louisiana Restaurant, perhaps doing a Saturday afternoon tea dance with Papa Celestine and his band.

Zutty's first drum set was the gift of a sympathetic aunt, and almost from the beginning his equipment (the basic components of his drum set) was set. He had considerably less paraphernalia than many jazz and popular drummers were using at that time, and a great deal less than show and pit drummers were using—unless he had to acquire something for a special effect. Singleton did not particularly like the several cow bells, wood and temple blocks that most drummers of the time affected, and he used them sparingly. Nor did he favor the array of triangles, chimes, gongs, and kettles that were often displayed. Not that he was always able to avoid them—and he is still fond of his woodblock—but the basic Singleton set consists of a bass drum; a snare drum; two tom-toms (the old-style, shallow kind); a woodblock; a couple of cowbells; and two, or more usually, three cymbals. He does not like the high hat, the two cymbals struck together by a footpedal, which most drummers have on the left ("it interferes with what the bass is doing").

Gene Krupa, in discussing his apprenticeship, once said that he had no idea at first what a wide range of effects a drummer could get. "I learned from Zutty Singleton and Baby Dodds the difference between starting a roll or sequence of beats with the left or right hand, and how the tone and inflection changed entirely when you shifted hands. . . . I punched holes in my tom-toms with an ice-pick, as Zutty told me, until they were pitched just right . . . learned from Baby Dodds how to keep the bass and snare drum in tune. . . . Then came the cowbell and the woodblock. . . . I finally was able to show that drums have a broad range of tonal variations so they can be played to fit into a harmonic pattern as well as a rhythmic one."

Singleton began using brushes instead of sticks rather early. Manuel Perez, the New Orleans cornetist, had become intrigued with drum brushes when he went to Chicago before the First World War, and he sent a pair back to New Orleans to his friend Louis Cottrell. But Cottrell, it seems, was a fastidious man, and when he discovered that tarnish from the metal brushes was dirtying his drumheads, he passed these new pieces of equipment on to Zutty Singleton.

We might note at this point that the listener is apt to get a rather false picture of how early jazz drummers actually played if he depends only on records. Drums presented a problem to recording engineers, and in fact they still do. But until the very late Twenties, jazz and popular percussionists in recording studios were encouraged to clop away predominantly on woodblocks, temple blocks, and on cymbals—dampened or choked by one hand while being struck by a stick held in the other. Early recording techniques simply would not absorb the low sound of bass and snare and the sounds of openly played cymbals in ways that made them reproduce effectively when played back. On the job, a given drummer might sound and play rather differently than he would on a record. Of course, listeners are not the only victims of this technical limitation. Young drummers who learn from phonograph records tried to imitate what they heard on the records. Indeed, this sort of misapprehension continued well into the late 1940s and early 1950s, when drummers of the New Orleans and Dixieland "revival" were variously clopping and popping away on an array of temple blocks in the belief that they were being strictly authentic.

It was in his very young years, drumming at the New Orleans theatres, that Singleton made one of his most important stylistic discoveries. He describes the event this way: "Ethel Waters came to town to play the Lyric, and she taught me the Charleston beat for one of her special numbers. I couldn't get it at first, but then I found out that if I played all *four* beats on the bass drum instead of two, that made it easy!"

Many New Orleans musicians found work on the riverboats, and in 1923 Singleton began drumming on the nightly excursion, including dancing, with Monday nights reserved for Negroes, of the boats the *St. Paul* and the *Capitol.* These boats were the enterprise of the Streckfus family, who had their headquarters in St. Louis. They would winter the boats in New Orleans. Captain John Streckfus had several famous, semi-famous, or famous-to-be musicians working for him, but one of the best was Zutty's leader, a man hardly known to the public at large, pianist Fate Marable.

Marable's story is almost as important as it is little known. Nearly everyone who has worked with him will call him a remarkable musician and a great leader. He began on the riverboats when he was only sixteen. He became—to deal with an aspect of his career that may seem minor to us today—so good a steam calliope player that every circus or carnival musician from the Middle West who was forced to undertake that boisterous instrument knew of Marable, sought him out, and watched and heard him with delight.

From among New Orleans players, Marable was perceptive enough to hire Louis Armstrong, the Dodds brothers, Pops Foster, Johnny St. Cyr, Singleton, Red Allen—and that is a scant list. Marable was still important and influential in the St. Louis area well into the late Thirties when his bands featured Earl Bostic and the crucially important bassist, Jimmy Blanton, for just two examples.

Fate Marable was well schooled and became an important teacher to almost every musician who worked for him. "When I joined him," Zutty Singleton attests, "I was replacing a drummer named Casey who not only read music but played bells, xylophone, and so forth. The best I could do was *try* to read, with my head buried in the music sheet, while I kept time. But Captain John Streckfus told Fate to get me to look up and stop keeping my head down.

"It was like being in the service to work with Captain John. He had Ralph Williams and Isham Jones leading the bands on his other two riverboats, and we had to go over and listen to them, and they to us. He would buy the newest records, by Fletcher Henderson or Paul Whiteman or someone like that, and if he liked a part of the arrangement, we would have to copy it. We started with a stock arrangement of the piece and had to figure out how to work that part in, but Fate was musical enough to do it. I remember I had to buy a gong to play Fletcher Henderson's *Shanghai Shuffle.*"

Incidentally, Zutty acquired his second nickname from Marable. The leader would call men passengers "Face"—if someone requested a number he would reply, "Okay, Face"—and women customers "Breath." The names were slightly disguised insults for Marable, but Zutty picked up the "Face" from him and carried it on just for fun, and as he called others "Face," they began to call him the same. Zutty's feature numbers in later years carried names like *About Face*, which he recorded with Pee Wee Russell, or, on another occasion simply *Face.*

It has been said by some jazz historians that Marable unfortunately never recorded. But Marable did record, although the label listed him as Fate Morable. Two sides were made in New Orleans in March 1924, and the drummer on them is Zutty Singleton. The titles were *Frankie and Johnny* and the leader's feature, *Piano Flage.*

Zutty's next move was perhaps a logical one, for he went to St. Louis, Missouri, which was, of course, the Streckfus headquarters. But there he worked for cornetist-leader Charles Creath, joining him in 1924.

The story of jazz in St. Louis is largely untold, but it is a story in itself, and it needs telling. The conventional jazz history will say that the city was a kind of stopping-off place as the New Orleans players carried their musical message north. But if a New Orleans player stopped there—even before 1900, when his own kind of music was not yet established—he would find St. Louis abustle with ragtime music, which decidedly *was* popularly established. Later, "they played a nice kind of jazz in St. Louis, and they improvised very well, with nice melodies," Singleton affirms. The musicians were apt to be, in some respects, more schooled and sophisticated, if less deeply passionate, than the New Orleans men.

St. Louis is a railroad town, and railroad jobs were available to Negroes. In *They Seek a City*, Arna Bontemps and Jack Conroy say that many a Negro would rather have been a lamp post on Targee Street in St. Louis than mayor of all Dixie; he could work the docks in a port or pick cotton inland. But in St. Louis his money was his own and so was more of his time. Scott Joplin's music had thrived here. St. Louis might even be the place where "Frankie" of the celebrated ballad shot "Johnny."

St. Louis also had one of the first symphony orchestras in the country and an activity of that sort is bound to set standards of musicianship which will permeate all aspects of local musical life.

The alliance of St. Louis musicianship plus New Orleans rhythm and feeling that was heard on the Streckfus steamship lines was apparently based on the intuitions of Captain Joseph Streckfus. In about 1910, he approached the secretary of the local colored musicians' union, and asked for a musician of technique and musical spirit. The union officials led him to Marable.

Another local leader who sometimes worked for Streckfus was Charles Creath, who was on the S.S. *St. Paul* in 1920.

Clarinetist-saxophonist Jerome Don Pasqual has remembered Creath this way:

"Charlie played with a rhythmic swing that just made you feel like dancing, and he had a piercing, brilliant tone that seemed to touch your soul. Why, many people in St. Louis would have bet their lives that nobody could play better. Charlie would play one note and hold it—and the people would start shouting. He would only sustain the note a few bars, but it sounded so pretty the people would go wild. Charlie Creath was so big at one time, around 1924–1925 he would have several engagements on one night. He'd send out maybe three or four bands under his name (Leonard Davis used to front one of them)."

Actually the cornet-trumpet tradition of St. Louis might make a fascinating study in itself. We could begin it with Charles Creath (although he himself undoubtedly had his progenitors) and with Creath's younger contemporary Ed Allen. At about the same time there was Dewey Jackson. And currently the tradition can brag of Clark Terry and Miles Davis.

The New Orleans musicians who found their way to St. Louis and the Marable and Creath bands were not the only players

moving north, up the river from the crescent city. White players like Tony Parenti came up from New Orleans; he played
on the Streckfus boat *The Capitol* and pianist Jess Stacy was
in the same group. Similarly Wingy Manone appeared at the
Arcadia Ballroom in St. Louis in 1924. And the following year,
Frankie Trumbauer had an orchestra there, with Bix Beiderbecke and Pee Wee Russell.

Beiderbecke's work would attract all musicians in those days—
Fate Marable, Dewey Jackson, the sidemen from a visiting Ted
Weems band, J. Gustat from St. Louis symphony circles.

So Zutty Singleton joined the leader, and by then only occasional cornet player, Charles Creath in 1924. The drummer's
reputation had already reached St. Louis. "Charlie Creath heard
me when we played a dance in Louisville while I was still with
Fate. My wife told me later that he came back saying 'I heard
the drumminest s.o.b. in the world.' Pops Foster was playing bass
with Creath then, and he had found out that I was from New
Orleans, but Pops told him, 'Yeah, I know him, but he's only a
kid.'"

There were, even then, some interesting alliances between
Creath's musicians and the local white players. "We knew
Frankie Trumbauer, Bix Beiderbecke, Pee Wee Russell, and
those fellows," Singleton says. "We used to jam with them at
the Westlake Dance Pavillion, where they played with Ted
Janson's band, every Wednesday night. I remember once the
Creath musicians were to play a benefit at the Booker T. Washington Theatre, and we got the idea to ask them to join us on
the stage. They just about screamed with delight."

The pianist in the Creath orchestra—it should certainly be
mentioned at this point—was often Marjorie Creath, the leader's
sister. She soon became Mrs. Zutty Singleton. And she still is.

In November 1925, the Creath band recorded four titles for
Okeh: *Market St. Stomp, Won't Don't Blues, Way Down in
Lover's Lane,* and *Grandpa's Spell.* And in May 1927, there were
two more Creath titles for Okeh, *Butterfinger Blues* and *Crazy
Quilt,* both again with Singleton.

Then, still in late 1925, Zutty and Margie Singleton decided
to go to Chicago. Actually, it was not Zutty's first trip to the
city. He had gone there in 1916 for six months, just to see the

town, and was there in the Navy the following year and got to know the drummer Jimmy Bertrad. The 1925 trip, however, was professional, but there were no definite prospects as he and Margie just packed up the Model-T Ford they owned and set out. Singleton remembers that his first job was substituting one night for Baby Dodds in a group that included brother Johnny Dodds on clarinet and Natty Dominick on trumpet.

By and large, the life of a musician in those days in Chicago was the way all the jazzbooks said it was: busy. So busy, in fact, that a good musician often did the work of two. Louis Armstrong has spoken of the days when he and Zutty worked and relaxed together this way:

"Things moved out further on the South Side of Chicago. The Metropolitan Theatre was running in full bloom with Sammy Stewart's orchestra out of Columbus, Ohio, holding sway. After Sammy, came Clarence Jones' orchestra. That's where I came in again.

"On the drums in this orchestra was my boy, Zutty Singleton. We would play an overture and then run into a hot tune. Sometimes Zutty and I would do a specialty number together. It was a scream. Zutty, he's funny anyway, would dress up as one of those real loud and rough gals, with a short skirt, and a pillow in back of him. I was dressed in old rags, the beak of my cap turned around like a tough guy, and he, or she (Zutty), was my gal. As he would come down the aisle, interrupting my song, the people would just scream with laughter. Zutty and I played together pretty nearly all our lives. Chicago and New Orleans. We have seen some pretty tough days right there in Chicago. Also my other boy, Earl Hines. But, we kept our heads up, believe that.

"The time the Savoy opened (1927), Earl Hines, Zutty, and myself had leased the Warwick Hall on Forty-seventh Street, just around the corner from the Savoy. They had such an opening that we never did get a chance to open our place. Ump! There we were with a year's lease on our hands and no place to get the rent. We decided to hustle. We gave a dance on the West Side of Chicago. The dance turned out to be a success. After all, the three of us were rather popular. With the three of us playing in those famous bands such as Erskine Tate, Dave

Payton, and Clarence Jones in those theatres, the folks came to hear us dish that mess out."

Hines went back to the Apex Club and Armstrong and Singleton joined Carroll Dickerson at the Savoy Ballroom, which had just opened. They did well and, with a break from the real estate people, paid off the lease at the Warwick.

Zutty's earliest important job in Chicago had also been a result of doubling. He was, first, drummer with Charles "Doc" Cook—Doc Cook and his Seventeen Interns was the billing then, believe it or not. It was with Cook that cornetist Freddy Keppard made most of the few records he made, and Jimmy Noone was Cook's featured clarinetist. But following their evenings with Cook, Singleton and Noone, with a pianist named Jerome Carrington, became members of a trio at the Nest, an after-hours club where the music began at 1 A.M.

The experience proved to be particularly fruitful and instructive for the musicians and for certain of the patrons. Zutty remembers, for instance, an attentive young Benny Goodman in frequent attendance. And an appreciative young Artie Shaw. There was also a very enthusiastic young poet named Carl Sandburg often at the Nest. And there was French composer Maurice Ravel, sitting in near-disbelief at Noone's clarinet. (The possibly apocryphal story from this period goes that Ravel wrote out a few of Noone's solos and later handed them to a classical clarinetist, who was unable to execute them.)

Jimmy Noone has not been one of the most written-about of the New Orleans clarinetists, but, along with Sidney Bechet, he was decidedly the most influential. The South Side audiences admired the earthy blues feeling of Johnny Dodds, and they bought his recordings. (There was even a late-Twenties contest to decide whether Dodds was the most popular, Dodds or the now largely forgotten Junie C. Cobb!) But the younger players—along with the audiences at the Nest and the Apex Club and the Eldorado—listened to Noone.

Benny Goodman always names him as his major influence. And in the early Sixties, the late, new-thing saxophonist Eric Dolphy often praised his work as he knew it from recordings. And questions of absolute influence aside, William "Buster"

Bailey of Memphis played a comparably arpeggiated style. The King Oliver Columbia recordings of *Chattanooga Stomp, London (Café) Blues, Camp Meeting Blues,* and *New Orleans Stomp,* long thought to feature Noone (and it certainly sounds like him), are now revealed to feature Bailey. (And both in Chicago and later in their days together with Fletcher Henderson, Bailey's techniques admittedly impressed Coleman Hawkins, who of course founded still another reed tradition.) It was Noone, furthermore, who most impressed the "third generation" of Creole reedmen like Albert Nicholas, Omer Simeon, and the rest.

Jimmy Noone was born just outside of New Orleans in 1895. He began to play clarinet when he was about fifteen, at first teaching himself. Later he took some lessons from Lorenzo Tio, Jr., the great Creole reed player who instructed at least two generations of New Orleans clarinetists. Noone was influenced also by Sidney Bechet. When the clarinetist "Big Eye" Louis Nelson was recorded in 1949 by William Russell, he bent his notes, made his runs, and placed his accents rather like Noone; perhaps he was also one of the founders of the style, unless, as is quite possible, Lorenzo Tio, Jr. himself was the founder.

Noone's best-known association in New Orleans was with the cornetist Buddy Petit in a Noone-Petit orchestra that was dissolved when Petit left for Los Angeles, briefly to join Jelly Roll Morton in 1917. Noone moved on to Chicago the following year, leaving with King Oliver to join Bill Johnson at the Royal Gardens.

By 1927, in a group with pianist Earl Hines, Noone established himself as a good attraction at the Apex Club and a good seller on recordings. (The Apex was actually the Nest, refurbished and catering to a "class" patronage.) The group offered an interesting and successful adaptation of the New Orleans style. With Joe Postom's alto saxophone carrying the lead melody, Noone would improvise complex, interweaving counter-themes in an elaboration of the clarinet's part in the New Orleans ensemble. Beneath this Hines provided not only harmony but sometimes a third melodic part as well. Each man, and other members of the group, also soloed. Thus, *I Know That You Know* and *Sweet Sue* became Noone showpieces. *Sweet Lorraine* became the Noone ballad—it used to gas everybody nightly, remembers Louis Armstrong, "and I was one of the everybodies." And *Four or Five Times* and *Apex Blues* became the Noone blues.

By late 1928, Alex Hill had replaced Hines, George Mitchell was in on trumpet, and a recording like *Let's Sow a Wild Oat* from this period is almost definitive for its ensemble swing.

Tommy Brookins remembered Noone at a club called the Eldorado: "Jimmie Noone was the 'sweetest' clarinetist who ever existed. He knew it and he often confined himself to the style to which he owed his success. But when Noone let himself go, using the high register of his instrument, his tone lost nothing of its beauty. Jimmie Noone was a calm man. His voice was gentle but he wasn't any the less energetic."

And clarinetist Joe Marsala has said, "Noone was the man who gave me the biggest kicks—holding the horn over that great belly of his and playing just like it was nothing."

Aside from his obvious proficiency, Noone played everything with personal feeling, and he was decidedly a blues man. He began his career on records with a profound blues solo on *Play That Thing* by Ollie Powers' Orchestra in 1923 and his lovely *The Blues Jumped a Rabbit,* from thirteen years later, is equally moving. Perhaps Noone's reputation today among some followers of jazz would be higher had he not remained in Chicago. But over the years there he continued to play excellently, as indicated on some still unreleased "location" recordings, made by jazz enthusiast John Steiner at the Yes Yes Club in 1941. On these, Noone was unhesitatingly undertaking the contemporary, sophisticated repertory of the time—*Body and Soul, Memories of You, Lady Be Good,* etc.

As New Orleans jazz began to experience a rediscovery, Noone began to be recorded again. And on the strength of a renewed career, Noone went to Los Angeles. There, to get well ahead of our story for a moment, he once again joined forces with Zutty Singleton. Capitol Records recorded them with men like Billy May on trumpet, Jack Teagarden, and Dave Matthews on tenor saxophone in November 1943. And Noone still excited the musicians who played with him and who heard the recordings.

On April 19th, just before he was scheduled to do a broadcast with the revived Ory band featuring Singleton, Jimmy Noone suddenly died. The group was able to get Wade Whaley as a last minute substitute, and they played a *Blues for Jimmy* on the air—a moving performance to all who heard it, still moving to anyone lucky enough to have an off-the-air recording.

Another 1920s visitor to hear Noone and Singleton at the Nest was a young drummer named Sidney Catlett. Indeed Catlett was more than a visitor: he did so much playing that Singleton frequently heard Noone request, "Let Zutty sit in for a while." And Noone's name for Catlett became "Lil Zutty."

Partly as a result of the pressures and late hours of the Nest engagement, Zutty hit upon one of his most important musical discoveries for jazz drums.

Up until this time most drum solos were brief "breaks" of a couple of beats, or at most a couple of bars; or they were rather formless and random interludes in which the drummer would perform all the tricks he knew. When he ran out, the horns would resume.

A trio of course has three players, and the hours for the Noone trio at the Nest were late and long ones. So more and more often the clarinetist and pianist found themselves spelling one another for long solo stretches. Then, logically, Jimmy Noone got the idea of turning to his drummer: "Why don't you play for a while? You take a chorus." And Singleton did exactly that: he offered an orderly drum solo, fitting it exactly to the form of the piece they were playing. He would hum the melody over mentally as he improvised, and not only finish at the end of twelve or sixteen or thirty-two bars, but also mark off the internal four- and eight-bar phrases as they came along. The young Sidney Catlett must have been deeply impressed; many younger drummers have said that Catlett was the first player they heard from his solos in this particularly musical manner. As for Zutty, if he is asked if he started the whole thing, he will say only, "I can't remember getting it from anybody."

Singleton did play differently. His drum set, as we have seen, was simpler than most, and had been for some time. He did not use the high hat, but he did play long passages, whole choruses on occasion, with his right hand striking the single ride cymbal. A modern drummer might use a slightly different beat, but the technique is similar to the one Singleton used in the Twenties.

Sometimes he plays the ride cymbal dampened by holding his left-hand drumstick under it while he struck it with his right. And sometimes he played it untrammeled. It provided a new and higher pitched sound to carry the basic beat on a cymbal this way. But it was not only the younger players who wanted it. "Even Joe Oliver liked that beat, with tom-tom offbeats too. Different guys wanted different cymbals. Some even liked the sizzle cymbals, with lots of rivets in them. Hardly anybody uses many rivets nowadays."

But of all Zutty Singleton's techniques, the one he was best known for was his brushwork on his snare drum. It is particularly fitting that he should have been one of the first drummers to record this effect, and it is even more fitting that it should have been done on the pick-up recording with Armstrong and Earl Hines. The producer of the dates for Okeh was the late Tommy Rockwell, who was determined to capture Zutty's brushes. Rockwell finally entered the recording studio himself, moved Zutty right on top of the microphone. He had Singleton stand up as Rockwell held his small drum right over mike while he played. The technique worked.

Zutty's choked cymbal sounds a bit odd, making a sort of "pock" sound, as the 1928 equipment was able to record it, yet it is effective as a semi-humorous device in introductions and breaks, and as a propelling accompaniment to Armstrong's solos. The very first Armstrong-Hines-Singleton date captured the choked cymbal on *Sugar Foot Strut*. A July 5, 1928, date, made under Carroll Dickerson's name, captured it on *Symphonic Touches* (on some issues titled *Symphonic Raps*). And the last date—now with Armstrong fronting what was really Dickerson's orchestra in New York, and without Hines—has Zutty backing Louis with a choked cymbal on *Sweet Savannah Sue*. Meanwhile, Zutty's open cymbal had accompanied Hines on *Skip the Gutter,* done at the very first session and the same open cymbal rings clear on *Savoyagers Stomp* from the July 5th Dickerson date.

By December 4, 1928, the Armstrong recording group had changed its name from the Hot Five (a holdover from Armstrong's early records under his own name, done with Kid Ory, Johnny Dodds, Johnny St. Cyr, and Lil Hardin Armstrong) to Louis Armstrong and his Savoy Ballroom Five. On their first date, and their very first two sides, on *No* (or sometimes it was called *No Papa No*) and on *Basin Street Blues,* we can hear the evenly played snare drum and the clear cymbal sound of Zutty Singleton, and on the latter, his celebrated brushes. On *Muggles,* made December 7, 1928, Singleton's brushwork contributed to a masterpiece. And from the session done in Chicago on December 12th, Singleton's brushes and choked cymbals complement Armstrong's superb three choruses on *Tight Like This.* On *St. James Infirmary* we hear a hint of his tom-tom work at the opening, a rustling of brushes behind Armstrong, and a very perceptive use of his bass drum toward the end.

Perhaps it is also fitting that a dispute over his drum set should have provoked Zutty Singleton into leaving Doc Cook. "I had just got a new set of pearl drums, with a twenty-eight by sixteen bass drum. He wanted a deep sound and a big drum, a twenty-eight by eighteen, and we fell out over this—I was asking myself, if I ever decided to leave Cook what would I do with a big drum like that." He joined the Dave Peyton Orchestra. And between 1927 and 1928, he was with Clarence Jones and Carroll Dickerson. This was the period that Armstrong described above, which culminated in a trip to New York. Zutty has described that event this way:

"When Louis was fixin' to make his next trip to New York (the first one on his own), Lil Armstrong loaned everybody in the band twenty dollars and off we went—without a job set or anything. I'll never forget that trip across the country in Louis's Hupmobile. I did most of the driving 'cause Louis spent most of the time sleeping in the back seat. And every big town we'd come to, we'd hear Louis's records being played on loudspeakers and stuff. Louis was surprised—he didn't know he was so popular. If we'd known that, we could have had an agent line us up one-nighters all the way to New York.

"We got to New York on Friday and by Sunday we'd lined up a job for that afternoon. Duke Ellington was playing the Audubon Theatre in the Bronx, but he couldn't make the first show because he had something else to do. So our band played it.

"The pit band looked pretty surprised when the curtain went up and there we were on stage. But then Louis played the St. Louis Blues and I saw something I'll never forget as long as I live. When he finished, even the band in the pit stood up and applauded for him. It was a wonderful, wonderful reception.

"We played the Savoy after that, then Connie's Inn. Louis got an offer then to play downtown and decided to break up the band. I wanted to go with him, but he told me he was breakin' up the band. 'Pops,' he said, 'you got a steady job, you better stay here.' "

Zutty went back to Chicago with a dance team.

The so-called "jazz club"—the nightclub that exclusively presents jazz music to patrons, most of whom want to listen or at least be around the music—is a phenomenon of the early Thirties, and specifically of the repeal of Prohibition. Previously, there was plenty of good jazz heard in dancehalls, speakeasies, and cabarets. Indeed, there was dancing in the so-called jazz clubs until the Second World War and the federal cabaret tax. But—to deal with the most famous location of jazz clubs—Fifty-second Street in New York City actually began as a collection of ex-speakeasies. Some of them had become musicians' hangouts. And some musicians had been hired to entertain other musicians and their friends. With repeal, these clubs simply opened up their doors (instead of merely opening the slots in their doors as they had been doing), set up canopies outside, and were frankly in business. Voilà, jazz clubs.

Fifty-second Street aside, however, one of the earliest jazz clubs in the country was in Chicago, and was called the Three Deuces. Zutty Singleton was well established there during the early Thirties. He led Zutty and His Band, for example, at one point (his reed man was Horace Eubanks, a St. Louis associate), and they recorded six sides for Decca. Zutty didn't play in-person drum solos much at that period, but record producer Dave Kapp wanted some for those records.

After the Deuces had to close temporarily, to repair water seepage which was flooding the basement, Roy Eldridge re-opened with Singleton as his drummer. And in 1937, they recorded *After You've Gone, Heckler's Hop,* and *Florida Stomp,* classic sides which proclaimed the major trumpeter's talent. At about this time also, Singleton was the subject of a profile in a then new music publication called *Down Beat.* The magazine's excited and youthful staff was discovering a "new" music called "swing," and had uncovered the fact that people like Singleton and Louis Armstrong had somehow been performing that style most of their lives.

In the mid-Thirties, Art Tatum came to the Three Deuces and brought along his own drummer. So Zutty Singleton again followed the history of jazz and moved to New York.

Zutty's first New York job was at the Lafayette Theatre—a since-closed but then illustrious Harlem vaudeville house—accompanying two popular singers, Katie Redd and Nina Mae McKinley, with a group that amounted to a cross-section of the earlier Henderson and Ellington orchestras, including Otto Hardwick, Bubber Miley, Charlie "Big" Green, and Hayes Alvis.

By late 1938, Zutty was a fixture at Nick's in Greenwich Village. He might be Sidney Bechet's drummer one week, lead the group himself the next, and be Bobby Hackett's drummer a month or so later. And he was very busy in the recording studios. He made four sides with Bechet's Nick's group which are a very interesting and largely successful effort to substitute the soprano sax and clarinet of Bechet and the tenor sax and baritone of Ernie Caceres for the traditional dixieland trumpet-clarinet-trombone frontline. And Zutty made Lionel Hampton recording dates, Pee Wee Russell dates, Mezz Mezzrow dates, Wingy Manone dates, Joe Sullivan dates, Art Hodes dates, Jelly Roll Morton dates, and so forth.

Zutty was also a member of the briefly lived and now-legendary "mixed" band of Negro and white musicians which Mezzrow formed at this period and which played one brief engagement. "Artie Shaw really wanted to take over that band," says Zutty. Max Kaminsky, in his book *My Life in Jazz,* spoke of the group:

> It was around this time, just before I worked in my first swing band, that I had one more whirl in one of Mezz's jazz bands. After his first adventure with a big band, Mezz was still trying, and he finally landed a booking for a band in the Uptown Lowdown Club, formerly Delmonico's, where I had worked for Joe Venuti. Mezz's second big band had, among others, Zutty Singleton, Dickie Wells, Frankie Newton, Sidney DeParis, and me. The two colored trumpet players, Frankie Newton and Sidney DeParis, were both six-footers, but since I was the only one who could read the arrangements, I

played first trumpet and sat in the middle. Frankie Newton solved our other problem of unequal height by putting an old automobile seat on my chair so the three of us would come out even on top.

This was a very fine band, and Zutty always tells how Artie Shaw was around there all the time trying to take over the band, but we decided we'd stick with Mezz. We made it an absolute rule, though, that Mezz must not be allowed to play the clarinet. We permitted him to lead the band, even though Zutty would always call out, "Don't *fan* us, Mezz, lead us!" for Mezz had a way of leading that looked as though he were trying to get a fire started. . . .

Shaw, however, did hire Zutty, but not as his band's drummer. Zutty went on a New England tour with Shaw more or less for the trip, but wherever fans recognized him, they would beg that he sit in with the band. Not that Artie Shaw avoided a mixed group. Even at this time he hired Billie Holiday as his singer, although constant pressure from certain entrepreneurs and audiences soon forced him to hire a standby white singer as well.

For the issue of *Down Beat* dated October 1, 1940, George Wettling wrote in his regular drum column,

> The other day I got to thinking what a good drummer my friend Zoot is and when he plays how you can feel his beat even when you are sitting at the far end of the room. It seems as though it comes from his bass drum right up through the chair you are sitting on. Zoot's real name is Zutty Singleton and he comes from New Orleans, but right now he is playing at the Village Vanguard in New York City with his own trio, including Albert Nicholas, a really fine clarinet player, and Eddie Heywood, Jr., a grand piano man. So I thought it would be a kick for the readers of this column if I had Zoot write out one of his famous breaks. Here it is and I hope you all will like it as well as I do.

Zutty had written "ETC." on a piece of music manuscript paper—which is a fairly accurate idea of what an improviser is going to play before he plays it. However, the column was accompanied by transcribed four-bar and eight-bar recorded solos played by Singleton.

In 1941, Zutty Singleton had become—as a then-young fan and amateur drummer recently put it—"the king of Ryan's." Ryan's is of course Jimmy Ryan's club on Fifty-second Street which, at this period, was turning to a policy of "traditional jazz" —a policy which, incidentally, it managed to maintain long after the strippers had taken over at the other Fifty-second Street clubs. (Indeed Ryan's maintained the policy until the club was torn down to make way for office buildings in 1962, and renewed it soon after when it reopened on Fifty-fourth Street.) Zutty was both a regular and an irregular at Ryan's and, beginning in the fall of 1939, to be an "irregular" meant to be a participant in the Sunday afternoon sessions, staged there by Milt Gabler of Commodore Records. Among drummers you might hear were Dave Tough, Kansas Fields, Sidney Catlett, Kaiser Marshall, George Wettling, Danny Alvin, Panama Francis, and, oh yes, Zutty Singleton. Among trumpeters Joe Thomas, Emmett Barry; Red Allen, Muggsy Spanier, Bobby Hackett, Hot Lips Page, Roy Eldridge, Charlie Shavers; among reedmen, Pee Wee Russell, Bud Freemen, Sidney Bechet, Albert Nicholas, Edmond Hall, Lester Young. Among pianists, Jess Stacy, Joe Sullivan, Sammy Price, a visiting Earl Hines, Meade Lux Lewis. And so it went. In 1942, incidentally, jazz made its first TV appearance as Eddie Condon led a band featuring Max Kaminsky, trombonist Benny Morton, Pee Wee Russell, Joe Sullivan, bassist Billy Taylor, and Singleton.

One evening at Ryan's Zutty was approached by representatives of Twentieth-Century-Fox pictures. They were planning an all-Negro musical to star dancer Bill Robinson and singer Lena Horne. A cross-section of Negro talent would appear in this "backstage" musical. For his sequence Singleton worked for one of his favorite musicians, Fats Waller.

There was a brief return to Ryan's after the 1943 *Stormy Weather* production, but Los Angeles soon became Zutty Singleton's headquarters and home—for nearly ten eventful and enjoyable years as it turned out. His first job was at a club called Billy Berg's, in the Sunset Strip area, then probably *the* chic and fashionable jazz club in the Los Angeles region. He worked with a group led by saxophonist Joe Eldridge (Roy's brother), and then he joined the trio of Slim Gaillard, for Gaillard's most successful period.

Gaillard is a guitarist, a sometimes parody pianist, a scat singer—and above all a comedian with a fine flair for casual nonsense and musical burlesque, and a rare ability to involve his audiences on occasion into his act. "Slim was going great!" Zutty recalls. "And what rhythm! There was Slim and Tiny Brown, the bass player. He had a hit record in *Cement Mixer,* and we had a Hollywood crowd almost every night—Marlene Dietrich, Oscar Levant, Betty Grable. Berg's stayed packed—you had to be somebody just to get in there. Slim's favorite trick was to do a take-off on the latest movie of everybody who came in. I remember one night he had Gregory Peck roaring by doing a spooky version of *Spellbound,* complete with music."

Another favorite Gaillard stunt was to announce every piece as *The Groove Juice Special,* played by "very special request." And Gaillard-recorded titles from the period also included *Vout Oreenee, Cuban Rhumbarini, Atomic Cocktail, Penicillin Boogie, Yeproc-Heresay, Ding Dong Oreenee,* and *Yahaha.*

It was in 1945 that Berg decided to import the new music called bebop from New York—actually trumpeter Howard McGee already had a good bop group in Los Angeles—in the persons of Dizzy Gillespie and Charlie Parker. It turned out to be a turbulent stay, the turbulence developing, first, between Parker and Gillespie and their audiences; in Parker's demeanor and state of health; and, eventually, between Gillespie and Gaillard backstage. However, the latter turbulence was not overt enough by December 1945 to prevent a Gaillard record date with Dizzy, Bird, Zutty, and others. And here Singleton was bridging another jazz era. For of course Gillespie and Parker were major innovators and their music determined the next twenty years for jazz, much as Armstrong's had dominated the previous twenty. Inevitably, they became controversial figures, but less so among musicians than among audiences, and Zutty said he had heard only good things about Parker before he actually heard him. Having heard him, Singleton knew that "he was the greatest. If you knew anything about music, you knew that right away."

Zutty's other California jobs included his presence at successful weekend "all-star sessions—the stort of "staged" jam sessions that were becoming popular in larger cities. Around Los Angeles these sessions were held by a local disc jockey who called himself the Lamplighter. Zutty also worked in the band at Ken Murray's sustaining comedy and music show—actually, a sort of middlebrow Minsky's—called *Blackouts.* And Zutty worked for ex-Bob Crosby guitarist Nappy Lamare at the latter's

Hollywood club, The 47. "*Everybody* came in there to sit in with us. And the Union was in favor of it. Nobody was hired but me and a pianist."

For a series of radio variety shows conducted by Orson Welles, and presented in the Southwest area only by CBS, Singleton was involved with Ory in a band of fellow New Orleans players. "I thought that people would appreciate his kind of music again. In fact, I never thought it had gotten a real chance with the public. Ory was off the trombone, playing bass. We got Mutt Carey on trumpet, Ed Garland on bass, Bud Scott on guitar, and my old friend Jimmy Noone who was then doing well in the jazz clubs in Los Angeles—the Streets of Paris and places like that." Not long after the series had begun, Jimmy Noone died. But Ory was into a renewed career. And a revival of interest in authentic New Orleans jazz was under way.

One result of that revival was an independently produced 1946 feature film called *New Orleans*. It was the second of two attempts by Hollywood to build a narrative around the history of jazz—or more or less the version of the history of jazz presented in the book *Jazzmen*—the first having been the earlier film called *Syncopation*, made in 1942.

For the early sequences of *New Orleans*, a special instrumental group was built around Louis Armstrong, and it included Singleton, Ory, clarinetist Barney Bigard, and, in some sequences, Billie Holiday. Many more musical sequences were shot and recorded than showed up in the finished picture. And as Singleton remembers it, the players spent much more time making music for the cast, crew, visitors from nearby sound stages, and themselves than they did in working on the film.

It was not long after this, and undoubtedly partly as a result of *New Orleans*, that Louis Armstrong finally broke up his last big band, and assembled a quasi-dixieland group of the sort he has led ever since. Zutty was not a member (Cozy Cole, Sidney Catlett, and a succession of replacements have drummed with the Armstrong All Stars) but many people have felt that Zutty should have been chosen, and many have made bold to suggest that Zutty himself has felt this way. It is a questionable theory to be sure, but bassist Milt Hinton's comments on the New Orleans hierarchy are provocative. (Hinton, it might be noted, first came to prominence with Cab Calloway, a job he got through Zutty's recommendation.)

"Even to this day these older musicians from Louisiana are like a cult unto themselves. A man like Zutty Singleton, for another example, he's always been considered the senior of the Louisiana musicians. Even over Louis. . . . I remember a big party one night·that was held a couple of years ago when Zutty had just come back from Paris. Mischa Resnikoff, the painter, threw this 'welcome home' party, and Louis and Bobby Hackett and a lot of the musicians were there. Zutty came in late and completely ignored Louis. Everybody was terribly embarrassed. Why did he? I think he feels . . . senior member of the jazz group (money or public recognition hasn't anything to do with it). . . . Louis' success hurt quite a few of his colleagues from Louisiana. They did feel he merited his success musically but they felt like Tony Spargo said once, 'Everybody seems to think Louis is the only thing from New Orleans.' You see, they feel they're all responsible for the music. His trumpet represents it but they all made it. They feel most people think Louis is it, but Red Allen, Wingy Manone, Punch Miller, and Guy Kelly all play the same type of thing and they're not copying Louis. They all play New Orleans but each has his own style. It's true that Louis was the greatest soloist."

In November 1951, Zutty Singleton was in Paris. He had been enticed there, along with trumpeter Lee Collins and several other American jazzmen, by Mezz Mezzrow, who had lined up a "traditional" concert at the Salle Pleyel, and who offered some grandiose assurances about a French tour, nightclub work, and so forth.

Zutty did play the Pleyel in February 1952 with Mezzrow and a dixieland group. And he was there in October of that year with expatriate American trumpeter Bill Coleman (who had lived in Europe variously since 1935) and trombonist Dickie Wells.

It was an important experience for Singleton. He was going to a country where his work had been praised by jazz critics for almost as long as there had been any jazz critics. And he was playing for audiences who were apt to know of his career and reputation in more detail than American audiences. And lurking around the fringes of the venture was the fact that at this period France seemed a refuge to a great number of American musicians who had been celebrated in the "swing" era. (Dickie Wells was one, Roy Eldridge, another.) At home, it seemed that modern jazz predominated; if that music had not exactly achieved the wide popularity that it soon would achieve, it was at least being widely heard. There was also the aforementioned dixieland revival going on in the United States, but by then it was dominated largely either by the antiquarian concept of Lu Watters and Turk Murphy, or by an overt commercialism. The players of the Thirties were caught in a squeeze, and many found refuge in Europe.

But a refuge dominated by the flamboyant Mezz Mezzrow, as was Zutty's, is apt to present problems of its own, and this one certainly did. The jazz press in France and the United States offered statements and accusations from the players and the journalists, followed by counterstatements and counteraccusations. Zutty would rather not hear or say any more about the whole affair. But he thinks that his personal reception at the Salle Pleyel and on the subsequent touring was wonderful and gratifying.

Zutty returned to New York. Lee Collins followed him, and they greeted each other one evening at a club called Lou Terassi's in a kind of public admission that they, at least, had no hard feelings over the French trip and were letting bygones be bygones.

Zutty was working at Tarassi's with Roy Eldridge in a kind of unofficial reunion. He later lost the job by exercising the Singleton temper—infrequently seen but strong when it appears—and walked out one night, not to come back.

Zutty and Margie Singleton live today in a comfortable, bright, two-room apartment at the Hotel Alvin, a favorite with musicians, at Broadway and Fifty-second Street. Their windows overlook the basement that was once Birdland, a club Singleton never played. For a long period, a trio, with Tony Parenti on clarinet, Dick Wellstood on piano, and Zutty on drums, drew in the people to the Metropole Café every afternoon from the bustling streets of the Broadway area.

And, soon after Jimmy Ryan's club had found a new home on West Fifty-fourth Street in late 1963, the booking was, appropriately, Zutty Singleton's, a job that became semi-permanent.

Zutty also had his share of weekend jobs at the public "jam sessions" around New York held, until the mid-Sixties, at the Stuyvesant Casino and the Central Plaza. Another thing that may occupy a weekend is the company of his good friend, comedian and mimic Larry Storch.

Singleton's more recent recordings in a sense come full circle and have included accompaniments to blues singers Victoria Spivey and Alberta Hunter on the Bluesville label, and some musical Fats Waller reminiscences, led by Dick Wellstood and featuring trumpeter Herman Autrey, on Swingville.

Singleton is apt to have heard all younger musicians. And he is, for one example, an admirer of Thelonious Monk; he and Storch attended Monk's first Town Hall concert with a big band. Asked about younger drummers, he may single out Rufus Jones, whom he first heard playing with Maynard Ferguson's orchestra and later with Count Basie, praising him particularly for his speed. He admires Max Roach but he confesses that he finds some of Roach's younger followers "a little out for me."

"I have read so many lies about jazz!" Zutty says. "I was a young drummer once. I took over. And everybody said they wanted to hear Zutty play." If there is pride in such remarks, it is a quiet pride and there is nothing of the braggart's self-righteousness. He is always modest in speaking of his contributions to jazz drums. But then, perhaps to be sure that he and his listener agree on what they are talking about, he may demonstrate a drum technique—on his drum set if it is at hand, or with his voice, hands, and feet if it is not.

At those moments Zutty Singleton is still a young drummer taking over.

Selected Recordings

Jazz Odyssey Vol. I, "The Sound of New Orleans," Columbia C3L 30.
Jazz Odyssey Vol. II, "The Sound of Chicago," Columbia C3L 32.
"Louis Armstrong Story Vol. III," Columbia CL 853.

"Sidney Bechet," Columbia CL 836.
"Pee Wee Russell," Mainstream 60026.
Lionel Hampton "Swing Classics," RCA Victor LPM 2318.
"Charlie Parker-Dizzy Gillespie," Savoy MG 12014.
"History of Jazz Vol. I," Capitol T 793.
"Wellstood, Dick, Uptown and Lowdown," Swingville 2026.
Victoria Spivey, Alberta Hunter, Lucille Hegamin, "Blues We Taught
    Your Mother," Bluesville 1052.
"The Real Fats Waller," RCA Camden CAL-473.
"Louis Armstrong," RCA Victor LPM-1443.
"New Orleans Jazz" (Armstrong, Bechet, Red Allen, etc.), Decca 8283.
"Jimmy Noone and his Apex Club Orchestra," Ace of Hearts AH 84.

Noone and trumpeter Freddy Keppard can be heard on one selection on Columbia's "The Sound of New Orleans" (C3L 30) and one
on Columbia's "The Sound of Chicago" (C3L 32). A Jimmy Noone
discography appeared in the French *Cahiers du Jazz*, No. 8. However, the best current opinion is that the four King Oliver Columbia
sides, once said to feature Noone, actually have Buster Bailey on
clarinet.

References

Balliett, Whitney, "Zutty," in *Such Sweet Thunder*. Bobbs-Merrill,
    1966.
Blesh, Rudi, and Harriet Janis, *They All Played Ragtime*. Grove, 1959.
Charters, Samuel B., IV, *Jazz: New Orleans 1885–1957*. Walter C.
    Allen, Belleville, New Jersey, 1958.
Crowder, Ed, and A. F. Niemoeller, "White Musicians of New
    Orleans." *The Record Changer*, November 1946.
Driggs, Frank, and Thornton Hagert, "Jerome Don Pasqual." *Jazz
    Journal*, April 1964.
Feather, Leonard, "Singleton, Arthur James." *Encyclopedia of Jazz*,
    Horizon, 1960.
——, "Jazz Giants: The Drummers." *International Musician*, Jan-
    uary 1964.
Kaminsky, Max, with V. E. Hughes, *My Life in Jazz*. Harper & Row,
    1963.
Rust, Brian, *Jazz Records 1897 to 1931*, second edition (1962). Pub-
    lished by the author, 38 Grimsdyke Street, Hatch End, Mid-
    dlesex, England.

Shapiro, Nat, and Nat Hentoff, eds., *Hear Me Talkin' to Ya.* Rinehart, 1955.

Simms, Bartlett D., "Jazz in St. Louis." *The Record Changer,* November 1945.

Williams, Martin, "Zutty Singleton, The Pioneer Jazz Forgot." *Down Beat,* November 21, 1963.

THE KID

In 1920, a songwriter-promoter named Perry Bradford approached Fred Hager, recording director for the Okeh Record Company in New York, and persuaded him to record a then well-established Negro cabaret singer named Mamie Smith, doing a song of Bradford's called *That Thing Called Love*. Hager's decision was not a clear-cut one because the company was under threat of boycott by Southern businesses if it dared to cater to Negro musical taste.

Mamie Smith was accompanied on that record by a white group, and sales were good enough. However, in getting the recording made, Bradford had taken only a preliminary step along a path he had thought out ahead of time. He next persuaded Okeh to record Mamie Smith doing an authentic blues piece accompanied by Negro music. *Crazy Blues* by Mamie Smith and Her Jazz Hounds sold three million copies (which would be a big sale even today); there was obviously money in the deal, including enough money to remove the threat of business boycott down South.

The success of *Crazy Blues* is, as is often said, the success of the first Negro woman singer to record an authentic blues. Unquestionably, it paved the way for recordings by even more artistically successful singers like Bessie Smith and Ma Rainey. But it also established the regular recording of Negro music of all kinds by Negro musicians. Therefore, because of Mamie Smith's *Crazy Blues*, King Oliver's Creole Jazz Band got recorded, as did "country" blues singer Blind Lemon Jefferson a few years later.

But one of the first instrumental jazz records to result was done in Los Angeles in June of 1922 by a band consisting of Mutt Carey, cornet; Kid Ory, trombone; Dink Johnson, clarinet; Fred Washington, piano; Ed Garland, bass; and Ben Borders, drums. The titles were *Ory's Creole Trombone* and *Society Blues* (not a real twelve-bar blues, by the way). It was the first time that New Orleans jazz had been recorded by Negro New Orleans musicians. The record was the promotion of the Spikes Brothers, the vaudeville team with whom Jelly Roll Morton had been associated back in the South and in California, and on its first appearance, on a label called Nordskog, the group was called "Spikes' Seven Pods of Pepper Orchestra." However, there were other issues, with a label called the Sunshine pasted over the Nordskog labels, and on these the group was more properly called Ory's Sunshine Orchestra.

We know something of Edward "Kid" Ory's story already, for his early career was involved with King Oliver's career, with Louis Armstrong's and Jelly Roll Morton's career. And Ory's later career is glimpsed in the stories of Zutty Singleton, Bunk Johnson, and Red Allen.

Ory is probably the best known of all the New Orleans trombonists. He is, by reputation at least, not the most technically adept. In that respect, Preston Jackson might out-play him. George Brunis could. Certain New Orleans musicians have spoken of Roy Palmer's knowledge of his horn, and there's no question about his spirit on the records we have by him. We have only two records by trombonist Zue Robinson (one of Ory's own favorites), so we can't say very much about how equipped he was. And who knows what we might think if there were any surviving records by Bolden's associate Frankie Dusen? But Kid Ory is perhaps the most expressive of all the "tailgate" trombonists [1] from New Orleans. And he is easily the most often recorded.

Ory has more technique, incidentally, than is generally supposed, or than he often shows. In a down-home ensemble con-

---

[1] Tailgate because, when a band rode through the streets in a wagon, to publicize a dance or picnic or other event, the trombonist sat to the rear so he could manipulate his slide over the lowered tailgate of the vehicle. Basically of course the style adapts the sliding figures of the trombone parts in marches.

text Ory may play more simply than in another style—and he has played in other contexts as we shall see. As a part of the picture Ory can also handle valve trombone, trumpet, clarinet, saxophone, piano, guitar, banjo, bass (he has played bass professionally), and drums.

In a music where a group's leadership usually fell to trumpeters, Ory has been a leader since the beginning, a sideman only occasionally and from time to time. Of the group that Ory had with King Oliver on trumpet, Louis Armstrong has declared that it was "one of the hottest jazz bands that ever hit New Orleans."

Edward Ory was born about thirty miles outside New Orleans at Laplace, Louisiana, on Christmas Day, 1886. He was decidedly of Creole background, his father with French heritage and his mother with partly Spanish and partly American Indian ancestry. French was Ory's own first language. His family was apparently fairly well-to-do and his father, with an uncle, was a landowner.

Weekend visits to the big city were regular events in the Ory family, and young Edward was fascinated by what he heard in the churches and in the street parades and at outings. He became not only a self-taught musician, he even made his own instruments—strings on sticks and cigar boxes—roughly imitating, first, a banjo and later guitars and basses. He formed a group among the local youngsters playing other homemade strings and a chair for drums and they used to practice outside the town on a bridge and then enter the streets and play for handouts. At about this time Ory's father, recognizing that his interest in music was serious, brought him home a real banjo from New Orleans, but the elder Ory died before he could hear his son perform on it, and the young man was taken in by an older brother.

Ory was becoming a first-rate promoter of his own music. By the time he was thirteen he had decided to hold picnics, offering beer, salad, and music for dancing, and charging a fifteen-cent admission. He would go down to New Orleans and hear what the bands, including Bolden's band, were playing, and come back home and reproduce the tunes.

Soon Ory had saved enough money to buy himself a horn, a valve trombone which he soon replaced with a slide trombone when the more conventional instrument began to attract greater attention with audiences. Apparently he first chose the trombone because when the other members of his group had finally settled on the instruments they wanted, the trombone was the only one left.

Ory and his men also sneaked in for some street-corner performing in the big city, and even made it into Storyville at night (something forbidden to anyone under age) by wearing huge overcoats that hid their size. "I talked to Bolden once when I was in New Orleans visiting at my sister's house," Ory has said. "I had just come from the music store where I bought a trombone and was trying it out. He was on the sidewalk and heard me playing and he knocked on the door. I answered the door and he said, 'Hello, young fellow, was that you blowing the horn?' I said, 'I just bought it.' He said, 'It's good.' I said, 'It's new, I just got it.' He said, 'I'm looking for a trombone, how would you like to come and play with me?' I said he'd have to ask my sister, so he asked her and she said I was too young. I had to go back home."

Soon Edward Ory was seriously searching for permanent work as a musician in New Orleans. His clarinetist, incidentally, was another graduate from the cigar-box strings of the earlier group, Lawrence Duhé (or Dewey), the man who later was to call King Oliver to Chicago. Ory's group played at Dixie Park, one story goes, and they encountered the Peerless Orchestra of Bob Frank in a cutting contest. When it was over, the Ory men were in music in New Orleans to stay.

Ory was a "kid," not so much because he was young but because he dressed sharply and smiled pleasantly, because he was the kind of bandleader and businessman who could sell his music on and off the bandstand, and because he liked the girls and they liked him. They began to ask for "the Kid" and the name stuck.

In 1914 cornetist Lewis Matthews left him to take a job at Pete Lala's Café and Ory hired Mutt Carey, the younger brother of trombonist Jack Carey. Bassist Ed Garland, virtually a lifetime associate of Ory's (until they had a permanent falling out when both men were in their seventies), was another replacement. And, when Duhé left for Chicago in 1917, so was clari-

netist Johnny Dodds, as well as (at various times) Big Eye Louis
Nelson, Sidney Bechet, Jimmy Noone, and others. When Mutt
Carey and Johnny Dodds left, headed for Chicago with a min-
strel troupe, Ory got Joe Oliver and, in the billing, crowned him
"King." When Oliver left, Ory's trumpeter was Louis Armstrong.

"I had a brass band, too. When I got a job I'd supply any
number of men they wanted. If I didn't have them, I could pick
them up. I had a sign on my house 'ORCHESTRA AND BRASS
BAND.' You couldn't miss it. At that time they used to advertise
dances and picnics by hiring a wagon with a big sign on the
side with the band playing in the wagon. I decided I'd try a new
idea and advertise my band that way. I rented a furniture wagon
and told a fellow to make signs 'KID ORY' with address and
telephone number. After that I got lots of calls for jobs and began
to get real well known."

Ory would play for private parties, and he remembers one
early occasion when both an Ory band and an Oliver band were
hired by a local banker. Oliver's ensemble played so loud the
host payed him off after one number.

Ory played in the work camps on Lake Pontchartrain at Milenberg, and these jobs ran from nine in the morning to six at night.
He worked short excursions on the boats. "I played in every hole
that could be played in."

He admired Alvin "Zue" Robinson's trombone very much (Robinson was then with the Olympia band and also working in
Storyville). "Smooth trombone—he was good. . . . He lived a
block from me. We practiced together. . . . He was a good piano
player and a good bass, too, studied piano, read music."

In 1919, Ory left New Orleans for California. He said years
later that "I asked my wife if she'd rather live in Chicago or
California. She thought she'd like California. I said, 'We're going
to leave Thursday.'" He knew only one man in Los Angeles
when he arrived, a carpenter who helped him find lodgings.
Then, a New Orleans acquaintance named Zack Williams, who
was working in films, helped Ory get a job at a Central Avenue
club, the Cadillac, at Fifth Street. He sent home for Armstrong;
he couldn't get him, but he got Mutt Carey.

The most celebrated local band was the Black and Tans, who
had more or less been copying the Freddie Keppard style after

the Original Creole Orchestra had visited the coast. Ory says he managed to cut the Black and Tans more than once in front of appreciative audiences, and his became the most talked about jazz band in the area.

Some insight into Ory's local success can be gained from the following notice by "Ragtime Billy" Tucker, a local promoter and also a Los Angeles correspondent in entertainment for the *Chicago Defender*. In his "Coast Dope" column during February of 1923, he wrote about the Black and Tan Orchestra and also of Ory's group as follows:

> KID ORY'S ORCHESTRA: Newcomers to this city, but who have made the town talk. Ory's Creole Band has distinction of being the only Negro jazz artists to make phonograph records to play for radio and to hold down a position in the largest white café on Coast, the Plantation Café. They were a feature of the Plantation Café for 14 weeks and have worked all the local white cafés and hotels in the city. They are in demand all times featured every Monday, Wednesday, and Saturday afternoon and night at Hiawatha Dancing Academy, the largest and cleanest place of amusement for the race in Los Angeles owned and operated by M. T. Laws and Ragtime Billy Tucker (the writer). Besides playing at the Hiawatha Academy the Ory Creole Band conduct their own dancehall at Normandie and Jefferson every Tuesday night. They are also a feature of the Wayside Park and Café every Sunday, the only park and café in the city owned by the Race. Personnel: Mutt Carey, cornet; The. Bonner, sax; Ed Garland, bass viol; Robert White, drums; Fred Washington, piano; Kid Ory, trombone and manager. Boy they are hot!

For the next five years Kid Ory jobbed around the West Coast mainly in Los Angeles and San Francisco. In order to record for Sunshine and the Spikes Brothers, he made a special trip down from Oakland. There were radio broadcasts in 1923, and at first the members of the group trembled so badly they could hardly play. (Would that there had been jazz fans doing off-the-air recording in those days.)

For some time King Oliver had been asking Ory to join him in Chicago (Ory had been the original trombone choice for the Creole Jazz Band), and the trombonist finally consented in 1924.

Thus Ory became the trombonist with the Oliver Syncopators. And, when Louis Armstrong, through the intervention of clarinetist Bud Jacobson, undertook a series of records for Okeh on his own, Ory became the trombonist with the Louis Armstrong Hot Five and Hot Seven. He also recorded with Jelly Roll Morton (and played an excellent solo on *Smokehouse Blues*), Tiny Parham, Luis Russell, Johnny Dodds, the New Orleans Wanderers, and others. Besides Oliver, he worked with Dave Peyton, Clarence Black at the Chicago Savoy (from this came the title of Ory's *Savoy Blues*), and with the Chicago Vagabonds at the Sunset Café.

On February 26, 1926, the Armstrong Hot Five recorded a piece called *Muskrat Ramble* which has since become a jazz standard. Outfitted with words, it also became a pop hit (as recorded by the McGuire Sisters, Andrew Sisters, and Dean Martin) in the early Fifties. It is a controversial piece. Ory says he originally conceived·it in Los Angeles, revising it out of an exercise in a saxophone study book. "I wrote it back around 1921 when I was playing in a taxi dancehall at Third and Main in Los Angeles. It had no name then. Lil Armstrong gave it that title at the record session." But Louis Armstrong told Dan Morgenstern in *Down Beat*, "I used to take a tune down to Okeh Records and sell it right out, like Fats Waller did. I'd get a little change so Zutty [Singleton] and I could go somewhere and ball. . . . I wrote *Muskrat Ramble*. Ory named it, he gets the royalties. I don't talk about it." On the other hand, Sidney Bechet once remembered *Muskrat Ramble*, or at least its second theme, as an old folksong he heard in his youth, *The Old Cow Died and the Old Man Cried*.

Ory was back in Los·Angeles in 1929, but there now seemed less of an audience for his own music. He worked a show called *Lucky Day* at the Pantages Theatre, and briefly went up to San Francisco with it. And that was about it. New Orleans jazz hadn't been rediscovered, and, to himself, Edward Ory was certainly no grand old man of a grand old music. He was just an out-of-work musician who had done his best work playing a style he grew up with and loved. After 1933 Ory sorted mail, ran a chicken farm with his brother, and tended the neat garden in front of his house. When New Orleans players like Armstrong came to town, one of the pleasures involved was a visit to the

Ory household and a Creole dinner prepared by Ory's first wife, "an utterly charming woman and a superb cook," according to one of his friends.

In 1942, in Los Angeles there was a record shop specializing in jazz called the Jazz Man, run by Dave Stuart and Marili Morden. Their taste had turned to early jazz, and Stuart was himself involved in Bunk Johnson's first recordings.

Marili Morden got a call from a photographer named Harry Tate who wanted to take some pictures of New Orleans musicians now living in the Los Angeles area. Soon she was leading Tate into Mutt Carey's house to photograph Carey and Ory. Kid Ory had not kept up his trombone practice, but he was asked to bring along his horn and to pose with it. He blew a few notes. Marili Morden said immediately, "I'm going to get you a job playing again."

Clarinetist Barney Bigard, recently departed from Duke Ellington's orchestra, was forming a small group to play in a downtown Los Angeles dancehall, and he was persuaded to hire Ory on bass. Gradually an occasional trombone specialty was introduced—some of the old-style numbers. Ory was back in music.

Stuart left the Jazz Man shop and it was run by Marili Morden with Nesuhi Ertegun, the son of a Turkish diplomat. Ertegun had become very much involved with jazz, in his youth in Turkey, in his student days in Paris, and subsequently in the United States (today he is vice president of Atlantic Records).

In February of 1944, Orson Welles had a half-hour weekly broadcast for Standard Oil on a regional CBS network through California and neighboring states. Welles loved New Orleans jazz, and, with the original idea of featuring one number on one show, asked Marili Morden if she could assemble a band. She called up Ory, Mutt Carey (who had managed to stay part-time in music although he spent twenty-two years as a pullman porter), Jimmy Noone (appearing locally with a more or less swing-style group), pianist Buster Wilson, guitarist Bud Scott, bassist Ed Garland, and Zutty Singleton. They were all delighted to be asked and jumped at the chance.

Their single rehearsal at the CBS Studio was quite an occasion, for some of the men hadn't seen each other since 1917. There were many amiable insults cast about, New Orleans style—

how old each of them looked and how they were falling apart. When things got more serious and more musical, the men decided to perform *High Society*.

Orson Welles walked in on the run-through, asked to be introduced, and was presented to the musicians. Edward "Kid" Ory stood aloof. When Ertegun presented Welles to the trombonist, Ory said, "What's that name again?" Welles, the star, the recent boy-genius, embraced Ory, and rattled off names of his records. He was clearly awed by these musicians, particularly with Ory, and the roles of star and public had clearly been reversed. Although very temperamental with his staff on occasion, Welles never said a cross word to the members of his New Orleans band.

When the show went on the air, the group sounded marvelous to its partisans. Apparently it sounded marvelous to Welles' audience too, because mail started to come in immediately after the show. Welles asked the ensemble to stay on as a regular weekly feature.

After a few weeks it became evident that this leaderless ensemble was having some internal problems. Singleton, after all, had been a continuing "name" drummer during the Thirties. Ory had been a leader for most of his career by talent and temperament, and had had several of these very men as his sidemen. Carey always felt that leadership should fall where it falls traditionally and musically in a New Orleans ensemble, to the cornet or trumpet player. And Noone, leading his own group elsewhere and experiencing something of a musical rediscovery, did not know exactly where he stood.

Noone came to Ertegun the morning of April 19th to talk out his problems. But late that afternoon, he suddenly died of a heart attack while shaving. It happened that clarinetist Wade Whaley, who lived in northern California, was in Los Angeles on a vacation, and he was quickly brought in. There was an effort at a rehearsal for the next broadcast, but almost no music was played or could be played. Before air time, Welles asked Ertegun for an outline of Noone's life. On the air he ad libbed a brief tribute, literally in tears, and the band, also in tears, played a *Blues for Jimmy*.

The ensemble continued on the Welles' show with Barney

Bigard as the clarinetist. Meanwhile, Ertegun had been trying to raise money to record what was by then clearly becoming "Kid Ory's Band." By early August 1944, a recording session had been set up with Carey, Ory, Wilson, Scott, Garland, and drummer Alton Redd. Ertegun felt, as did several others, that Barney Bigard's clarinet style, developed in the Ellington orchestra, was not really suited to New Orleans ensemble playing. He heard that Jimmy Lunceford's orchestra was in town and he called Omer Simeon, who was appearing with Lunceford on alto saxophone and who had been such a superb ensemble improviser on recordings with Jelly Roll Morton. Simeon said he would brush up his clarinet and make the date.

There was a fine atmosphere in the studio on August 3rd, and with no previous rehearsal, Kid Ory's Creole Jazz Band did *South, Creole Song, Blues for Jimmy,* and *Get Out of Here.* Ertegun was then totally inexperienced at recording, but he saw to it that there were only two microphones and that the ensemble was physically grouped together, the way they played best.

When he finally had copies of the first pressing, Ertegun sent a few to friends, including jazz historian Frederick Ramsey, Jr., in New York. Ramsey knew some men at *Time* magazine whom he approached, and the music page of the January 1945 issue featured a story titled "The Kid Comes Back."

Now nearly everyone knew about the New Orleans revival and about Edward "Kid" Ory. During the next two years Ory recorded for a label called Exner (set up by a Seattle dentist), for Decca, and three more times for Crescent. In 1946, he did the first of two Columbia albums. Along with certain of Bunk Johnson's records (and most of them are personal rather than ensemble triumphs) these Kid Ory records, and particularly the 1944-1945 sides, are the soundest and most durable recordings to come out of the New Orleans revival.

The next event that affirmed Kid Ory's rediscovery and renewed career was an extended run by the Ory band, beginning in 1945, at a club on Hollywood Boulevard, called the Jade Room. Again, Marili Morden had been instrumental in setting up the job. She had also found Minor "Ram" Hall, once King Oliver's drummer, working in a southern California aircraft factory, and he joined the group. On clarinet, Ory used Darnell Howard, whom Ertegun had located in Chicago, or Joe Darensbourg, or (doubling from his own swing-style ensemble) Barney Bigard.

The Jade Room was a pseudo-Oriental bar, relatively large and more relatively garish. The bandstand was on a raised platform behind a horseshoe-shaped bar, and on the weekends in this wartime period, Ory and his men usually packed them in three deep. Ironically, at about the same time Dizzy Gillespie and Charlie Parker opened at Billy Berg's club on Sunset Strip and virtually outraged a segment of the jazz public. Gillespie and Parker were outlining the next twenty-plus years of jazz music; Ory and his men were showing how much beauty and vitality the music still had to offer in one of its earliest styles.

For most of those who heard Kid Ory at the time, it was a first experience with live New Orleans music authentically played. One's first impression was of a beautifully integrated ensemble performing with rare and deep but often understated conviction. The individual parts were simple, to be sure, but the ensemble had an effect of relative complexity and graceful momentum. And the style was so direct that one's impression of its beauty was immediate. The rhythm section was, according to Ertegun and others, "the best New Orleans rhythm section I ever heard. It floated. Buster Wilson was the key man. He had a very light, loose touch."

The atmosphere at the Jade Room was relatively informal for a nightclub, and between sets one or two young fans might go upstairs where the band rested to chat. The most gracious listeners and talkers were Mutt Carey and Buster Wilson. Pappa Mutt, as he preferred to be called, might explain how in his day in New Orleans there were no solos; if a man put his horn down during a number he would be considered an inferior musician who couldn't hold his own. Or he would say of the lyric to *Black and Blue*, a piece he often sang with the band, "that's the truth, you know." Or Wilson would reminisce about Jelly Roll Morton; he would end each of the band's sets with a few bars of *The Pearls*.

Ory stood aloof. He was somewhat cold, somewhat authoritative, and beneath it, somewhat awkward and shy. On the stand, he would "sell" the music with gestures, brief comments, and encouragements. His manner, however, was unobtrusive, and he was actually giving the proceedings a touch of old-time show biz. But physically and psychologically, Ory sometimes seemed somewhat awkward, as if he were forcing himself a bit.

"He was stiff or standoffish with everyone," says an associate from this period. "But if you had a pretty girl with you, a kind of Creole graciousness would come out. He would warm up to her, and then to you too a little. Apparently it was hard for him to be otherwise.

"He was always a frugal man, you know. He always saved money and lived well. And he usually did his own business management and booking. Ory has the mentality of a French peasant, with all the charm that that implies, and all the shrewdness and stinginess and caginess too." He smokes little, drinks less, and stays in excellent physical shape.

However, when Ory plays, all the emotion, all the warmth, the joy and humor and pain, all the things he usually hides, come out. As a bandleader, he is a boss and many of his sidemen have actively disliked him. But as an ensemble player Ory is all discretion, deference, support, and soulful cooperation.

The evening sessions at the Jade Room usually involved the standard Dixieland repertory of *Muskrat Ramble, High Society, Down Home Rag, Didn't He Ramble,* and the rest. But Ory added *Maryland, My Maryland,* borrowed *South* from Benny Moten, did the Bob Crosby-Bob Haggard New Orleans pastiche, *South Rampart Street Parade,* and did a couple of Creole melodies. Then there were surprises, for the Ory band liked to play *Sentimental Journey.* The Ory band played the *Missouri Waltz* in ¾ but with jazz feeling. The Ory band did *Organ Grinder's Swing* and *Tuxedo Junction* and *Mood Indigo* with fine ensemble dynamics. And they might do a riff blues like *C-Jam Blues.*

Even more revealing were the more casual Sunday afternoon sessions at the Jade. Perhaps it was because there were not too many rabid New Orleans fans present, but Ory, who had been taking trombone lessons again, might do a medley of standard ballads, beginning with *Marie,* as a tribute to Tommy Dorsey (one of his favorite players), and including *Sophisticated Lady.* And the whole thing might come off respectably, but with a touch of moaning Ory blues.

Harold Drob has remembered the way this band rehearsed.

"They started with a stock arrangement and rehearsed that until they could perform it flawlessly. Then they put the music aside and began to take liberties with it. But they did not attempt to insert their own ideas until they were sure that they knew exactly how the tune went."

A split began to develop in the ranks of the "inside" New Orleans fans. New Orleans jazz was obviously not an old repertory of dixieland tunes played at more or less fast tempos and with a touch of bravura. It was a way of playing music, almost any music. It was relaxed, it had a deep passion and aesthetic mystery to it. But at the same time, some felt, if properly presented, it would be immediately appealing to any audience—perhaps most particularly an audience who did not care to hear *That's a Plenty* shouted out once more.

At times, the Ory ensemble was so relaxed that it must have seemed slick. But to hear the group play the same number several times was to realize that the players understood each other's style so well that spontaneous collective changes could go on constantly. To hear them was therefore also to understand some very basic things about New Orleans jazz. Musically, Mutt Carey was clearly the leader, as the trumpeter must be in such music. He was not a great trumpeter (his lip had never been strong apparently, even when he was young), nor even a great jazzman. But he was a superb New Orleans ensemble leader. He set and altered pace, dynamics, and mood. And with the slightest sketch of a melody, with a minimum of notes, he could hold the music together and encourage all its subsuming parts. The band approached each piece on different terms, but it could play anything and make it its own.

In San Francisco meanwhile, a kind of cult had grown up around Bunk Johnson, and one wonders what Johnson himself made of it. Its leadership apparently went to a man named Bill Colburn, who had been involved with the Lu Watters revivalist band. Also participating were William Russell, a jazz critic and historian and classical percussion composer; Eugene Williams, ex-editor of the "little" jazz magazine, *Jazz Information;* jazz journalist Ralph Gleason, Williams' one time co-editor; and a few others. They had discovered that New Orleans jazz was after all basically a people's dance music. They had been shocked at first when Bunk Johnson wanted to play some topical favorites like *Mairzy Doats* instead of an old New Orleans repertory, but they soon understood his position as valid. The music was not a set repertory but a way of playing. And it should have a wide popular audience.

However, as if to protect their discoveries, some of these men suddenly wanted to shut the music off from its avid fans, with their somewhat know-it-all attitudes of "purity" and shouts for favorite pieces, and reach a general public that could enjoy it without preconceptions about what it *ought* to be.

Bunk, they felt, was a great player, but Ory had a band. With Eugene Williams providing financial and managerial leadership, they opened Ory in a relatively obscure place called the Green Room. There was absolutely no commotion about the booking, no publicity, no advertising; the public was to discover the great music for itself. And Kid Ory, one may be sure, was not working for low fees. He must have been quite puzzled by the whole thing. Some nights the place was virtually empty. On other nights ten people made a good crowd. Williams, who had sold his very valuable jazz record collection to help pay for the enterprise, must have lost thousands. But some home recordings, made in the room before Ory discovered a recording microphone hung from a pillar, show what moving, easy, quietly passionate music this band made at medium tempo.

A couple of years later there was a similar event when Chicago jazz fan John Schenk flew the group to New York and hired Carnegie Hall for a concert. By this time, Mutt Carey had left and would soon be dead; and Buster Wilson was dead. Schenk brought in Lee Collins and pianist Little Brother Montgomery from Chicago. There was no promotion—there was not even a sign outside of Carnegie Hall. Schenk probably lost $3000.

Ory himself continued to do very well, however. Along with Barney Bigard and Zutty Singleton he had been chosen as a member of the band especially assembled for the Louis Armstrong film of 1946, *New Orleans*. The producers themselves were apparently wrapped up in the New Orleans revival; they had sent a crew to New Orleans to do some location recordings and had the results transcribed. They had also brought some revival-inspired records by New Orleans old-timers. Armstrong and his men were instructed to learn from the transcribed and the recorded music. Leonard Feather remembers visiting the *New Orleans* set during one of these sessions of "instruction." "Soon the men listened to some of the records they were supposed to 'learn' from. As Armstrong, Bigard, and the others gathered around the machine, they erupted in roars of laughter at the welter of wrong notes, out-of-tune horns . . ."

The producers, of course, had made the same error as had many another New Orleans fan and devotee, which was to equate any and all New Orleans music that echoed a certain era. They felt that the players still in the city were more "authentic." The bands on these recordings and transcriptions were uneven amalgams and mélanges of players who were capable and players who were not. The one thing most of them had in common is that they had not ventured forth from New Orleans to enter music in other places.

There is of course another side to the story. Placed beside Kid Ory, a New Orleans trombonist who hadn't left home might be an amateur who is capable of executing only a few repetitious and grunting ideas. But that same trombonist may have rhythm and guts and (his great limitations being granted) a really authentic musical spirit and an obvious joy in playing.

With departures and deaths like those of Carey and Wilson, Ory's music inevitably changed, and the changes are instructive. Mutt Carey's second successor was a very good trumpeter, an Armstrong follower named Teddy Buckner. But with Buckner's broadly solo-esque style leading it, the band's old ensemble balance was gone.

But such changes did not alter the course of Ory's career. From 1949 through 1953, he was at the Beverly Cavern. And from 1954 to 1961, he was in San Francisco, operating his own club called On the Levee. Meanwhile, he had done a role in *The Benny Goodman Story* in 1955, as a New Orleans musician who had inspired the young Chicago clarinetist. It was a speaking part and had some fairly important turns of plot in its lines.

He had two tours of Europe in the Fifties. In a story in the *International Musician*, he said:

They're crazy about dixieland over there. We met Mayors and dignitaries of so many cities, including West Berlin. We played about fifty cities in ten countries each time. In Copenhagen there was such a big crowd they wanted us to play an extra show. We'd been on the road so much that the fellows started crying about it. But I told them, "Come on now, boys, we're just warming up!" I didn't feel tired.

Ory came back to Los Angeles permanently in 1961, playing his seventy-fifth birthday during another long stay at the Beverly Cavern. But by 1964, after sixty-seven years of playing, he undertook a kind of semi-retirement. He keeps in shape, keeps his lip up, and keeps a house full of instruments, but he appears only occasionally, most often at Disneyland, where a riverboat on an artificial "Mississippi" features jazz. As befits a man of his lifelong frugality, he still lives well, off Sunset Boulevard in the Brentwood area of Los Angeles. In 1966, he announced he was moving to Honolulu.

The New Orleans revival obviously served Ory well, and by 1946 he had already served it superbly. Trummy Young, Louis Armstrong's long-standing trombonist has said, "Ory is a great dixieland player and many guys who play in that style could learn a lot from him because he has the timing for it and he *knows* the tunes . . . Dixieland trombone is punch. It's got to come on out and it's got to build. I don't think anyone really knows it outside of Ory."

Recordings

The 1921 *Ory's Creole Trombone* has appeared in Vol. 11 of the "History of Jazz" series on Folkways FP75.

The Ory-Johnny Dodds New Orleans Wanderers and Boot Blacks recordings are on Epic 16004.

Ory with Oliver's Syncopators is on the British issue "Ace of Hearts" AH34 and AH91.

Louis Armstrong and his Hot Five and Hot Seven on Columbia CL 852.

Kid Ory's Creole Jazz Band, "Tailgate" on Good Time Jazz 12022; this LP includes the 1944–1945 Crescent recordings.

A superb example of the integrated relaxation of the mid-Forties Ory band is the version of *Savoy Blues* which the group did for the Armed Forces wartime label V-Disc.

References

Blesh, Rudi, "Listen to What Ory Says." *The Jazz Record,* October 1945.

Bradford, Perry, *Born with the Blues.* Oak Publications, 1965.

Dance, Stanley, "Trummy Young: Style, Sound, and Soul." *Metronome,* November 1961.

Drob, Harold, "Bunk Johnson, An Appreciation, Part I." *Record Changer,* November 1952.

Feather, Leonard, "Life with Feather, Part V." *Down Beat,* July 15, 1965.

Marne, Geoffrey (pseudonym), "The Kid Ory Story." *International Musician,* December 1964.

Len Kunstadt, "Some Early West Coast Jazz History." *Record Research,* July 1964.

Kid Ory, "What Did Ory Say." *Record Changer,* November 1947.

BUNK

I'm descended from Congo royalty.
Nobody can take advantage of me.

On a warm spring evening in the mid-1940s, a thin, white-haired Negro man walked along New York's Fifty-second Street. He may have had a couple, but he carried his lanky, well-dressed frame with dignity and dispatch. He paused in front of one of the Street's well-known jazz clubs, observed a sign that announced that the place featured trumpeter Roy Eldridge, entered, and walked directly to the bandstand. There he picked up Eldridge's horn from a rack, put it to his mouth, blew the highest note he could (which probably wasn't very high), turned on his heels, and marched out of the place, grabbing an empty wooden crate en route. On the sidewalk in front of the club, he planted himself on top of the crate and began to make a speech to the small crowd that had quickly gathered. "You see that? No wonder the man can blow high. Got a mouthpiece no bigger than a soda straw! You heard what I blew on it and I was born in 1879! Anybody can blow high on a horn like that." The crowd, aware that the whole thing was an elaborate and somewhat inside joke, was vastly amused. And none was more amused than Roy Eldridge himself.

Probably everyone present knew, along with Eldridge, that the speaker was Willie Gary "Bunk" Johnson, New Orleans jazzman, and once second cornetist to Charles Buddy "King" Bolden.

Johnson was into his second career, and by the mid-Forties, at a time when the new bebop, or modern jazz, of Charlie Parker and Dizzy Gillespie was controversial, nobody's music became

more controversial than that of Bunk Johnson. And some of the
controversy was going on among Johnson's most avid admirers.

The controversy goes on still. When Johnson's first recordings
were reissued on LP in 1963, a reviewer in one of the national
hi-fi magazines wondered once again why anyone had bothered
to resurrect the old man in the first place, beyond purposes of
satisfying a certain scholarly and historical curiosity. Immediately, a Johnson defender wrote a long piece in a jazz magazine
to suggest once again that Johnson's might be some of the
greatest jazz records ever made. Immediately, others of Johnson's
partisans declared that these records, after all, are not the *real*
Bunk. For the *real* Bunk one should hear such-and-such other
records. Or one had to have been there at such-and-such a place
on such-and-such a night while he was still playing—then you
heard the real Bunk.

The continuing arguments about Bunk Johnson are by and
large the same arguments that raged during his later life, after
he was rediscovered and became something of a national figure.
One is hard put to know how Johnson himself felt about it all,
or to decide exactly what he hoped for in the new career he was
having. For all the calm and deliberate dignity and independence
that his partisans saw and respected in most of his actions, Bunk
Johnson was a man given to firmly indicative acts when he
thought he had been badly dealt with. On one occasion, a group
of musicians—an assemblage of established professionals more or
less of his own choosing—was set up for him, a hall hired, and
members of the show-biz and music-biz hierarchy were invited
and had promised to attend. Johnson arrived deliberately late,
angry that the trombone player was being paid more than
Johnson thought he ought to be paid. He then played badly deliberately; he not only blew out of tune but skipped beats and
whole bars of music, made bad chords, and did everything he
could to confuse the group. When he had finally driven every
newspaperman, manager, booking agent, and trade-paper reviewer out of the hall, Bunk Johnson settled down to play magnificently for the small clique of adoring Johnson fans who would
have remained at any cost.

He drank, many people attest, and he sometimes missed jobs
because he drank. But he would delicately and ostentatiously eat

half a pound of candy, piece by piece, with his little finger crooked in mock elegance, to prove he was not an alcoholic. "You don't see no whiskey-head eating candy," he would say, pronouncing the latter word with a deliberately false broad A.

He was rather formal and even inhibited on stage. But off stage he was a superbly funny mimic, vocally and physically, taking off with deadly accuracy on public figures, friends, and the members of his compulsive coterie. "If he had ever done that in public," says one man, "he could have had a great career as a comic."

He was subtle, as only an intelligent Southern Negro can be subtle. "Uncle," a redneck accosted him on the streets of New Orleans, "you don't think colored folks ought to be allowed to vote, do you?"

"Not until they're educated," Johnson would answer with a straight face and the sure knowledge that he had much more schooling than the cracker who had questioned him.

Johnson was once kept waiting in a midtown New York drugstore. He had gone in to buy a particular brand of cough syrup which he considered a good hangover remedy. When the clerk had ceased ignoring him in favor of white customers, and finally fetched what he wanted, Johnson slowly picked up the bottle, carefully examined its stopper, turning it slowly, and launched into an endless discourse: a few years before, he had worked in the factory that filled these bottles and he knew they were not always carefully sealed. And that if they weren't, a certain form of bacteria might develop inside the liquid, and that if it did . . . etc., etc.

Before he stopped talking, Johnson gave a detailed account even of which streetcar lines he took to get to work at the drug plant, blandly ignoring both the clerk's obvious impatience and the line of waiting customers which by now half filled the store. Then he calmly put the bottle in his pocket, handed the clerk some money, and ended his discourse with, "For a minute there I thought I was down home."

He was always sure what his music was about. He once sat in with Dizzy Gillespie's big band (a possibly apocryphal story has it) and asked the leader what his music was for, while explaining, as he always did, that his was to make people happy. And he would shock the fans who thronged around him to voice endless requests for *High Society* or *When the Saints Go Marching In* by saying that he certainly did enjoy Louis Jordan's record of *There Ain't Nobody Here But Us Chickens.*

When Johnson died, the critical argument shifted a bit. Academic scholarship was even invoked to prove that (a) Johnson was not as old as he said he was, (b) did not do what he said he did, play with whom he said he played, (c) did not influence whom he said he had influenced.

On the question of influence, Bunk himself had long since begun to use his own hyperboles. He told an interviewer from *Collier's* magazine that he had blown "charge" for Teddy Roosevelt's Rough Riders at San Juan Hill ("them soldiers went up San Juan Hill like cats with mustard on their seats"). But he fell into the habit of saying to others' questions, "Who was that? Does he play trumpet? He does? Then I taught him!"

He also elaborated for *Collier's,* "My grandma, Rose Jefferson, lived to be 114 years of age. My mama, Theresa Johnson, passed a hundred. Grandma Rose had eleven boys and eleven girls. My Mama had seven and seven. I got six and six. My pap skin me by two so far. But I can't tell yet . . . I only start shavin' when I was sixty-two."

At times he was the soul of patience with inferior musicians; he once spent the better part of an hour trying vainly to teach an unschooled trombonist how to play the simple two-note pick on *Royal Garden Blues* correctly.

After Bunk Johnson's death, Louis Armstrong disclaimed that he had been "his teacher" and declared that Joe Oliver was still his idol and "the King." But New Orleans players knew that if Bunk was in no formal sense Armstrong's "teacher," and if Armstrong had learned basic lessons from Oliver, nevertheless Armstrong had heard Johnson, followed him, and tried to emulate him, his tone, his vibrato, his ideas, as Armstrong himself said. They declared that Armstrong's first recorded solo, on *Canal Street Blues* with Oliver, came from Johnson's blues playing. And they knew, more importantly perhaps, that Bunk Johnson had brought an important technical knowledge of music, of the cornet, of harmony (particularly inverted and diminished chords) into New Orleans jazz at an early stage. And they knew that the more relaxed, legato phrasing of Armstrong, of Buddy

Petit, and of Oliver himself when he was using it rhythmically, reached back, not so much to Buddy Bolden and Freddie Keppard, but to the tradition of the *second* cornet founded by Bunk.

"If it wasn't for Louis Armstrong," a New Orleans musician has remarked, "everybody would be phrasing like Henry Busse." If it hadn't been for Bunk Johnson, one might add, perhaps Louis Armstrong would too.

Willie Gary Johnson ("William," some still say, but Bunk said it was Willie) was born in New Orleans in 1879 in the section called Assumption Parish. He had thirteen brothers and sisters; his father, William, and his mother, Theresa, had been slaves.

When he was six years old he was sent to school. The music instructor, who was also the chapel organist, was a man of Mexican extraction named Wallace Cutchey (or so the name is usually given). He gave Bunk basic instruction in music, and later in playing the cornet. When he left school in 1894, Johnson was, as he put it, "fit for orchestra."

The name Bunk: it came, according to some old-timers, from a youthful Bunkie; according to others it was adapted from an Irish drayman named "Bunk" Flynn who had admired Johnson's stamina as a youngster. It stuck, probably, with a note of irony. His memory remained phenomenal and exact nearly all his life, and he told the truth—unless he decided that his listeners needed a little putting on, in which case he might fabricate wildly and outlandishly.

At sixteen, Johnson joined the largely colored Creole orchestra of Adam Olivier (the name is sometimes written Oliver). They read their music. But like nearly everyone else in the city, young Willie Johnson loved the music being played by King Bolden's band at Lincoln Park. Bunk not only wanted to hear it, he wanted also to play "that head music."

Johnson was probably instructed by Cutchey through *solfège;* in later years, he said that the best instruction taught the pupil to whistle and read before he picked up an instrument. And he said of Bolden that everything Bolden could whistle, he could play. Bunk wanted to play Bolden's blues and his quadrilles like *Tiger Rag.* Some say that Olivier, playing at the rival Johnson

Park, had simply been put out of business by the crowds that flocked to hear Bolden. In any case, one evening after Johnson had finished playing with Olivier, he went to Lincoln Park and approached the bandstand, carrying his cornet in a green felt case his mother had made from a pool-table cover.

"What you got there, boy?" said Bolden from the bandstand.

"A cornet," replied Johnson looking up at him.

"Can you play it?"

"I can play it."

"Can you play the blues, boy?"

"I can play the blues."

"What key do you play the blues in?"

"Any key you got."

And Bunk Johnson became the second cornetist in Buddy Bolden's Olympia band, or the cornetist in one of Bolden's bands when Bolden was holding down several jobs at once.

Johnson was not with Bolden after 1898; he had begun a period of wandering in and out of New Orleans (he was in Texas in the early 1900s and got as far as California in 1905), in and out of bands—eventually, in and out of the country. He worked on boats that sailed to South America, China, Australia, France, Japan. He said he led bands in the army in both the Spanish-American War and the First World War. He said on one occasion that he had gone to England with a circus band and played before Queen Victoria who laughed and "had hysterics." With the Hagenbeck-Wallace circus, incidentally, Bunk met the father of swing-period trumpet star Harry James.

Back in New Orleans, he worked some in Storyville halls and honky-tonks. He worked with Frankie Dusen's Eagle Band, an outgrowth of Bolden's group and his band's first successor as the local favorite. Or, conversely, he would work society jobs with John Robichaux's orchestra. He drank Jack Johnson, a cheap New Orleans wine, and reverted to the honky-tonks. Louis Armstrong heard him playing blues in the back room with the wine dripping out of his horn. He quit Pete Lala's because the management told him not to wear a blue shirt to work. "A man tells you how to dress and the next thing you know he's telling you how to play."

In these Storyville years, Johnson knew and played with Jelly Roll Morton, King Oliver, Sidney Bechet, Freddie Keppard, King Oliver, and Tony Jackson. He recreated an encounter with the latter on one of the recordings he did for William Russell:

"I were working right across the street from Johnny [Pete?] Lala's which is called '25' and I would knock off around four o'clock. Tony would wait around the barroom until I'd knock off, and then after I'd knock off, why we'd go into a private room we called the wine room where they had a piano, had a few chairs and a sofa for the musicians to sit down in and relax, discuss music or to try out new piano scores or entertain themselves . . . and—

"The waiter would serve them with the cold beer just as they would order it and he would ring the bell. No one was permitted in that room but the musicians.

"On one morning Tony and I sat down in there—he was to the piano. We were playing blues (and) from one song to another . . ."

Johnson toured with traveling shows like "Georgia Smart Set, No. 1" or the "Vernon Brothers and Davis Show" and went to Chicago, New York, went into Montana and went mostly through the South and Southwest. If a show was stranded, he might turn cigar maker (as he did in Chicago) or work sideshows at a county fair or get a job in in local honky-tonk. For awhile he also played saxophone but gave it up when slap-tonguing became fashionable, because he considered such effects illegitimate. He got an offer to join King Oliver in Chicago and he turned it down. Off and on from 1923 to 1925, he was in the orchestra at the American Theatre in Houston where he would play for touring dancers and singers, one of them Ma Rainey. Trumpeter Orin "Hot Lips" Page, of Dallas and Corsicana, Texas, remembered that it was a youthful privilege to carry Bunk Johnson's bags and horn for him from the railroad station when he came to town. In 1931, Johnson was in Kansas City in a place called the Yellow Front Café, working with pianist Sammy Price, singer Julia Lee and drummer Baby Lovett, a lifetime favorite of Johnson's.

That same year Johnson returned to New Iberia, Louisiana. He found what musical work he could in those depression days.

His teeth were going bad on him and one night at a dance in Rayne, Louisiana, under leader Evan Thomas:

"We were playing in a hall, and this bastard John Gilbey came in with a big knife. He was drunk and swearing he'd kill Evan for foolin' with his wife. Evan hadn't been, but no matter. Gilbey jumps up on the stand and Evan, a big man, ducks behind little George Lewis. Gilbey reaches right over George and slices Evan's throat, and the blood pours out all over poor George. Gilbey runs out of the hall, and we're trying to get our things together and get the hell out of there when he returns with a gun. Man, he's gone crazy! So we went out headfirst through the back windows. From outside we heard him roaring and swearing and all of a sudden a terrible crashing and banging. He was wrecking our instruments. He stomped my cornet—wrecked it forever."

That experience very nearly ended Bunk Johnson's career in music in 1931.

He worked in 1940 and 1941 in the local school system teaching music under the WPA program. But soon he was hauling sugar cane in the fields at $1.50 a day, or working in the New Iberia tabasco "Louisiana Hot Sauce" plant. He was not a young man, although he felt and acted like one, and he had lived hard. Perhaps his life was just about over.

In the later 1930s, swing was the thing. And yet there was a Dixieland revival going on, as there often is. In order to explain the origins of swing, several national magazines, along with the "March of Time" film series, had declared it, as we have seen, "another name for jazz." The Original Dixieland Jazz Band of Nick LaRocca found itself reassembled and playing again. Of course, the Bob Crosby orchestra had featured the Dixieland style in the small group called "the Bobcats," and featured an adaptation of it, in a sense an extension of the style of King Oliver's Dixie Syncopators, in the big band. Indeed, key members of that group, like drummer Ray Bauduc, clarinetist Irving Fazola, guitarist Hilton "Nappy" Lamare, and tenor saxophonist Eddie Miller, were New Orleans musicians. Undoubtedly something should be made of that fact, and something should also be made of the fact that the Crosby orchestra was an offshoot of a mid-Thirties Ben Pollack ensemble. But one should also be clear that, for example, Eddie Miller's style is much indebted to Bud Freeman's.

The Crosby band, of course, achieved national fame. A few years later, so did Eddie Condon, with his variant of Dixieland. For a while, Tommy Dorsey featured a Dixie-style ensemble-within-the-band, the Clambake Seven. Woody Herman held to a more or less Dixielandish line during the late Thirties. There were others. Even quasi-hillbilly comedy groups like Freddy Fisher and his Schnicklefritzers and (a bit later) Spike Jones offered German band music crossed with Dixieland and laced with mountain dew.

Beginning also with the appearance of the first Louis Armstrong autobiography, the largely ghost-written *Swing That Music,* and of Hughes Panassie's *Jazz Hot* from France, there was evidence of a more serious and somewhat more scholarly digging into the musical traditions of New Orleans. It took the form of record collecting and of research. And in the late Thirties, Louis Armstrong was advising Frederick Ramsey, Jr., co-editor of a work-in-progress called *Jazzmen,* and concert composer and jazz historian William Russell, one of the book's major contributors, to look up a man down in Louisiana named Bunk Johnson. Clarence Williams confirmed the suggestion by naming Johnson too.

When *Jazzmen* appeared in 1939, jazz record collecting, research, and simple antiquarianism achieved a rallying point in its early chapters. And the book was prefaced by a quotation from a letter to the editors from Willie G. "Bunk" Johnson.

The Commodore Music Shop in New York had already begun to reissue older records where they were kept in print. Before long, Columbia and Victor had reissue programs at home. The Hot Record Society put out reissues from its New York shop, and published a magazine, the *HRS Rag,* that was anything but hostile to traditional jazz. And there were "hot clubs," devoted to jazz around the country from the mid-Thirties on.

Now there was a book, an apparently scholarly and authoritative book. And on the heels of *Jazzmen* appeared a magazine, *Jazz Information,* edited by a group of Columbia students,

Eugene Williams, Ralph J. Gleason, and, for a while, Ralph de Toledano. Record collecting, scholarship, and promotion of earlier jazz idioms had its "little magazine." It became avid, it became radical, and gradually it became rather anti-modern— or at least quite pro-traditional.

In late August of 1940, Heywood Broun, son of the news-paperman,[1] went down to New Orleans to record the traditional idiom firsthand. Getting Negro musicians a place to record in that city in those days was a problem in itself, but Broun took down eight titles by trumpeter Kid Rena's Jazz Band with two clarinets, probably because one of the pictures in *Jazzmen* had shown a Buddy Bolden group that happened to have, perhaps by accident, two clarinets on view. One of the clarinetists was Alphonse Picou, who, by adapting a written piccolo variation on *High Society* to the clarinet, had provided New Orleans play-ers with a test piece. The other was "Big Eye" Louis Nelson. The trombonist was a then largely unknown player named Jim Robinson.

When the Kid Rena recordings appeared on a label called Delta, the great revival was on, although it was slow in forming at first. And being on, it was perhaps inevitable that Bunk John-son would be a part of it.

When Willie Johnson had heard from William Russell and Frederick Ramsey, Jr., and had provided *Jazzmen* with material, he had also provided the information that if he could get some teeth and a horn he was sure he could play again, and that he still had "what it takes to stomp 'em down."

In early 1942, chiefly through the efforts of William Russell, Johnson had his new teeth, made for him, by the way, by Sid-ney Bechet's dentist brother, Leonard Bechet, and he had an instrument. In the spring, he wrote to his friends up North that he had been practicing on his horn with his new teeth and he was ready to play again. Along with the letter he sent a small acetate recording of his playing. No one was particularly im-pressed with the performance on that disc, but David Stuart, then proprietor of the Jazz Man Record Shop in Los Angeles, got in touch with jazz follower Bill Colburn and disc jockey Hal

[1] Broun is now an actor and broadcaster and uses the name Heywood Hale Broun.

McIntyre, both in San Francisco, to ask them to accompany him to Louisiana to see Johnson and make arrangements to record him.

Stuart already had a small "Jazz Man" label operating out of his shop, on which he had issued some sides by the San Francisco group led by trumpeter Lu Watters, known as the "Yerba Buena Jazz Band." This group was an amalgam of record collecting semi-amateur musicians and professionals. They had made a serious effort to revive the early New Orleans style—or, at least, what they could learn of it from the old records. They were not in the strictest sense Dixielanders, because they sought to relearn and reemploy the idiom of King Oliver and of Jelly Roll Morton, at least as much as (probably more than) that of the Original Dixieland Jazz Band. Colburn had been manager for the group, and McIntyre an avid follower who played their records over the air.

After getting enthusiastic response from Colburn and McIntyre, Stuart called William Russell, then living and working in Pittsburgh, and Eugene Williams in New York, both of whom agreed to meet Stuart in New Iberia.

These men expected that they would be recording a document of early jazz, and at that they did not expect the document to be much more than a faint echo of what early jazz had probably been like. In Johnson they expected to find an old man probably playing weak trumpet that might give an inkling of what the music was like in 1900. In their first evening with him in New Iberia, the visitors encountered a lively, energetic, articulate man, with a remarkable memory, a fascinating capacity as a conversationalist, and, as he demonstrated, an ability to play the trumpet that simply thrilled them all.

Stuart's memory of the discussions and planning that went into those first recordings is one of full cooperation among himself, Russell, Williams, Colburn, McIntyre, and Johnson. Bunk Johnson's version, imparted to later associates, was somewhat different.

In the first place, he wanted to play *Deep in the Heart of Texas*, a recent hit, a tune he liked. They wanted to play old blues and stomps. Bunk felt the blues was one number, and there was no point in doing it twice. The visitors probably thought of Bunk as playing *only* "head music." But when they visited the home of pianist Walter Decou (who had been suggested for the date but not by Bunk) they were surprised to see Johnson sit down at the piano and rip off an accurate version of *Maple Leaf Rag;* they did not know he played the instrument. But Johnson's real motive, one may be sure, was to reveal to them by example what it meant to play really musical piano.

The visitors had heard the trombonist on the Kid Rena records, Jim Robinson, and wanted to use him. Bunk knew of him and, since they were insisting on him, recommended Robinson's usual partner, George Lewis. Johnson had originally wanted "Big Eye" Louis Nelson on clarinet but when his visitors heard him, they had been disappointed.

There seems no question that the jazz enthusiasts were somewhat misguided about the kind of musician Bunk Johnson was. And they were misguided, too, about the kind of musicians George Lewis and Jim Robinson were. Johnson, nevertheless, was delighted to be recorded again. And rehearing those first records, technically poor as they are, one realizes that Johnson plays exceptionally on them. And that sometimes he is trying to ignore, use, and even instruct a group of musicians who were not his kind of musicians.

That is not to question the energy, the enthusiasm, the feeling, or the sincerity of the music of the sidemen on the session. But technically they are gifted amateurs compared to Johnson, and that frequently the ensembles on these and subsequent records are spirited and passionate chaos. Hearing them in the Forties, thousands of avid jazz fans were immediately convinced that early New Orleans jazz had been just like this, and as cacophonous and harmonically makeshift. It is highly unlikely that it was; but, the truth is that we simply cannot know whether it was. But Sidney Bechet, Freddie Keppard, Jelly Roll Morton, Jimmy Noone, or King Oliver probably would not have developed out of a musical tradition represented by this kind of playing.

Getting those records made at all was for Stuart and his associates possibly a worse task than young Heywood Broun had had getting the Rena records. Stuart was turned down by all the studios in town who weren't allowing any Negro musicians in. He relates that, searching for some acetate blanks on which to do the recording, the visitors went into Grunewald's Music Store. A young clerk proudly told them that he had a box of twelve acetates, the only ones in New Orleans. On further acquaintance, he said he had a small Presto home recording machine he would lend, and that they could use the third floor of the shop, a piano storeroom, to work in.

Thus they had three hours in which to work, twelve acetates, a makeshift studio, intense heat, and, through the windows, sounds of automobile horns, streetcar bells, and barking dogs. Stuart continued, "To get the affair started Bunk picked a tune everyone knew—*Yes, Lord, I'm Crippled and Cannot Walk.* The Presto's mike, we discovered, was just large enough to feature one or two instruments and pick up most of the others. So Bunk stood front with George at his side, and the others made an arc around them. Turned out to be a happy solution. The band went over the number once, then Bunk stomped off and the legend was under way. Some of it got on the acetates. Some of it escaped through the windows and splashed down on the street below."

Shortly after this initial date, Eugene Williams was again in New Orleans and recorded Johnson a second time. Lewis was present once more, but not Jim Robinson. They worked in San Jacinto Hall above Canal Street, rehearsing three times before the discs were made. Johnson's intentions emerge in the choice of some of the tunes like *When I Leave the World Behind, Yaaka Hula Hickey Dula,* and a version of *Shine,* on which Bunk plays some pretty wild stuff, including a phrase he obviously borrowed from Louis Armstrong's version. (Armstrong, by the way, had sent a trumpet. Perhaps Johnson was using it this time.) "Musicians don't go to hear other musicians to enjoy the music," he once said. "They go to find out things to steal." Further, Johnson's choruses on *Franklin Street Blues* typified a relaxed lyricism of his approach. At other times Bunk simply drops out of the ensembles, however. He was probably disgusted with the group.

By this time Eugene Williams and William Russell had begun spreading the word that Bunk Johnson was the greatest. Not that Bunk was still a very fine New Orleans trumpet player and musician, but that Bunk was the greatest of *all* living jazz musicians; before long, Bunk had become "greater than Louis Armstrong." Bunk had also somehow become a fount of wisdom, a man of profundity who could solve all the world's problems, all its ills, rid the human race of hate, of war—indeed abolish evil from the world.

One story will perhaps illustrate the attitude of his idolaters. One afternoon Johnson approached the modest shack of a New Orleans friend. Like most shacks of the sort in New Orleans, this one was built on blocks above ground level, and had no porch but had four or five steps leading up to its front door. In order to knock on the door, Johnson did not climb the stairs; he simply stood at ground level, reached up with his fist and gave a knock. Around him, a group of white men looked with awed and nervous admiration. By thus logically conserving his energy, ingratiating "old man Bunk" had somehow become a kind of demigod to them. Soon in almost everything he said and did they were finding cryptic profundity—a situation which he probably not only did not encourage but was perhaps not even fully aware of.

The next event in the Bunk Johnson rediscovery took place in San Francisco, a hotbed of New Orleans revivalism despite the fact that by this time Lu Watters himself, and some other members of his band, were in the service.

In the spring of 1943, at the San Francisco Museum of Art, Rudi Blesh was giving a series of four lectures on jazz—the jazz he was then particularly interested in and championing, the early New Orleans style. Blesh wanted to culminate the series in a live concert and had the idea of bringing up Johnson for the occasion. A call went out for contributions to raise the money to get him there, and also to William Russell, who was in town and who knew how and where to get in touch with Johnson. Johnson, then working in the tabasco sauce plant at New Iberia, said he'd come. Blesh had also located a pianist named Bertha Gonsoulin, who had played with King Oliver in San Francisco, who had known Jelly Roll Morton at "Mary's Place," but who had now given up jazz for church music. She was persuaded to play with Bunk. The rest of the group was to be former Lu Watters sidemen and their associates.

Johnson didn't arrive on train after train. New Orleans trumpeter Mutt Carey, then working as a porter, spotted a man sitting on an upturned trumpet case in a crowded wartime coach headed for San Francisco. Carey paced back and forth a few times and then approached him.

"Say, don't I know you?"

"Yes, and I knew your father and grandfather and brother. . . ."

On his arrival, Johnson explained that his luggage had been stolen and his reservation disappeared with it. There was a hurried rehearsal, followed by a concert. Johnson was ingratiating and the audience loved it. "I am honored to be with you," he began, "and I know you are to have me." They even liked his fluffs, according to one observer.

Blesh relates, "He was just the right mixture of confidence and charm. He never Uncle Tomed anybody. And he was very conscious of being Bunk Johnson, an important person. His drinking, by the way, was no problem then."

Almost immediately, a public concert, with an NBC Pacific network broadcast (transcribed and rebroadcast by the Office of War Information), was set to follow at the Gary Theatre in San Francisco in May. The theatre happened to be playing *Lavender and Old Lace* with Boris Karloff; the "dark" day, Sunday, was scheduled. The concert was to be an elaborate affair for which Kid Ory and Mutt Carey—along with Ed Garland, Buster Wilson, and drummer Alton Redd—were brought up from Los Angeles. Locally, clarinetist Wade Whaley was found.

To prepare for the concert with Ory and his sidemen, William Russell, Bill Colburn, and the others played for Bunk some Ory recordings, including *Ory's Creole Trombone*. Johnson listened a bit and then commented, "Ory's trying to play the Carbarlick Rag." Russell remembers being dubious, and thinking that perhaps the old man was mispronouncing *carbolic* as well. But a few years later he ran across a piece of sheet music from 1904, "*Car-Barlick-Acid*, Two-Step-Cake Walk composed by Clarence Wylie." And there, to put it discreetly, was the origin of Ory's piece. Later, when Ory arrived for the Gary Theatre concert, Johnson recalled their first meeting in New Orleans, the exact street corner, and the tune Ory's band was playing. Ory at first disagreed but later approached Bunk to tell him he had been precisely right.

Almost from the beginning there were hassles and troubles with the musicians' union, the stagehands, the ushers. And some of those troubles were Jim Crow troubles. There had to be a standby band hired in the orchestra pit, and the local white musicians' union had theatre bookings sewed up. Finally, there had to be two groups, and no mixed groups. But there was a concert. The audience was delighted. And when, on *Maryland, My Maryland,* Johnson and Carey exchanged phrases from the stage to the balcony, back and forth (something they had secretly worked up on their own), both the audience and the producers were bowled over. Al Zohn, trumpeter associate of the Watters men, sitting in the pit band alongside Watters trumpeter Bob Scobey, joined in too. The finale featured both bands.

Johnson stayed on in San Francisco, and several things happened to him. The publicity, which was to continue for the rest of his active years, began to get under way. A great deal of it had a basis in sound musical respect for Johnson's playing. Blesh set up an audition especially for *New York Herald Tribune* music critic Virgil Thompson, who happened to be in town on vacation; it was held at the Dawn Club, Watters' old place which he later reopened. The occasion was Virgil Thompson's first encounter with Johnson, but not his last. And Thompson's best-known essay on the trumpeter became highly influential:

> He is an artist of delicate imagination, meditative in style rather than flashy, and master of the darkest trumpet tone I have ever heard. He is also the greatest master of 'blue,' or off-pitch, notes it has been my pleasure to encounter. The degrees of his deviation from the normal pitch are infinite, and the taste with which he exploits this variety merits no less a word than impeccable. His timbres, his intonations, and his melodic inventions are at all times reasonable, and at all times completely interesting. His work takes on, in consequence, and so does that of those working with him, depth, ease, and lucidity. Nothing could be less sentimental or speak more sincerely from the heart, less jittery, or move around more freely. Certainly no music was ever less confused.

Johnson's most sustained activities in San Francisco took place leading the remnants of the Watters band, in the CIO hall of the longshoremen's union headed by Harry Bridges, and sponsored by the San Francisco Hot Jazz Society. The trumpeter was not fully happy with his sidemen. They, in turn, were shocked when he wanted to play *Mairzy Doats*. And the Watters men found Johnson's playing puzzling. When he once made a suggestion to a drummer, one of the player's wives commented aside, "What does he mean by telling us about New Orleans jazz? We've made a study of New Orleans music."

Squire Girsbach, later Gersh, the bass player who subsequently played with Armstrong, has said, "It was foreign to us. We didn't like the way he played but he didn't try to yell at us what to do. He just went on playing his own way and we got to thinking this old nut must have something. Then suddenly at rehearsal one day we were jogging along with that old rambunctious rhythm section we had and I heard him! He was playing straight down the middle, not wavering, and putting in some lovely little things. He was hitting it, as they say. I started to laugh and I couldn't play for laughing. It was the same when I first played with Louis. They were both calling us home."

At the same time, Johnson was having a fairly full social life. He was an ingratiating, talkative, and witty dinner guest, and usually expressed his appreciation of his hostesses' meals by cleaning his plate and showing it as he spoke his thank you's.

Dining one evening at Bertha Gonsoulin's, he conducted an elaborate and, according to some, seductive flirtation with a lady choir leader, entirely using Biblical quotes and pastiches; he had some of the guests completely deceived and others attempting to repress their laughter.

Nesuhi Ertegun had said of Johnson, "He was extraordinary. He had the best manners, he was the most urbane and sophisticated of all the New Orleans musicians I have ever met. He was intelligent and gracious and sensitive. And *he's* the one who ended up working in the rice fields!"

His drinking was only intermittent but it was detrimental at times. He was once set up with the Watters men to do a show for the BBC to be called "Portraits of American Cities," using Herbert Marshall as the narrator. Johnson didn't show up. And at the last minute clarinetist Ellis Horn and pianist Paul Lingle got a studio trumpeter, wrote out a Johnsonlike line, and had him play it on the air.

Blesh says, "Like that of many artists, his life was partly fantasy. He had no great sense of reality. And he could be ornery and cantankerous at times.

"He could charm almost anybody. Later, when Harriet Janis and I went to New Orleans to do interviews for *Shining Trumpets*, we dropped by a neighborhood bar. It was one of those places with a white and a colored entrance, and inside were two sections to the same bar partitioned off. When we realized Bunk Johnson was on the other side, and he recognized our voices, it was obvious we wanted to join each other. In deference to Bunk the bartender simply left the room, and we did."

Of his playing, Blesh, who did not really stay a member of the Johnson cult, has said, "He was uneven. He had moments, not quite of brilliance, but of realizations, I think, of the way he had played. Of the records he made at this time, I like best the version of *Careless Love* with some of the Watters sidemen. It has his relaxed phrasing and his tone, and the way he would play after the beat and then momentarily hurry up to the beat, and then back again. And his favorite downward figures—remember that he said, 'when my boy Louis makes it up, I make it down.' I felt that at his best he was a greatly expressive player, highly melodic. His blues were very moving. Louis, Oliver, and Bunk each had his own way on the blues. On the recording of *Bunk's Blues*, from his first record date, you can hear the trick he had of opening a half-tone dissonant. The effect was blood curdling."

The records of Bunk with the Watters associates, including *Careless Love*, were made through the efforts of David Rosenbaum who had founded the San Francisco Hot Jazz Society. They weren't issued for many years, and barely got made in the first place. Bunk's actions suggest he didn't want to make them, but as was often the case, still wasn't quite willing *not* to make them.

There were a few rehearsals; but when Johnson arrived for the first recording date he had no trumpet. There were several dates following over several weeks, for some of which Johnson had to be tracked down. The last was to feature the San Francisco gospel singer, Sister Lottie Peavey. According to banjoist Clancey Hayes, who played drums in this group, she put Bunk on his mettle. "He was very contrite as only he could be, and he really played."

There were more hassles about Bunk and his white band. Johnson took local nonmusical jobs. He lifted oil cans on the waterfront for a while and worked in the storerooms of McKesson and Robbins, the drug firm. By midsummer 1944, he was on his way back to New Iberia, once again a disappointed man.

En route, however, he did some recordings in Los Angeles for the World Transcription Service, a Decca subsidiary servicing radio stations. The date was set up by Bill Colburn and used largely seasoned professional personnel; the drummer, for example, was Lee Young, Lester Young's brother. Most of the musicians began the date with the idea that they were tolerating a tired old man. Bunk remarked, "Lee, I used to take you to school in New Orleans," and gave him the exact street address and the name of the school. Young, who at first remembered none of this, was astonished. After an hour, Johnson had the personal respect of the group.

Down home there was further recording. William Russell brought drummer Baby Dodds to New Orleans and recorded sides with the George Lewis group, Bunk, and Dodds. Russell used his own home recording equipment, but he was careful to set up a single microphone in front of the band to capture its sound and allow it to make its own dynamics. To release these and other documents, William Russell eventually set up his own record label, American Music. Bruce King has written an interpretation of Bunk Johnson's style which is largely based on these and other recordings done for Russell.

> His tone is clear, and fairly legitimate. He plays each note separately, without smears, or running them together. His technique is essentially that of a trained brass band musician; many of his runs could have been taken from a correct exercise book. . . . He will begin a tune by playing straight lead as written; then he will play it "hot" by "vamping" a new melody on the chords (a ragtime piano technique). While Bunk could play many beautiful variations on the blues, he was less imaginative in his treatment of faster numbers. Bunk claims he introduced the diminished chord into jazz

(AM 643), and many of his variations consist of runs on diminished, minor and inverted chords. On the trio sides he made in New York (AM 644) this is his primary means of varying his solos from chorus to chorus. Bunk, however, had a good understanding of the New Orleans ensemble style. He left lots of room for the clarinet and trombone; and he varied his lead on his sessions with Lewis and Robinson by shifting his part, or introducing new variants of the melody. Bunk also learned to play a "hot" second trumpet part, which was fashionable in the twenties; and while this is not the same thing as creating perpetual melodic variations, it got exciting. Bunk only occasionally varies the way he attacks notes. He often delays the first note of his phrase, but only occasionally bends notes, or runs his phrases together. Bunk's best playing is on an untitled nine-minute blues (AM 638), *Careless Love* (AM 647), and *After You've Gone* (AM 647). His recordings of *All the Whores, You Always Hurt the One You Love, Golden Leaf Strut* and *827 Blues* (all AM 644) are also good, with Bunk maintaining a very high standard of disciplined ensemble lead. They are a happy contrast to the dull trio numbers on the other side of the record.

One of the most tantalizing documents of Johnson's career also comes from this period. New Orleans was beginning to recognize the value—at least the commercial value—of the city's jazz heritage. A New Orleans Jazz Foundation had been set up, and arrangements were made to rename the old Basin Street, which (in an effort to disguise its former history) had for years been called North Saratoga. A concert was arranged at the Municipal Auditorium for January 17th. Louis Armstrong, Sidney Bechet, and trombonist J. C. Higgenbotham were to be featured. There was to be a broadcast, part of the tri-city "All-American Jazz" broadcast sponsored by *Esquire* magazine. It was to be climaxed by a performance of *Basin Street Blues* featuring the Armstrong group plus Johnson. Alas, the speeches by local pundits and the announcer dragged on, and there was time only for a few fast choruses by the ensemble. But Bunk's moments on them, revealed on off-the-air recordings, and including interplay with Armstrong and a partial accompaniment to Armstrong's vocal, are treasured by all those who have copies. After the show went off the air, the two trumpeters continued to play together, but nobody recorded it.

Bunk had given Sidney Bechet one of his earliest jobs and in the spring of 1945, Johnson went North to join Bechet, with

Fred Moore, drums; Pops Foster, bass; and Ray Parker, piano, for a job at the Savoy Café in Boston. It was very nearly disastrous, and off-the-air recordings made at the time reveal Johnson playing with sour intonation and many fluffed notes.

The way Johnson later told it, he felt that Bechet's soprano saxophone (he called it his "fish horn" but not necessarily in disparagement—it was the common nickname for the instrument in New Orleans) competed with the trumpet, and had asked him to play only clarinet. Also, Johnson had brought along some music in the interests of making it a good job, but Bechet felt he was trying to take over the band. Johnson began drinking, and when Bechet instructed the bartender to serve him no more, the trumpeter announced, "I'm not a child. I'm sixty-five years of age and if I want to drink some whiskey I know how to find the nearest bar."

Bechet had quite a different version. He felt that Gene Williams, particularly, was sabotaging things, possibly to protect the recordings that he had made with Bunk and with the musicians he was apparently convinced were "Bunk's band." When Johnson arrived in New York and he and Bechet prepared for the trip North, Williams was always around. Bechet continues, "I had an apartment at the time and Bunk was staying there but this Gene wanted Bunk to stay with him. I had no idea that what he really was planning, it was to keep Bunk away from me so *we* couldn't record. . . . This Gene, he came right over to the apartment and asked Bunk to move over with him. Old Bunk, though, he was a funny one. He was the damnest fellow for mimicking; he could act anybody on out. And there was something real shrewd about him that dug out in a way what it was a person was after, and if there was the slightest thing he could mimic, that person, he was gone. So Bunk stood there listening to this Gene talking and talking, and when he'd finished, Bunk he pulled his mouth sort of funny and stuttered kind of, something the way this Gene had been talking, and he said, 'Well, you'll have to move out then to make room for Sidney, Gene; I'm here with him.'"

Williams wasn't through yet, Bechet continued. He kept prodding Johnson to be his own boss. He gave him too much to drink, and he encouraged him in general carousing.

The next events in Johnson's new career brought him the widest publicity, greatest success, and greatest frustrations of his life. Chiefly through the work of Eugene Williams, it was arranged that Bunk would lead a band for dancing in the Stuyvesant Casino, a Lower East Side catering building which rented out meeting and banquet and dance halls. But the band was to be the Lewis-Robinson group, and to include Baby Dodds.

Johnson agreed to this, but he tried in various ways to persuade and to indicate that, although he wanted to play for dancers, he wanted to play a different kind of music than these men played. He came up to New York by train separately. Later, he sometimes slept on the bandstand. After two weeks, he wanted Sandy Williams in place of Robinson. He did not like Dodds's explosive style. But his coterie did not understand or did not agree. At first, the sponsors filled the hall by passing out free tickets at servicemen's centers. But soon the publicity swirled around him ("as cultural an activity as any and more so than most," said Virgil Thompson in the *Herald Tribune*), and there were recordings for major companies, Victor and Decca.

Soon after the job ended and Eugene Williams had gone to California to hear the Ory band, the manager of the Stuyvesant Casino himself arranged to bring Johnson back, but he too insisted on the "regular" band. Johnson did get Don Ewell, perhaps the best "revivalist" pianist of them all and an excellent musician, and he got Kaiser Marshall and later Alphonso Steele on drums.

It began to sink through to Johnson's immediate followers that he was more than a still capable old-timer who was interested only in reviving old music—or a record collector's idea of what the New Orleans tradition was like—and using whatever available musicians, of whatever talents and competence, in order to do it. Johnson wanted a group of technically capable musicians who could learn through reading, who would take leadership, who would rehearse carefully, and who would undertake any kind of repertory, and who were aware that their first purpose was to provide good dance music and develop an ensemble style. And at about this time a young New Yorker named Harold Drob, fresh from the army, decided to try to help Johnson form just such a group. Eventually he succeeded.

Johnson, meanwhile, worked around town—sometimes in makeshift concerts and jam sessions, sometimes accompanied by pathetic young amateur musicians who were, or thought they were, Bunk Johnson fans.

On one occasion, Chicagoan John Schenk set up a concert in Orchestra Hall in that city, asking Johnson to pick his own group. The trumpeter said he didn't know any Chicago musicians, but that he did not want to play with Baby Dodds. When he received a copy of the program, Johnson noticed that Dodds was also to appear during the evening. His reaction was to show up two hours late and play badly.

The consequences of such actions were of course complex. As a musician Johnson worked at better pay than in the Louisiana rice fields or hot sauce factories, and any musical job was hard to resist. When he wanted it, Johnson also had his revenge for what he considered business deception. And some of the fans in the audience proved to be too foolish to know whether he was playing badly or not. But some people who knew better about bad playing decided that Johnson could play no better, and declared, often in the public prints, that they simply should have left the old man alone.

Harold Drob now approached Bunk Johnson and offered to set up a job with whatever band he wanted to hire, and with rehearsals guaranteed. When Eugene Williams heard about it, he wanted to share the costs. Bunk said he wanted to go back to the Stuyvesant Casino, and the hall was booked for Friday and Saturday evening dances on November 7 and 8, 1947. He picked Garvin Bushell, an excellent clarinetist who had worked with Mamie Smith, Chick Webb, and others; trombonist Ed Cuffee, who had worked with McKinney's Cotton Pickers, Fletcher Henderson, and Count Basie; pianist Sammy Price, later replaced by Don Kirkpatrick who had worked with Chick Webb and arranged for Basie and others; guitarist Danny Barker, from New Orleans, who had been with Cab Calloway; bassist Wellman Braud, also from New Orleans and who had been pivotal in the Ellington orchestra in the Twenties; and drummer Alphonso Steele.

Johnson never played loud but he could project his horn powerfully, and he was at his most powerful the first night in this group, in a set which lasted just over an hour. He even played softly behind the other solos in counterpoint. He had told the group nothing except "just play and we'll see how you do."

The ensemble continued to perform for various dances for two weeks, with steady improvement and a gradual acquisition of a character of its own. Not all the fans were happy with it, of course, and Eugene Williams, for reasons of his own, withdrew his support after the second dance.

The sessions were costing Drob money. He offered a proposition: he, with his friend Bob Stendehl, would record Bunk Johnson with a band of his own choosing and tunes of his own choosing, up to twelve. Johnson wanted to use the same band that Drob had been sponsoring. He said he wanted to use some of the arrangements in the old *Red Back Books of Quality Rags* —Johnson felt strongly about ragtime, its musical quality, its influence, and the technical lessons it could still teach. Otherwise he would like a list of the pieces Drob had enjoyed hearing him play.

At the suggestion of Bill Loughborough, with whom Johnson was staying at the time, Carnegie Recital Hall, a small auditorium in the Carnegie Hall building was picked as a studio, and a single microphone arrangement was set up for the afternoons of December 23, 24, and 26, 1947.

There were rehearsals two afternoons of the preceding week. At these, Johnson distributed parts from the *Red Back Book* and then left the room on a pretext for fifteen minutes, asking the men to look them over. They soon began to run down the rag pieces, some of which are difficult. At one point, after a suggestion from Bushell, Bunk said, "If you have something better than what's written, go ahead and use it—that's what I'm doing."

When they ran across a particularly difficult piece called *Kinklets* while leafing through the books, Bushell remarked jokingly that they might as well forget that one because Bunk would never be able to play it. Johnson retaliated by running off Bushell's clarinet part on his trumpet, and *Kinklets* became one of the pieces eventually recorded.

The recording sessions themselves went off smoothly except

that on the third and last one, on the day after Christmas, the musicians trudged through a twenty-six-inch snowstorm to get to the Hall. At the end of a fruitful session, the snow was still coming down, and as Johnson turned down the brim of his homburg and raised his coat collar, he repeated, "I left Louisiana for this! I left Louisiana for this! Oh no! Oh no!"

The original plan with these recordings was to put them out as singles, get them into jukeboxes, and see if the response of the lay public to Johnson's music would not be favorable. The release would not be directed at jazz fans. The music would not be presented as jazz or as old New Orleans, or as anything but just some titles available in jukeboxes, by the band of a man named Bunk Johnson.

The test was never made. And the records were unreleased until 1952, when Columbia, at the instigation of George Avakian, brought out an LP collecting them. Without them, the heritage of Bunk Johnson on records would be poorer, and the quality of their music, individually and collectively, is such as to change one's whole idea of the music of Bunk Johnson, and make one hear all his other records differently. In them, one can hear the quiet strength of his lead and the response of relatively knowledgeable and sophisticated musicians to his presence. One can hear a group style emerging. One can hear Johnson's swing. One can hear his particularly moving, blues-derived work on *Chloë*. And one can hear his solo and following chorus-lead on *Some of These Days*—an entirely inventive solo, by the way, made on the chords, and not a paraphrase of the melody—one of the best "classic" trumpet statements on records.

A week after the recordings were made, Johnson went home. And toward the end of 1948 he had his first stroke. It was perhaps the first time in his life he had been sick, and he was determined to recover. He was fond of calling himself "old man Bunk," but he never acted old and thought of much younger men as getting along pretty well for oldsters. But he died suddenly in July 1949.

Johnson's story, told strictly from his own point of view and from the point of view of the best music he made, may seem to be (perhaps necessarily) hard on others. It is hard on a great figure: drummer Baby Dodds. Dodds' style is superbly suited to certain kinds of music and certain groups, and his contribution to King Oliver's orchestra, certainly to Jelly Roll Morton's records, and to jazz history is unquesitonable. How dismayed Baby Dodds must have been, after building up the climax of one soloist and rolling into the opening of the next, or after interplaying with the ideas of an improviser, to be told by Johnson to "stop making them explosions" and "just play time"! But Johnson felt that in the cool, understated, swinging brushwork of Baby Lovett in Kansas City (for one) he had found a nearly ideal kind of drumming for his music.

The story is also necessarily hard on George Lewis and his associates. Lewis is a simple musician, simpler, I am sure, than the old-timers like Keppard. Simpler obviously than Bechet and Noone, who were schooled and skillful clarinetists—simpler even than Johnny Dodds, who was a gifted, self-taught follower, and an important one. Some of Lewis's fans and champions of his authenticity would probably be surprised that he has named Artie Shaw as a favorite clarinetist, and shocked to learn that his *St. Philip Street Breakdown* is actually an attempt to play Woody Herman's *Chips Boogie Woogie* plus the Count Basie-Benny Goodman *Gone with 'What' Wind*.

But when George Lewis plays his slow blues or improvises on a simple structure like *Ice Cream,* one is aware that this man is deeply and passionately in touch with the essence of music; and one is enlightened by hearing him. Garvin Bushell is an excellent musician but, compared to George Lewis, a jazzman only by the acquisition of a style, not by innate calling or conviction.

Johnson's story is unique in jazz history not only for his rediscovery but also for the fact that the nature of that rediscovery and subsequent career was partly determined by a group of jazz fans and scholars. There is no doubt about the sincerity of these men, and one should be cautious in generalizing about them, for their understanding of him and his music and their participation in his career differed from one to the next. We may question their motives—at least their unconscious motives—however, and question how far their own egos and self-esteem were involved in their promotions and decisions. Up to a point, they knew, or thought they knew, what the music was like in the old days and how it should be revived and preserved. But of course they did not know, or could not really be sure that they knew. Nor, by now, can anyone except the few remaining men who heard it then. Nor did they know the best kind of music that Bunk Johnson had to offer, at least not at first. They realized that he still had a great deal of music in him, but they did not know the nature of that music, and apparently would not listen to what he had to say about the musicians he was thrown together with or the kind of music he wanted to make.

At the same time, however, they projected into this man a godhead of infinite justice and wisdom whose every utterance and action implied insight into man's great problems and their permanent solution. To one member of his cult, Johnson, despite his vast insights into the nature of human evil, was himself a man of pristine innocence without a malicious impulse or motive —a man without a shadow!

Johnson wanted his comeback, he wanted the recognition and success that he felt he deserved but that had never come to him. He was a sophisticated and intelligent Negro, raised in the South, surrounded by white men from the North—and that is a relationship that is seldom as straightforward as many Northern white men would like to think it is. Still, one is tempted to believe that, all else being said, there were times when Johnson consented to things he did not want to do when he perhaps did not have to consent. And there were times when he might have made his demands heard and intentions and principles better understood. He did have, as Blesh says, the impracticality and sometime vagueness of a gifted and creative man. But in general he was innately polite and ingratiating and perhaps those qualities also got in his way. In any case, it is not easy to be adored, and by his cult, Bunk Johnson was indeed adored.

Despite the bad records, the bad music, the missed chances, despite the times he was the victim of his rediscovery, Johnson's belated notoriety did draw attention to New Orleans music and its importance. And I think it helped keep that heritage alive, although it did produce detractors as well. It preserved *Bunk's Blues, Weary Blues, Shine, Franklin Street Blues, Careless Love, You've Got to See Mama Every Night, Chloë, Some of These Days,* and those performances will answer for Johnson's stature as a jazzman.

If clarinetist Albert Nicholas is right that Johnson's records are but the pale echos of the past of a once-fine musician who drank too much to keep playing well, how glorious that past must have been.

Recordings

"Bunk Johnson and His Superior Jazz Band," Good Time Jazz M 12048, offers Johnson's first recordings plus the "talking records" made at the same session.

Johnson's second series of recordings, originally made for the Jazz Information label, are currently available on Mainstream 6039.

Johnson's last date, the one with his "New York Orchestra," is on Columbia ML 4802, "The Last Testament of a Great Jazzman."

One half of Good Time Jazz L-12024, "Bunk and Lu," offers the music Johnson recorded with the members of the Yerba Buena Jazz Band in 1944. It includes *Careless Love* and a very interesting Johnson vocal accompaniment on *Ace in the Hole*.

William Russell issued briefly several ten-inch LPs on American Music featuring Bunk. Among the most important were "This Is Bunk Johnson Talking" (AM 643), including an exposition of Bolden's style with Bertha Gonsoulin ("just to hear that man talk sends me," Louis Armstrong said of him); "Bunk 1945–46" (AM 644), including quartet performances with pianist Don Ewell, one of them *You've Got to See Mama Every Night*. American Music 638 has "Blues and Spirituals." And American Music 647 is "Bunk, New Orleans, 1944."

Some of the Johnson music done for William Russell's American Music label has appeared in England, issued by Storyville Records on LP and EP.

References

Avakian, George, "New Orleans Rebirth." *The Needle*, vol. II, no. 1.
Bechet, Sidney, *Treat It Gentle*. Hill & Wang, 1960.
Charters, Samuel B., "Willie Geary 'Bunk' Johnson." *Jazz New Orleans*, 1958.
Drob, Harold, "Bunk Johnson: An Appreciation." *Record Changer*, November 1952.
———, "Bunk Johnson: His Last Date." *Record Changer*, December 1952.
Dugan, James, "Old Man Jiver." *Collier's*, February 9, 1946.
Gleason, Ralph J., liner notes to "Bunk Johnson and His New Orleans Band." RCA Victor album H J 7.

————, liner notes to "Bunk Johnson and the Yerba Buena Band." Good Time Jazz L 17.

————, "Bunk's Amazing Story." *Down Beat*, August 26, 1949.

Harrison, Max, "Bunk Johnson American Music Titles." *Jazz Monthly*, 1963.

Hodes, Art, "Bunk Johnson at Stuyvesant Casino." *Down Beat*, February 28, 1963.

King, Bruce, "A Reassessment of New Orleans Jazz on American Music Records, part 3." *Jazz Monthly*, April 1959.

————, "Albert Nicholas: Artist in Exile." *Jazz Monthly*, September 1961.

Mangurian, David, "George Lewis: A Portrait of the New Orleans Clarinetist." *Down Beat*, August 29, 1963.

Martin, John, "Bunk or *Bunk?*" *Jazz News*, October 17, 1962.

Shipman, Jerome S., "Two from Mainstream." *Sounds and Fury*, July-August, 1965.

Squibb, Francis, "Bunk Johnson, the Legend and the Music." *Jazz*, September 1963.

Stuart, Jay Allison (Dorothy Tate), *Call Him George*. Jazz Book Club, London, 1963.

Thompson, Virgil, "Music at the Golden Gate." From *The Musical Scene*, Knopf, 1945.

HENRY RED

HENRY "RED" ALLEN, JR., has been making records as a trumpeter-leader with his own groups since 1929. But he still approaches a recording date with apprehension, and with a sound but slightly nervous determination that everything should go well. His reaction to his apprehension—unlike that of many another professional in jazz—is neither to show up slightly late, nor to affect a casual attitude. He is usually early and he is usually frankly busy.

At least he was very early for some recording he did in the summer of 1962. Allen had been using a quartet for successful appearances in such semi-posh lounges as the Embers in New York, the London House in Chicago, the Theatrical Grill in Cleveland, and on college tours with comedians Shelley Berman and Bob Newhart, and he was asked by Prestige Records to make an LP with the group. Prestige, like several New York jazz record companies, uses the studios of an ex-optometrist named Rudy Van Gelder, who began high-fidelity recording as a hobby and ended up with a successful business on his hands. Van Gelder's studios are located just across the George Washington Bridge from Manhattan Island in the New Jersey suburbs, and Red Allen pulled up his shiny black Cadillac in front of Van Gelder's large, backyard brick building early—almost forty-five minutes before the date was to begin. Van Gelder is more used to show-business lateness than earliness, and he was not only surprised but dismayed at the arrival of Allen and his quartet. However, once he had made the firm announcement that recording would not begin until the scheduled 1 P.M., he opened the studio door and let the players wait inside.

Allen soon regained the composure he was so determined to preserve, and inside the high-ceilinged, wooden-beamed studio he found plenty of time to prepare. "Early?" muttered Jerry Potter setting up his drums, "This group is always early!"

It was better to be inside. The day was overcast; there was a drizzle which turned into a heavy rain by late afternoon.

Allen donned a pair of glasses that gave him a studious air, an air that few people who have watched the exuberant and powerful Red Allen on a night club bandstand would recognize. He leaned over the back of the studio piano, studying his list of repertory with the quartet and going over some of his lyrics.

Before long there was a casual exchange of players at the piano bench—first the group's bass player, Frank Scaate, and then Allen. Lanny Scott, the quartet's pianist, is the professional, of course, so it would not behoove him to play for such casual amusement. Musicians take this sort of thing for granted—nearly everyone plays a little piano and enjoys it, but it is often surprising to outsiders.

A little before 1 P.M. Esmond Edwards arrived. Edwards had set the date up and he was to supervise it for Prestige. (In other fields of endeavor he would be called a producer; in recording, he is called an A & R man—meaning artists and repertory.) He was frankly surprised to find the musicians all present and ready to go. He took his place inside Van Gelder's control booth, behind the large glass panel which is broad and high enough to take in the whole barnlike studio at a glance. Van Gelder soon had his machines threaded with tape and was seated behind his complex control panel. The date was officially ready to begin.

On the other side of the glass the musicians began running through the first piece, *Cherry*, to warm up and to check the placement of the microphones. Red Allen was swinging from the first bar, and his very personal, often complex phrases rolled off his horn with an apparent, almost casual ease. He was also showing his fine control of the horn; he would begin with an idea at a mere whisper of trumpet sound, and develop it to a powerful shout at the end of his phrase—the kind of dynamics that few other trumpeters know how to employ.

After the run-through, Edwards suggested that drummer Jerry

Potter try sticks instead of brushes. Everyone agreed. Then *Cherry* was going onto the tape, take #1—an inventive opening by Red, but he stopped after his vocal. "I goofed the words all up." Another take, but the bass wasn't balanced. First numbers on a record date usually go this way.

Then, *Cherry* #3. Everyone was working; the group was concertedly alive. Allen was truly inventive, for he used only one brief phrase that he had played in any previous version of *Cherry* so far. "That man really improvises," someone in the booth said, as Edwards and Van Gelder nodded. "I wonder if he could repeat himself, even if he wanted to." As the ending rang out through the wooden rafters and across the mikes, echoing the power and drive of the performance, Edwards laughed, "They don't play like that any more!"

"Can we hear that back?" Red asked—"How do we sound in here?"

A bit later they began running through *Sleepy Time Gal*. Allen's lines were weaving in unexpected directions and he was beginning to show his command of the full range of his horn, with the perfectly played low notes that are almost his exclusive property. His melodies were still gliding over the rhythm section and basic time, with sureness and inner drive, and no excess notes.

The first take of *Sleepy Time Gal* was much simpler than the run-through, and there was some trouble with the introduction. Allen is still more used to recording for the old flat acetate record blanks rather than tape, and he had been counting off the tempos to the group at a whisper. But with tape it's easy to cut, splice, and remove a downbeat or a count-off. "You can count it off out loud, Red," Edwards reminded him.

At the end of another take, Edwards apparently saw something was about to happen, and he reached for his mike to say over the studio loudspeakers, "How are the chops? Can we do one more right away?"

"Yeah, sure, my man!" immediately from Allen. And then they did the best *Sleepy Time Gal* yet.

This time Allen came into the engineering booth to hear the playback and sat beside Van Gelder's elaborate array of dials and knobs. He raised and curved his eyebrows at a particularly lyric turn of phrase in his own improvising, pretty much the way any listener would in following the music.

By 2 P.M. they were into *I Ain't Got Nobody;* on his vocal Red was gliding through as many as six notes in singing just the opening word "I." After the run-through, Edwards suggested that Allen blow another trumpet chorus on the final take. Again, Allen's ideas were fresh and different each time they ran the piece down, and he still glided over the basic one-two-three-four of the rhythm with perfect poise. His trumpet alone might make the whole group swing. He counted them off loudly now for the final take, "ONE! TWO!" And at the end, after the reverberations had settled, there was the inevitable Red Allen genial cry of "Nice!" Almost his trademark.

Then, a short break as some visitors arrived. Van Gelder immediately gave them a firm invitation to sit quietly in the studio and stay out of the booth. Jerry Potter came in to ask for a little more mike on his bass drum. "Can you bring it up a little? Then I can relax. I have to keep leaning on it otherwise."

"Okay, we'll try. It's not easy to do."

In the studio, designer and photographer Don Schlitten, there to get a picture for the LP album cover, had his lights and shutters going. Allen wasn't bothered. Nervous or not, Red Allen had been strictly business from the beginning. And he was obviously impatient to get back to work.

Later, they were well into a new version of one of Allen's early recordings, *There's a House in Harlem,* and Red was getting deep growl effects the way he does on his open horn, without a plunger. Again, every version was different. Van Gelder remarked for about the third time that they should be recording everything including the warmups and run-throughs. And again, he shook his head in appreciation of how well Red was playing. Edwards stopped the take, remarking on the intro, and drummer Lannie Scott and bassist Frank Scaate worked it out together before the tape was rolled again.

They began *Just in Time,* a more recent show tune, from *Bells Are Ringing.* "Everybody plays that thing now," a visitor remarked. "I guess it's become a jazz standard already. I heard Art Farmer do it the other day." There was some trouble again with the intro so Red took it himself unaccompanied. They went through the piece once and Allen was after Jerry Potter again, "Let me hear a little more of that bass drum, please." The ending was "up," loudly and broadly signaling the finish of the piece, just as the group does to a club audience.

Another break, this one officially called by Edwards. Red was still anxious to get back to work and he toyed around on his horn, playing the next piece he wanted to do, *Nice Work if You Can Get It*. "Johnny Hodges has a record of that," remarked Lannie Scott, "Did you hear it?"

By the time Edwards suggested they go back to work, Red had relaxed at least long enough to be showing a visitor a color picture he has of his mother, himself, and his granddaughter—his "gran" as he calls her—four generations of the Allen family. But he broke off abruptly and was back at his mike at the suggestion they resume playing.

On the take of *Nice Work*, Edwards encouraged, "Make it clean." Red's variations rolled off easily and with a rare and very personal asymmetry.

In the studio, the quartet then began to run down a piece that seemed both familiar and not familiar, a piece that sounded like the blues and was not exactly the blues, and was thirty-two bars long. When they get the routine set, Edwards asked for the title. *Biffly Blues* said Allen—a new version of the first record he ever did under his own name. One take and for the time being everyone agreed with Edwards' comment, "That's it. It won't go down any better than that."

As they were running through *St. Louis Blues* in the studio, there was talk in the booth about "still another record of *that one*," but Edwards decided that if they did something different with it, then it should be recorded. They did, of course.

It was getting late, nearly 4 P.M., and Edwards did some quick calculations from the timings recorded in his notes on the session. "Red, why not stretch out with a few more choruses on this," he said into the studio mike. "We will have enough time for it on the LP." While the tapes were rolling, Allen suddenly went down very low on his horn again, growling out notes for almost two choruses. One take, as usual, did the blues.

The date was nearly over now. Edwards made more calculations on timing, and then stepped into the studio to suggest to Allen they do a longer version of *Biffly Blues*. Agreed. "What does that title mean, Red?" a visitor asked hurriedly, hoping to get his question in before the tapes rolled again. "My nickname— when I was a kid," he smiled. "My folks used to call me Biffly Bam when I wanted to be a baseball player. You know—biff, bam—hit. Wham!"

After a rough start—Red had placed his horn and chops in too much of a hurry—they got through a long taping on *Biffly Blues* with Edwards conducting and encouraging through the glass of the booth—waving his arms emphatically at the rhythm section, as Allen concentrated on his solo choruses. (Creative A & R work, it's called.)

"You know," offered Potter at the end, "that *Biffly Blues* is the kind of piece that could hit."

"Maybe," said a visitor. "You can never tell about those things. Anyway, it sounds just as fresh as when he first did it thirty years ago."

"No. Fresher. Because Red is fresher," said another onlooker softly. "You can't date that kind of talent. And he's himself, and that means he's got things nobody else could pick up on."

Henry James Allen, Jr., is probably the last important jazz trumpeter to come from New Orleans, the final link in the chain of that city's jazz development. The chain begins in the misty near-myth of Buddy Bolden. Its second link was rediscovered in the Forties when Willie G. "Bunk" Johnson was found in New Iberia and recorded. Stylistically, it first materialized on records in the handful of pieces made by Freddie Keppard. In the work of King Oliver, the New Orleans cornet-trumpet heritage startled all jazzmen and affected all jazz. It reached its fullest develop- ment in the genius of Louis Armstrong. And, along the way, it carried such important talents as those of Tommy Ladnier in a style slightly predating Armstrong's, and Kid Rena, Punch Miller, and Lee Collins in styles contemporary with or slightly postdating Armstrong's. But of all the styles to come after Arm- strong's the most fully developed was Red Allen's.

Especially because he is from New Orleans, Allen has often been associated with contemporary quasi-dixieland playing. And what with the constant revivals of the style, so have most trumpeters of the Thirties. Good New Orleans-dixieland jazz is primarily an ensemble style, and Red Allen is not really an ensemble player. Coming after Armstrong, he is of a generation of soloists, and the differences between Red Allen's style and Freddy Keppard's are greater than the differences between Red Allen's style and, say, Lester Young's. Allen's best melodic lines are perhaps too active and exploratory to be lead parts in an ensemble.

He can play the dixieland repertory, of course, and play it well. One of his best solos of recent years was on a recording of *Frankie and Johnny*. But he also finds a challenge in tunes of more complexity, in various medium and slow ballads, in their melodies, in their harmonies. When Louis Armstrong began to turn away from the then-standard jazz repertory of the Twenties and improvise on more sophisticated popular songs and ballads of the Thirties, he laid down a kind of challenge for the future to other jazz musicians. Red Allen was one of the first players to meet that challenge successfully; his 1935 *Body and Soul* is a classic example.

Like Lester Young's, and like Thelonious Monk's, Red Allen's music depends on quick discoveries and surprises. And besides the thrusts of dynamics and range, his use of the unexpected includes rhythm. His rhythmic sureness is exceptional at times. There are many players of his own generation who still use repeated notes and other phrases with the more or less mechanical function of rhythmic reminders, of maintaining or reestablishing the basic pulse. Allen goes directly to the melody he is improvising, with an easy phrasing that doesn't need such signposts. His relaxed sense of tempo, of the "time" as musicians put it, and his use of dynamics and the range of his horn breaks his lines up provocatively. Probably no horn man who arrived between Armstrong and Lester Young sounds less mechanical in his phrasing or has developed more rhythmic flexibility and variety than Red Allen.

In 1965, the very able young trumpeter, Don Ellis, who has worked both with George Russell's avant garde jazz group and Lucas Foss's improvising "classical" ensemble, paid tribute to Allen in *Down Beat* in these words: "What other trumpet player plays such asymmetrical rhythms and manages to make them swing besides? What other trumpeter plays ideas that may begin as a whisper, rise to a brassy shout, and suddenly become a whisper again, with no discernible predictability? Who else has the amazing variety of tonal colors, bends, smears, half-valve effects, rips, glissandos, flutter-tonguing (a favorite on a high D), all combined with iron chops and complete control of even the softest, most subtle, tone production? . . . No one has a wider scope of effects to draw upon, and no one is more subtle rhythmically and in the use of dynamics and asymmetrical phrases than Henry (Red) Allen."

The real pleasure of listening to Red Allen is melodic and it is to the line he is improvising that he is always committed. Perhaps, some people say, Allen's melodies sometimes get adventurous enough to become disorderly. But such people may be hearing him the wrong way. His exploratory twists of melodic line and trumpet sound are often personal enough to establish standards of their own; his playing is often personal enough to create its own aura, uniting the plaintiveness of a blues man and the lyricism of a fine ballad player. His melodies are frequently less exuberantly extraverted than his stage manner.

Order and balance are deeper pleasures only when one has dared and won them, and Red Allen sometimes shows a daring that may turn up a kind of order not known before him. Certainly one of the major achievements of the best jazz improvising has been to affirm that melody need not obey mechanical notions of form, that it need not use traditional repeats, but can be continuous linear invention and still be a satisfying aesthetic entity.

It is for that rare kind of order that Red Allen modestly searches.

One of the earliest known photographs of New Orleans musicians is (according to the lettering on the bass drum in the center of the picture) of "Allen's Brass Band of Algiers, La." It preserves the person of trombonist Jack Carey (for a while, remember, *Tiger Rag* was known as "Play Jack Carey"), a youthful Oscar (later Pappa) Celestine, William Young (father of Lester Young), and the leader Henry Allen, Sr. On the left, about three-quarters visible and in slightly foggy focus, is a

young boy kneeling behind the band. He was Henry Allen, Jr.,
born January 7, 1908.

Algiers might actually be called West New Orleans. In several
senses it is removed from the brothels and barrooms of the
Storyville district; it is removed from the poverty of the uptown
Negro section of New Orleans; and it is removed from the particular snobberies of the colored Creole section.

Allen Senior is remembered today for his brass band, but in
those days he did very well on the docks. "He was what you
would nowadays call a waterfront boss," says a fellow New
Orleans musician and a member of Red's generation. "He did
very well for his family. Red didn't have to scuffle around
peddling coal, carrying newspapers like the rest of us when he
was a kid. And he got a good education, too."

"I love my son," Red Allen told Graham Boatfield, "and I
guess my father loved me."

The Allen home might have been the envy of several of Red's
contemporaries, but according to Red himself it was not all that
exceptional. "They could get a house in those days much easier.
A man would throw a party and all of his friends, who'd be
carpenters, bricklayers, slaters, plasterers, and so forth, would
come. They would all eat and drink and build a house. Of course
nowadays the Unions won't allow that kind of thing."

Allen's Brass Band was available for parades, funerals, picnics,
even dances. And during its most illustrious years, King Oliver
and Oscar Celestine both joined the senior Allen on trumpet.
Allen had cards printed up and he used the telephone in a nearby
grocery store for his bookings; sometimes that phone would hang
for a long time off the hook before he could be found. The personnel of the group inevitably fluctuated from job to job, depending on who was available. But he had one good way of
keeping his repertory from other groups. Whenever he used a
stock arrangement (which young Red passed out to the players)
he carefully tore off the tops of each music sheet to keep its
name a secret.

Everyone agrees that Allen Senior was a good military cornet
player. "I had the great advantage that my father used to hold rehearsals in our home," Red Allen told Sinclair Traill, "so I had
a chance to hear anyone that was coming on up. Although my

father's band was what they call these days a marching band, they had a lot more than just 6/8 time. They could really swing, and that was where I came in! My father would let me play the jazz numbers. I started first on the upright alto horn. My mother wouldn't let me play trumpet as she thought it was too strenuous for one of my years. She'd see the guy's blowing with their necks all swollen out and she said I was too young for that. She also gave me a violin, but it had a very short stay with me. But my father he wanted me to play trumpet, so it came along slowly, and that is perhaps why I don't have the ball in my cheeks that some other trumpet players do. Because of my mother's wishes and my father's, I played trumpet, but I took to it easily and slowly."

The elder Allen brought up his son in the Catholic Church and in music. He protected him, but he did offer him respect for the New Orleans musicians whose life was far rougher than anything the young Red Allen experienced. To discourage his son from smoking and drinking, he told him that a good trumpet player could ruin himself that way; that King Oliver and Bunk Johnson, they didn't smoke and drink. The lesson took, and it held even after Red became better acquainted with the facts. He did not drink or smoke at all until the late Forties, when he began to have an occasional social beer.

Red at first had played drums, like his older brother George. He developed a good wrist movment and admired Louis Cotrell for his rolls and paradiddles. He also studied violin with Peter Bocage. Some of the trumpeters he admired are only names to us now, names like Henry Rene and Richard Alexis and Chris Kelly, the white player Emmet Hardy, and Buddy Petit. Others, like Kid Rena, recorded only in their later years.

And then, of course, there was Louis Armstrong. "But not so much when we heard him. Louis wasn't an influence to us until he started making records. We got Louis from records, like all the other jazz musicians in the country, I suppose. Except of course we knew where his music came from better than others."

The Allens had a wind-up phonograph, and by changing the speed at which the old 78-rpm records were played Red Allen pitched each piece into a variety of keys, and learned to play in

them all—an experience which stood him in good stead for the
rest of his life.

Henry Allen, Jr., had passed through the Storyville district
only to go to summer school in the Bienville section. But when
he was still a youngster, he briefly took a job there, playing a
benefit at the Elite Café. He couldn't play for long; for one thing,
he was still so young he couldn't stay out late. But the pianist,
Walter "Fats" Pichon, could pass for a man and that gave the
group a certain air of maturity.

It was such occasional jobs that gradually introduced Red
Allen to the musical life of New Orleans, and to the jobs available
on Mississippi excursion boats that ran, sometimes for an evening's outing and sometimes for a trip, as far as St. Louis, with
music in the lounge generally provided by the leader and entrepreneur Fate Marable.

Through such appearances, Guy Kelly and Red Allen became
rivals among the younger New Orleans trumpeters. Once there
was a public "cutting" contest between Allen and another rival,
Kid Thomas. The crowd awarded Allen the prize but Thomas
went and got the police to take it back, claiming that Red's gang
was doing more hollering for its size than it should have. The
rivalry, nevertheless, was friendly. And Allen, by the way, became "Red" because his face lit up when he blew his horn, and
his light skin showed it.

Allen's growing technical knowledge of music complimented
his growing ability as a jazz improviser. One event he remembers, laughing, "made me a star!" Ethel Waters came to town
singing a little vaudeville piece which later became a Dixieland
standard, *That Da Da Strain*. Most of the local groups picked it
up, but they harmonized it wrong. Allen found the correct second
chord for *That Da Da Strain* and, "overnight I became a celebrity!"

At the Elite Café, pianist Luis Russell heard Red Allen, and
drummer Paul Barbarin heard him. In Chicago, King Oliver was
still sending down home to New Orleans for replacements when
band members left him: he acquired both Russell and Barbarin
that way. And in 1927, when he needed another trumpeter, they
recommended Allen.

Oliver was on his way to try New York when he sent for

Allen, and Allen met the group in St. Louis. He was nineteen, still a boy, the product of a protected childhood, now among men, and he became incurably homesick. Oliver put him up briefly in New York, he worked some jobs in and out of town with the King, and made a record date for Clarence Williams. But Allen was soon on his way home, despite a second offer to stop off again in St. Louis and play with a band there called The Missourians, which was building a reputation (and which later became Cab Calloway's orchestra). He described the experience this way to Sinclair Traill:

"I had the pleasure of working with 'King' when I was a kid—he played in my Dad's band on the parades and things. And it was King Oliver who made me the first offer to leave home (what you call New Orleans, but what I call New Or'lins). Paul Barbarin was the instigator behind that, and I left and joined the band. . . . I stayed only a short time in New York and then returned home. As a matter of fact this was the time that Barney Bigard left Orleans to join Duke Ellington. King Oliver had been offered the job at the Cotton Club, but had held out for better finance or something. But I guess he held out too long, and Ellington got the job. So I caught the next train out. I wasn't used to going on my own and I didn't get with it in New York too much—I was used to my mother doing for me, so I made out quickly."

Back home, Allen again worked the district with Fats Pichon at a club called the Pelican. In 1928 and 1929 he was again on the riverboats, sometimes on the *Sidney*, a rival to the Strekfus boats, with leader Sidney Desvignes. His reputation was spreading.

In 1929, record producer Loren Watson, who had heard Allen on the riverboats, asked him to come to New York again. The inducement was a recording contract, and Watson was obviously putting a great deal of faith in Allen's future. He was to be Victor Record's singing-trumpeting "answer to Louis Armstrong."

Allen's first record date after he arrived in New York this time, however, came about almost by accident. Eddie Condon and Fats Waller had commandeered Jack Teagarden, Gene Krupa, Albert Nicholas, and several others into a recording studio for a date under Waller's name. They needed a trumpeter in a hurry, and somebody said, "I heard a guy down the street, plays something like Louis Armstrong. Let's get him." They did, and under Waller's ever-jubilant guidance, they sketched out an arrangement for *Lookin' Good But Feelin' Bad* and *I Need Someone Like You* and put them on wax (the trumpet on this date, incidentally, has been credited to others, but it is Allen).

Allen's first records on his own were made with the Luis Russell orchestra under Allen's name—"Henry Allen and his New Yorkers" recorded *It Should Be You* and *Biffly Blues* for Victor on July 16, 1929. He continued to record for Victor for a year and the company also made a "team" of Allen and blues singer Victoria Spivey. Later, beginning in 1933, he worked for Perfect and Vocalion steadily through 1937.

The records were primarily directed at an urban Negro audience, and, during those depression years, were largely bought for jukeboxes. They also sold well in Europe. The selections, particularly on the later series, would include some standard popular songs, some Allen originals, and some ad lib blues, but the general fare was the latest tunes—a "cover" recording of a hit tune or of a new tune the companies thought had promise. For the new material, the players may have come into the studio cold, probably never having seen or heard the pieces before. They would work up slight arrangements, probably using only a publishers "lead sheet," with melody, simple harmony, and lyrics. Sometimes the repertory got pretty odd. Not only was Allen working with such deathless gems as *The Touch of Your Lips* and *I'll Sing You a Thousand Love Songs,* but he recorded *On the Beach at Bali Bali* and *Take Me Back to My Boots and Saddles.* The best of them still come back to him; Allen gets requests for *When Did You Leave Heaven* fairly regularly, and a fan in Dayton, Ohio, dubbed him off a complete set of a series on tape.

One rather famous Allen number got recorded first in this series—he worked up a little exercise run into a piece called *Rug Cutter's Swing,* but those who know it from the Fletcher Henderson or Benny Goodman versions know that Horace Henderson's name is on it as composer.

Allen was offered a job with Duke Ellington in 1929, but he

decided to go with Luis Russell instead (although fellow New Orleaneans Barney Bigard and Wellman Braud were in the Ellington band then and it was probably Bigard who recommended Allen) because the band had more of Allen's friends. His choice was a typical Allen choice, and friendship and loyalty, as well as more obvious friendliness and geniality, are still the centers of his life. Ellington took Cootie Williams instead, a Mobile man most New Orleans players believe was heavily influenced by Red's old rival Chris Kelly. Allen still proudly keeps Ellington's telegram which offered him the position.

The late Luis Carl Russell, the pianist-leader whose career was so closely bound for long periods to King Oliver's and to Red Allen's, was born on a small reef island called Careening Cay, off Panama. His father was Alexander Russell and he played church organ, did choir directing, and taught piano. The son Luis became a professional cabaret pianist at sixteen. Only a year later, in 1919, young Luis won a lottery and, using his $3000 prize, came to New Orleans with his mother and sister the following year. There he entered the musical life of the city. Storyville was officially closed down, but the bars were still wide open. Russell became leader of the "house band" at Tom Anderson's and there worked with men like Louis Armstrong, Albert Nicholas, Paul Barbarin, and Barney Bigard, then a slap-tongue tenor saxophonist.

Five years later, Russell had moved to Chicago and was working in Charles Cook's orchestra with Freddie Keppard and Jimmy Noone. Later in the same year he joined King Oliver, and in late 1927 Russell took over what had been the Oliver band as his own. The group held some fairly illustrious jobs—at the Savoy Ballroom, the Saratoga Club, and Roseland Dance Hall. After Allen joined in 1929, they went on to the Arcadia Ballroom and Connie's Inn.

Red Allen remembers Russell's success as deserved. "I think it was the most firey band I ever heard. There was more group spirit, more friendliness, and star temperament was never a problem. It had the finest rhythm section, with Pops Foster on bass and Paul Barbarin on drums especially inspiring to the soloists along with Will Johnson's guitar and Russell's piano.

Why, the rhythm section used to rehearse alone!" Pops Foster's work with Russell had every New York tuba player switching to string bass and pursuing him for lessons.

The chief soloists besides Allen were Albert Nicholas on clarinet, Charlie Holmes on alto saxophone, J. C. Higgenbotham on trombone, and Russell. In a sense, the band was a final development of the New Orleans style, for Russell began with Oliver's late style, his adaptation of Crescent City style to the "big band," and Charlie Holmes (from Boston) helped polish it. Many of the arrangements were "heads," invented and gradually changed and evolved by the musicians as they played them, on standard chord sequences (on the blues, of course, and pieces like *I Ain't Got Nobody*), and some were never written down. On its recordings the unique rhythmic spirit of the band and its soloists shone best on comparatively simple scores like *Louisiana Swing* or *Case on Dawn*. It was, by the way, the first band Allen knows of where the players stood up for their solos, and the first he had played in that used an exchange of four-bar phrases, "chasing" from player to player, later a common practice.

Between his work with Luis Russell and the recordings he was making under his own name, Red Allen became one of the most celebrated jazz trumpeters in New York, and one result of this celebrity was that he was in constant demand to work on recordings with other leaders. King Oliver used Allen on occasion, and it is Red Allen, not Oliver, who contributes the often-praised solos on *Mule Face Blues* and the second trumpet solo on Oliver's *Stingeree Blues*.

Allen also worked with the Reverend Gates, a preacher who recorded terse versions of his sermons. Toward the end of the records, Gates and his congregation would burst into song and the musicians were required to follow them—a sometimes difficult proposition since Gates had little concept of pitch and might fall into a very difficult key. Allen recorded some celebrated sides in 1932 with the Billy Banks Rhythmmakers, a racially mixed group also featuring Pee Wee Russell's clarinet.

Indeed, everyone from the Washboard Rhythm Kings to composer-arranger Don Redman tried to get, and got, Red Allen on records. The Kings, usually given to simpler pieces, did *I Cover the Waterfront* with Allen. And it was Allen who played the virtuoso passage that begins Redman's *Shakin' the African*—a kind of bravura jazz trumpet that almost every accomplished player since has echoed, and which has caused one of Allen's friends to exclaim in hyperbole, "Man, he invented bebop!" That intricate opening on *Shakin' the African* is one of the achievements of which Allen is most proud.

By late 1929, it had become obvious that Louis Armstrong was to be a great popular artist with a national audience, and he expanded his format to include a large band. At first he used Luis Russell's band on recordings as his own, and subsequently there was a brief tour. In one of the Armstrong-Russell recordings from this period, the 1929 *I Ain't Got Nobody*, Louis and Red split a chorus and nobody realized for over twenty-five years they had done it.

Lil Hardin Armstrong, incidentally, remembers one evening when her husband came home from work to discover her playing records by one of her own favorites, Red Allen. "He just stood there for a minute, with an angry expression on his face," she once told Robert Levin. "Then after a bit he smiled and said, 'Yeah, he's blowing.'"

Soon Allen left Luis Russell for the job which was in some ways his most famous and most influential. It came about partly because of Allen's early home training with that wind-up phonograph. Fletcher Henderson was reorganizing. He still had his star tenor saxophonist, Coleman Hawkins, but he needed a trumpet soloist to replace the departing Rex Stewart. Henderson dropped by one of the jam sessions at The Rhythm Club, the uptown spot where the best New York jazzmen could be heard. He was there to hear Allen, and both Benny Carter and trumpeter Russell Smith were in Allen's corner. Henderson's test was fairly direct. He sat down at the piano and tried some difficult keys. "When he hit those black keys, I followed him. 'You're my man,' he said," Allen remembers, and Henderson hired him then and there.

Allen's first job with Henderson was a record date and his first piece was a difficult one for the time, Coleman Hawkins's *Queer Notions*, on which Allen also had a solo. Soon the saxophonist and trumpeter were not only featured with Henderson but, on records, as a duo with the "Allen-Hawkins Orchestra," a small group variously using some of the best Henderson sidemen. It was these records that led to Allen's second major contract on his own, the one with Perfect and Vocalion which continued from 1933 through 1937.

Allen was pleased to be a part of so celebrated a band as Henderson's, of course, and it was this version of the Fletcher Henderson Orchestra that recorded *Down South Camp Meetin'*, *King Porter Stomp, Wrappin' it Up,* and *Rug Cutter's Swing* with solos by Allen. When Benny Goodman later played these pieces, trumpeter Harry James often paid Allen the compliment of building his own solos around Allen's originals. Allen's solo on *Minnie the Moocher's Wedding Day* was later written out and became a section part for all the trumpets. And, as we have noted, Allen's little composition was scored by Horace Henderson to become *Rug Cutter's Swing.* Allen also introduced the fanning trumpet mutes that the Henderson section used on *Honeysuckle Rose;* originally, fanned back and forth, up and down, in front of the brass instruments were quart and gallon beer containers making varied accents. The effect, usually executed with metal "hats," was later a part of every swing band's repertory.

Despite the fact that he had one of the best jazz bands in the country, and was playing a style which only a few years later was to become an international craze, Henderson found these mid-depression years rough going, and in late 1934 Henry Allen joined the Blue Rhythm Band under Lucky Millinder.

The Blue Rhythm Band was one of the enterprises of manager Irving Mills, whose chief client was Duke Ellington. It had been in existence for several years, and had only recently acquired Millinder as its singer and (in the parlance of the business) front-man. J. C. Higgenbotham joined along with Allen. Ex-Henderson clarinetist Buster Bailey was also a member, and many of the arrangements were done by the band's tenor saxophonist, Joe Garland, who had a hit on his hands a few years later with a riff he called *In the Mood.*

It was with the Blue Rhythm Band that Allen did a highly successful recording, a *Tiger Rag* variant called *Ride, Red, Ride.* The record very nearly wasn't issued. Allen and the band played it in the studio and it was waxed, but the record company men didn't like it and finally released it only because they had to have something to put on the back of a number they did like. It hit.

In 1935 Louis Armstrong returned from a European tour and permanently took over fronting the Luis Russell orchestra for eight years. Allen rejoined as a kind of relief to Armstrong. He was a featured soloist on the bandstand (if not on the records) and received billing in the announcements and advertising.

Otherwise, the band was there chiefly as a backdrop to Armstrong's talent—or Allen's when he spelled the nominal leader—and it had moments by other soloists (trombonist J. C. Higgenbotham, who had been traveling from band to band with Allen in a kind of unofficial team, clarinetist Albert Nicholas, plus some moments from pianist-musical director Luis Russell).

It was a disorganized ensemble, and its recordings show a careless kind of musical disagreement, in ensemble, in intonation, in rhythm—in almost all aspects of group discipline. Armstrong did not seem to care. He performed. The musical direction was not up to him, but he showed only fleeting concern that it should be up to anyone. But, one should remember, these were not the days of Armstrong's greatest public popularity; the early days of young Louis were drawing to a close, and the later days when genial Satchmo could pack them in had not yet arrived. A booker of Negro dances in the South might take Armstrong only because he had to, through some sort of block-booking "package deal," in order to get a Jimmy Lunceford for a dance a couple of months later.

In 1940, Henry "Red" Allen left the Armstrong orchestra. For a brief time he worked with Benny Goodman, but Allen was actually on his way toward leading his own group. A booking at the Café Society Downtown gave him his opportunity, and Allen formed a sextet. He has been on his own ever since.

The Cafés Society, one downtown and a later and more pretentious one uptown, were a phenomenon of a certain level of New York taste. For many years, the more advanced soloists of the swing style had been able, if they left the big bands and struck out on their own with small groups, to find work along Fifty-second Street in the many small cellar clubs strung out between Fifth and Sixth Avenues. But by the very late Thirties this swing period music (or "mainstream jazz" or "middle jazz"

as it has been more lately called) had been around long enough
so that it was beginning to be fashionable among the somewhat
better heeled. The downtown, then the uptown, Café Society
was largely a result of this upper-middlebrow popularizing of
swing music. The clubs featured Billie Holiday, the boogie-
woogie pianists (Albert Ammons, Meade Lux Lewis, and Pete
Johnson, with blues shouter Joe Turner), Teddy Wilson, and
others, and (inevitably) quasi-jazz artists like Hazel Scott.,

As its recordings demonstrate, Red Allen's 1941 sextet was in
some ways one of the most advanced groups around. Allen
picked Ken Kersey as his pianist, and Kersey was one of the
brightest and freshest of young pianists. Allen brought along
the robust Higgenbotham, and he used Edmond Hall, a Louisiana
clarinetist who retained much of the feeling of his heritage but
who also had the musical respect of more sophisticated players.
Years later, Allen told Nat Hentoff, "That's one of the reasons
jazz stays so absorbing, it's always changing, and I like to hear
those changes. I've changed some myself. And that's why I have
no fear about the future of jazz. This music can't die out while
there are always new generations of musicians trying new things.
I only hope that they also combine their innovations with listening to some of the players who have gone before them."

Red Allen stayed at the Café Society through 1941. There
was a brief trip following to Boston, and between 1942 and 1946
he held forth in Chicago, with a slightly modified personnel—alto
saxophonist Don Stovall in for Hall, Bill Thompson on piano,
and Kenny Clarke on drums. This booking was at the Down Beat
Room of ex-boxer Joe Sherman. Allen recalls the lady washroom
attendant there. He kept telling Sherman she was a fine singer,
and she sometimes substituted for the club's regular singer
Billie Holiday. Her name was Ruth Jones but Red's nickname
for her was "dynamite." One evening *she* didn't show up for
work. She was over at the Sherman Hotel at the Panther Room,
singing with Lionel Hampton as Dinah Washington.

The years 1948 and 1949 saw Allen on Fifty-second Street at
Kelly's Stables and the Onyx Club. The street itself was dying
as an institution. It had grown up to harbor the advanced players
of the Thirties, and had provided work for the early modernists.
There was still good music to be heard even to the end, but most

clubs had put in the strippers, who held out until the wrecking crews moved in during the Fifties and tore all the buildings down.

When modern jazz did arrive in the mid-Forties, it had a small and dedicated audience at first. But the style that had the greatest popular following at the time was a revival of Dixieland, and most of the players from the Thirties who were still active, but who no longer had many big bands in which to play or which to lead, either embraced the revival or left music. It was perhaps even more inevitable that Red Allen, as a "New Orleans musician" and as a hard-working showman, should become identified with this style. Even Louis Armstrong joined the revival, and thereby received the greatest popular success he has ever known.

Allen played next at a "traditional" spot in San Francisco called the Hangover. And in the early Fifties he was at a midtown New York bar, in the heart of the theatre district, Lou Terassi's. He had clarinetist Buster Bailey in his group. The repertory was varied, but more and more often it featured Dixieland tunes and fast crowd-pleasers. But Allen would also play a ballad—a revived *Body and Soul*, or another—and show his range as a jazz soloist.

By the late Fifties, after stays in Minneapolis and Chicago, Red Allen had become a fixture at a New York "show" bar called the Metropole.

The Metropole is another New York phenomenon. It juts onto Seventh Avenue just off Times Square. Its wide front is almost all glass doors and windows which reveal the long, narrow interior to a passerby in the street. It is a brassy, bold presence, and one of its aims is to attract and pack in just as many strolling tourists as it can. Before the Metropole took up jazz, it featured stout, aging females with whisky contraltos, dressed in costumes with lots of feathers and sequins and boas, belting out *She's Only a Bird in a Gilded Cage*, *Mother Machree*, or *Melancholy Baby* with every ounce of strength they had left.

For the performer, the Metropole takes a lot of strength. The stage is a high, narrow platform, above and behind the bar and running almost the entire length of the place. Directly across the narrow width of the room is a huge mirror, which again runs almost from the front to the back of the club. The performer, even on the most crowded and noisy of nights, hears his every note (even his every breath) bouncing back and forth across the narrow distance from one side wall to another. And if he looks up he will find himself staring into his own face, constantly reflected from a few feet away. At the Metropole a horn-man is apt to find his bass player or his drummer or his pianist (who strikes a tinny and frequently out-of-tune spinet) several yards away from him, and all but inaudible over the din.

With the dixieland revival, the Metropole put in dixieland. Then it put in Red Allen. Things continued to catch up, and the Metropole put in other swing period players like Roy Eldridge, Coleman Hawkins, and Charlie Shavers. For a while, the management opened up a separate room upstairs for modernists and hired Dizzy Gillespie, Horace Silver, and others. By the Sixties, the downstairs Metropole had rock-and-roll twist bands in the afternoon, and in the evening might feature Woody Herman's big band strung out along the bandstand, or Gillespie, or (more often than not) Red Allen.

Red Allen Jr. meanwhile had also moved on to a different milieu, and there he was playing a somewhat different and sometimes more appropriate repertory. He began at first at the Embers in New York, where he appeared with piano, bass, and drums, in a repertory of standards, ballads, and blues, in slow, medium, and occasionally fast tempos.

The Embers was still another phenomenon in the presentation of jazz in night clubs, a relatively posh East Side club which began as a result of the early popularization of modern jazz (or sometimes "almost modern" jazz) in the groups of George Shearing, Oscar Peterson, etc. But the Embers achieved its greatest success when it put in swing-style trumpeter Jonah Jones, with his horn always muted (it's in the club's contracts) to accommodate the sometimes high-pitched buzz of animated after-theatre conversation from the customers. To spell off Jones' successful engagements, the club used swing-era trumpeters like Charlie Shavers, Cootie Williams, Erskine Hawkins, Rex Stewart, trombonist Tyree Glenn, and Red Allen. As a result, Allen has also played what might be called the Embers circuit of similar clubs in Chicago, Cleveland, Toronto, etc.

In the fall of 1959, Red Allen' took momentary leave of American engagements to tour Europe with Kid Ory, Red's first trip to the continent. (He had been supposed to go in 1934 with the Henderson band, but as things worked out, Coleman Hawkins went alone.) Ory's style and repertory are, of course, older than Allen's, and European audiences were apparently expecting a tottering old trumpeter in Allen. What they got was an energetic and forceful musician, an individual stylist, and a man whose music is still immediate, personal expression, not—as with many jazzmen of Allen's and subsequent generations—an imitation of glories past.

Allen is proud of the strong impression he made in Europe on audiences and on European critics. He was also deeply moved when he walked into Fatty George's club in Vienna and found the wall decorated with his father's picture. (What American jazz club would show that sense of tradition?) He is proud of the letters he still gets from Europe, and, unlike some jazzmen who lack his straightforward approach to an audience, he is pleased when a fan or collector wants to talk old, long out-of-print records.

In early 1964, Allen made it overseas on his own, and, according to the reviews he received, "made it" is putting it mildly. In Manchester, England, he appeared in a most remarkable, complex establishment called The Manchester Sports Guild, a three-floor building, with "live" mainstream jazz in the basement, jazz records in the bar, and modern jazz by a big band in residence in a large hall—there is even a "folk" lounge. One reviewer declared that Allen, working singly with local musicians, had done more to revitalize British jazz in his brief stay than several touring American big bands.

At Manchester, Allen received the citation for his contribution to jazz, an event which he numbers among the three things in his life that he will always remember. "It has nothing to do with finance. It is a feeling that you're wanted. That helps a guy very much."

The other two things include a parade he participated in on one of his yearly trips to New Orleans. (He still makes them, incidentally, to visit his mother and other relatives—"down there, a fifth cousin is a relative; up here I'm very lucky to have grandchildren.") This one took place while his father was still alive. Allen Senior sat in his son's car. Henry Allen III, the grandson, drove. And Henry "Red" Allen led the parade playing his father's horn.

The other was when he first joined the Luis Russell band. "It has been a good life—a happy life."

Allen is generous to a fault in his viewpoint of others—"Better not ask me what trumpeters I like. It would be easier to name those I don't like. I know them all and I go around with them for pleasure. Different styles and schools and that sort of thing don't mean much to me. After Charlie Parker died I went to pay my respects at the benefit concert for his children that was held in Carnegie Hall." It was Allen who broke through a long stage wait toward the end of the concert, while Thelonious Monk and Dizzy Gillespie were verbally and musically sifting through old numbers to pick one to finish off the evening. Allen picked the slow blues and started to play. "We made it. It turned out all right," he says.

"Playing," he told Whitney Balliett, "it's like somebody making your lip speak, making it say things he thinks." And he added, "the blues is a slow story. The feeling of the beautiful things that happen to you is in the blues. They come out in the horn. You play blues, it's a home language, like two friends talking. It's the language everybody understands. You can inject into people with the instrument, I think."

Most of the musicians that Allen knew and respected when he was young were musicians only part of the time. "My father worked on the docks, and the others were plasterers, roustabouts, cigar makers, and painters, some were household servants. And so forth. When I started playing, I never really expected I would be able to devote my life to it, and I am very grateful."

Thus in his feelings about music Red Allen remains a communal performer. There are no squares to him, there are only listeners whom he seeks to entertain with what he sings and plays. The fact that what he offers them reaches them directly, but cuts more deeply than mere entertainment, shows that Red Allen is a gifted man. He knows that he is gifted, to be sure, but he uses his gifts with a kind of innate charity that might well be the envy of all men.

Recordings

Allen's own playing on the quartet date described in the opening of this piece can be heard on Swingville 2034, "Mr. Allen."

Otherwise, Red Allen on LP is somewhat scattered. Columbia's "The Fletcher Henderson Story" (C4L 19) has *Queer Notions, Yeah, Man, Can You Take It?*, and *King Porter Stomp*, and RCA Victor's "A Jazz Autobiography of Coleman Hawkins" (LPV-501) has Henderson's *Hocus Pocus*. Victor's King Oliver set (LPV-529) has Allen's solos on *Mule Face Blues* and *Stingaree Blues*.

Specialty shops may have the European reissues of the Luis Russell band on Odeon XOC 145, and "Henry Allen Jr. and his New York Orchestra" on RCA Victor 430.602 (which has *Swing Out, Feeling Drowsy, It Should Be You*, and the original *Biffly Blues*). The same shops may have EP, 45-rpm reissues of some of the Allen-Hawkins sides. (Also try proprietor Bert Bradfield's Treasury of Jazz, 8 Rue Albert Laurent, Chatillon-sous-Bagneaux, Seine, France, for such overseas issues.)

If you can find a copy of the recently out-of-print Red Allen-Coleman Hawkins LP "Ride, Red, Ride" on Victor LPM 1509, you will have especially good Allen on *I've Got the World on a String, Sweet Lorraine, Love Is Just Around the Corner, 'S Wonderful*, and *I Cover the Waterfront*.

Columbia has, from 1936, *Lost* and *Every Minute of the Hour* in its "Swing Street" album (SN 6042), and Allen is briefly represented in Columbia's Billie Holiday set (C3L 21), Victor's Sidney Bechet set (LPV 510), Victor's Lionel Hampton "Swing Classics" (LPM 2318), and Columbia's "The Sound of Harlem" (C3L 33).

Columbia promises a Red Allen album, which will include sides from the Thirties and early Forties. Meanwhile, that label has Allen's "live" LP, recently recorded, "Feelin' Good" (CL 2447).

References

Balliett, Whitney, "The Blues Is a Slow Story," a profile of Red Allen. *The New Yorker*, July 8, 1966.

Boatfield, Graham, "Henry Allen from New Orleans." *Jazz Journal*, February 1960.

Ellis, Don, "Henry (Red) Allen Is the Most Avant-Garde Trumpet Player in New York City." *Down Beat*, January 28, 1965.

Grut, Harald, "Luis Russell." *Jazz Journal*, March 1964.

Hentoff, Nat, "Henry 'Red' Allen: Jazz as Rejuvenating Joy." *International Musician,* June 1963.

Hoefer, George, "Luis Russell." *Down Beat,* November 8, 1962.

————, "Red Rides Again!" *Down Beat,* January 8, 1959.

Levin, Robert, "Lil Armstrong." *Jazz 'n' Pops,* April 1957.

Lucas, John, "Reminiscing with Red." *The Record Changer,* December 1954.

Traill, Sinclair, "In My Opinion," an interview with Red Allen. *Jazz Journal,* September 1964.

Voce, Steve, "Red Allen at the Manchester Sports Guild." *Down Beat,* June 18, 1964.

Williams, Martin, "Some Words for Red Allen." *Metronome,* October 1961.

INDEX

INDEX

ADAMS, Stephen, 30
African-American music, xii-xiii
Alexis, Richard, 260
Allen, Ed, 110, 185
Allen, George, 260
Allen, Henry, Sr., 258-260, 273
Allen, Henry Red, Jr., xiii, xv, xvi,
   xvii, 55, 74, 81-82, 107, 114, 141,
   183, 197, 200, 206, 251-275
   recordings, 274
Allen, Henry, III, 273
Allen, Ray, 138
Allen, Richard, xvi
Allen, Shep, 52
Allen, Walter, 104
Alvin, Danny, 153, 197
Alvis, Hayes, 195
Ammons, Albert, 269
Anderson, J. Lee, 162
Anderson, Tom, 16, 173, 264
Ansermet, Ernest, 136, 144
Armstrong, Clarence, 169
Armstrong, Louis, xi-xvi, 32-34, 56,
   57, 68, 79, 88, 89, 92-100, 102,
   106, 109, 110, 117, 121, 126, 130,
   138, 142, 145, 162-180, 183, 190-
   200, 206-211, 218-226, 230, 234,
   235, 238, 241, 256, 257, 260, 264,
   266, 268, 270
   background of, 164-165
   on Bolden, 14
   King Oliver's influence on, 169-
   170
   recordings, 176
   on Singleton, 187-188
   on Storyville, 18, 85, 168-169

Armstrong, Mrs. Louis, 56, 86, 87,
   89, 91, 92, 94, 95, 97, 174-176,
   192-193, 211, 266
Armstrong, Mayanne, 165, 167, 172
Asbury, Herbert, 5, 6, 15
Austin, Lovie, 88
Autrey, Herman, 202
Avakian, George, 246

BAD Sam, 51
Bage, Agnes, 111
Bailey, William "Buster," 80, 99,
   110, 188-189, 267, 270
Baker, Josephine, 111, 146
Balliett, Whitney, 45, 179, 273
Banks, Billy, 265
Baquet, Achille, 27
Baquet, George, 20, 21, 82, 140
Barbarin, Paul, 22, 86, 101, 103, 112,
   262, 264
Barker, Danny, xvi, 17, 68-69, 244
Barnes, Paul, 116
Barry, Emmett, 197
Basie, Count, 34, 158, 202, 244, 247
Bauduc, Ray, 128, 229
Beauregard, P. G. T., 6
Bechet, Albert, 141
Bechet, Homer, 141
Bechet, Joseph, 141
Bechet, Leonard, 141, 231
Bechet, Sidney, xii, xvii, 14, 22, 32,
   49, 74, 85, 87, 110, 126, 136-161,
   163, 166, 188, 189, 195, 197, 209,
   211, 228, 231, 233, 241-242, 247
   background of, 140-141

death of, 160
recordings, 160-161
Beiderbecke, Bix, 34-35, 121, 123, 126, 186
Benny Goodman Story, The (movie), 219
Berg, Billy, 197, 198, 215
Berman, Shelley, 251
Bertrad, Jimmy, 187
Bigard, Barney, 59, 101, 103, 105, 199, 212, 213-214, 215, 218, 262, 264
Black, Clarence, 211
Black, Lew, 125
Black, Louis, 123
Black Code of 1724, 5, 9
Blanton, Jimmy, 183
Blesh, Rudi, 44, 235-239
Bloom, Marty, 55
Blythe, Jimmy, 88
Boatfield, Graham, 259
Bocage, Peter, 260
Bolden, Charles Buddy King, xi, xiv, xvii, 1-15, 26, 92, 108, 142, 167, 222, 226, 227, 231, 256
 birth of, 11
 disrespect for propriety, 2-3
 mental illness of, 11, 12, 14
 music evaluations, 14-15
 recordings, 23
 religious background, 10
 traditions of, 3-10
Bonano, Sharky, 36
Bonner, Theodore, 210
Bontempts, Arna, 41, 184
Bontempts, Willy, 181
Bookins, Tommy, 190
Borders, Ben, 206
Bose, Sterling, 153
Bostic, Earl, 183
Botley, Buddy, 11
Botley, Dude, 13, 17
Bradford, Perry, 138, 205
Braud, Wellman, 49, 75, 86, 244, 264
Brice, Fanny, 48
Bridges, Harry, 238
Brookins, Tommy, 87, 88, 174
Broun, Heywood, 231, 233
Brown, Boyce, 128

Brown, Lillyn, 72
Brown, Steve, 27
Brown, Tiny, 198
Brown, Tom, 27-29, 123
Brunies, Albert Abbie, 123, 131, 134
Brunies, Henry, 131
Brunies, Merritt, 131, 134
Brunies, Richard, 131
Brunis, George (Brunies), 121, 123, 131-134, 206
Brunn, H. O., 33
Buckner, Teddy, 219
Bushell, Garvin, 90, 244, 245, 247
Busse, Henry, 173, 226

Cable, George W., 7
Caceres, Ernie, 195
Cahill, Albert, 47
Callahan, Albert, 131
Calloway, Cab, 200, 244, 262
Capone, Al, 124
Carew, Roy, 16, 47, 66-67, 73
Carey, Jack, 181, 208, 258
Carey, Mutt, 10, 14, 19, 84, 88, 104, 199, 206, 208, 209, 210, 212, 215, 217, 218, 219, 236-237
Carrington, Jerome, 188
Carter, Benny, 266
Casaras, Ernie, 149
Catlett, Sidney, 138, 151, 157, 178, 191, 197, 199
Celestine, Oscar (Papa), 109, 116, 172, 173, 181, 258, 259
Cesares, Ernie, 139
Charles, Robert, 42
Charters, Samuel B., 21
Christian, Buddy, 144, 170
Christian, Emil, 31
Clarke, Kenny, 138, 157, 159, 269
Clayton, Buck, 139
Cless, Rod, 133, 153
Cobb, Bert, 100, 105
Cobb, Junie C., 100, 188
Colburn, Bill, 217, 231-232, 236, 240
Cole, Cozy, 199
Coleman, Bill, 153, 200
Collier's (magazine), 225
Collins, Lee, 56-57, 100, 200, 201, 218, 256
Collins, Wallace, 1

Condon, Eddie, 92, 197, 230, 262
Congo Square, Sunday dances in, 6-9
Conroy, Jack, 41, 184
Cook, Charles Doc, 22-23, 188, 193, 264
Cook, Will Marion, 49, 143-144
Cottrell, Louis, 179, 182, 260
Courlander, Harold, 4
Cox, Ida, 88
Creath, Charles, 53, 184, 185, 186
Creath, Marjorie, 186
Creoles, background of, 4-10
Cricket, The (gossip sheet), 2
Crosby, Bob, 35, 128, 216, 229-230
Cuba, 5
Cuffee, Ed, 244
Cutchey, Wallace, 226

DARENSBOURG, Joe, 215
Davis, Leonard, 185
Davis, Miles, 185
Davis, Peter, 166
Davis, Victoria, 81
De Paris, Sidney, 151, 195
De Paris, Wilbur, 68, 153
Decou, Walter, 233
Dédé, Sante, 5
Defender (newspaper), 106
Desvignes, Sidney, 262
Detroit, Paul, 179
Dickenson, Vic, 138, 139
Dickerson, Carroll, 188, 192, 193
Didimus, Henry, 7
Dodds, Johnny, xv, 85-90, 95, 99, 103, 105, 126, 178, 187, 188, 192-193, 209, 211, 247
Dodds, Warren Baby, xv, 59-60, 87-90, 93-94, 97, 99, 160, 172, 173, 178, 181, 187, 240, 243, 244, 246-247
Dolphy, Eric, 188
Dominguez, Paul, 1, 173
Dominick, Natty, 187
Dominique, Natty, 88
Dorsey, Tommy, 216, 230
Douglas, Louis, 146
Down Beat, 73, 93, 196, 211, 257-258
Drob, Harold, 216-217, 243, 244, 245

Duhé, Lawrence, 86, 143, 208-209
Duncan, Hank, 242
Dunn, Johnny, 67, 68
Durante, Jimmy, 32
Durell, Henry Edward, 7
Dusen, Frankie, 11, 13, 53, 82, 206, 227
Dutrey, Honoré, 82, 87, 88, 90, 95

EDWARDS, Eddie, 28, 29, 30, 31, 35, 36
Edwards, Esmond, 252-256
Eldridge, Joe, 197
Eldridge, Roy, 178, 194, 197, 201, 222, 271
Ellington, Duke, 71, 107, 126, 145, 156, 193, 212, 262-264, 267
Ellis, Don, 257
Erskine, Gilbert, 91
Ertegun, Nesuhi, 212-215, 238
Esquire (magazine), 241
Eubanks, Horace, 194
Evans, Carlisle, 123
Evans, Stomp, 100
Ewell, Don, 243

FARMER, Art, 254
Fazola, Irving, 128, 229
Feather, Leonard, 219
Ferguson, Maynard, 202
Fernandez, Butchy, 173, 180
Fields, Julius Geechy, 68, 72
Fields, Kansas, 197
Filhe, George, 100
Fisher, Freddy, 230
Fletcher, Lucy, 109-110
Foss, Lucas, 257
Foster, George Pops, 82, 87, 153, 172, 183, 186, 242, 264-265
France Musicale, La, 8
Francis, Panama, 197
Frank, Bab, 21
Frank, Bob, 208
Freeman, Bud, 93, 121, 122, 127, 128, 197, 230
Frenchy, Benny, 51
Frisco, Joe, 27
Fritzel, Mike, 124

GABLER, Milt, 197
Gaillard, Slim, 197-198

Garland, Ed, 85, 86, 87, 90, 199, 206, 208, 210, 212-214, 236
Garland, Joe, 267
Garrison, Ben, 65
Gates, Reverend, 265
Gennett, Oliver, 94
Gilbey, John, 229
Gillespie, Dizzy, 178, 198, 215, 222, 224, 271, 273
Girsbach, Squire, 238
Gitler, Ira, 93
Gleason, Ralph J., 217, 231
Glenn, Tyree, 271
Gold, Lew, 64
Gonsoulin, Bertha, 235, 238
Gonzalez, Antonia P., 16
Goodman, Benny, 35, 132, 188, 247, 263, 267, 268
Gottschalk, Louis-Moreau, 7-9, 11
Green, Charlie Big, 195
Greer, Sonny, 145
Guriffre, Sonta, 130
Gushee, Larry, 96
Gustat, J., 186

HACKETT, Bobby, 149, 195, 197, 200
Hadlock, Richard, xvi, 64, 137, 141
Hager, Fred, 205
Haggard, Bob, 216
Haiti, 4
Hall, Edmond, 197, 269
Hall, Minor Ram, 86, 87, 89, 143, 214
Hammond, John, 149
Hampton, Lionel, 195, 269
Handy, W. C., 55, 63-64
Hardaway, Diamond Lil, 100
Hardin, Lil, 56, 86, 87, 89, 91, 92, 94, 95, 97, 174-176, 192-193, 211, 266
Hardwick, Otto, 195
Hardy, Emmet, 260
Harrison, Jimmy, 65
Harrison, Max, 152
Hawkins, Coleman, 189, 266-267, 271, 272
Hawkins, Erskine, 271
Hayes, Clancey, 240
Heard, J. C., 138

Henderson, Fletcher, 68, 74, 100, 101-102, 110, 126, 173, 183-184, 189, 244, 263, 266-267
Henderson, Horace, 263, 267
Hentoff, Nat, 269
Herman, Woody, 230, 247, 271
Heywood, Eddie, 196
Higgenbotham, J. C., 112, 138, 241, 265, 267, 268, 269
Hilaire, Andrew, 23, 62
Hill, Alex, 190
Hines, Earl, 53, 138, 151, 178, 179, 187, 188, 189-190, 192, 197
Hinton, Milt, 199-200
Hodeir, André, 180
Hodes, Art, 153, 195
Hodges, Johnny, 145, 147, 156, 255
Hoefer, George, 16, 73, 107
Holiday, Billie, 160, 196, 199, 269
Holmes, Charlie, 112, 265
Horn, Ellis, 238-239
Horne, Lena, 197
Howard, Darnell, 59, 103, 214-215
Howard, Joe, 166
Hunter, Alberta, 49, 86, 202

International Musician, 219-220
Irvis, Charlie, 144, 145

JACK the Bear, 51
Jackson, Charlie, 99, 126
Jackson, Dewey, 185, 186
Jackson, Preston, 130, 167, 206
Jackson, Rudy, 99
Jackson, Tony, xv, 16, 38, 47-50, 63, 109, 110, 143, 228
James, Harry, 28, 29, 227, 267
Janis, Harriet, 44, 239
Janson, Ted, 186
Jazz, origin of the word, xii, 28
Jazz: A History of the New York Scene (Charters and Kunstadt), 21
Jazz Hot (panassie), 230
Jazz Information (magazine), 230-231
Jazz Masters of the Thirties (Shih), xvi
Jazz Masters of the Twenties (Hadlock), xvi
Jazz Review, The, 148

Jefferson, Blind Lemon, 126, 205
Jefferson, Rose, 225
John, Dr., 5
Johnson, Bill, 20, 22, 23, 85-86, 94, 189
Johnson, Dink, 20, 206
Johnson, Jack, 69
Johnson, James P., 51-52, 69, 111
Johnson, Pete, 269
Johnson, Theresa, 225, 226
Johnson, William, 226
Johnson, Willie G. "Bunk," xvi, 2, 11, 13, 80, 81, 92, 142, 163, 166, 167, 175, 206, 212, 214, 217-218, 222-250, 260
    background of, 226-227
    controversy over, 222-223
    influence of, 225-226
    recordings, 23, 249
    recreates Bolden's style, 14-15
Jones, Billy, 31
Jones, Clarence, 193
Jones, Clifford Snags, 99, 100
Jones, David, 87, 89
Jones, Isham, 183
Jones, Jonah, 271
Jones, Joseph, 166
Jones, Richard M., 83, 84
Jones, Ruth, 269
Jones, Spike, 230
Joplin, Scott, 21, 26, 185
Jordan, Louis, 225

KAHN, Gus, 48
Kaminsky, Max, 195-196, 197
Kapp, Dave, 194
Kelly, Bert, 28
Kelly, Chris, xv, 260, 264
Kelly, Guy, 200, 261
Keppard, Freddie, xv, 15, 19-23, 49, 57, 80, 83-85, 88, 126, 143, 167, 188, 209-210, 226, 228, 233, 247, 256, 257, 264
    background of, 20
    recordings, 24
    refusal to record, 21-22
Kersey, Ken, 269
King, Bruce, 97, 240-241
Kirkpatrick, Don, 244
Krupa, Gene, 181-182, 262

Kunstadt, Leonard, 21

LADNIER, Tommy, 101, 126, 139, 146-150, 256
Laine, George Vitelle (Jack), xv, 27
Lala, Pete, 208, 227
Lamare, Hilton Nappy, 128, 198-199, 229
Lambert, William, 27
Lannigan, Jim, 127
LaRocca, Dominic James, 28-36, 229
Latrobe, Benjamin Henry, 7
Laveau, Marie, 5
Laws, M. T., 210
Le Menthe, Ferdinand Joseph, 41
Leadbelly, 158
LeClerc, Erwin, 47
Lee, Julia, 228
Levin, Robert, 266
Lewis, George, 163, 229, 233, 240, 247
Lewis, Meade Lux, 197, 269
Lewis, Steve, 181
Lewis, Ted, 32, 132-134
Lindsay, Johnny, 61-62
Lindsey, Joe, 170
Lindsey, John, 99
Lingle, Paul, 238-239
Lippincott's Magazine, 3-4
Lomax, Alan, 41-42, 73
Lomax, Louis, 42, 44
London *Daily News*, 31
Lopez, Ray, 27
Loughborough, Bill, 245
Lovett, Baby, 228, 247
Loyocano, Arnold, 27, 123, 124, 125
Luke, Charles, 64
Lunceford, Jimmy, 214
Luter, Claude, 159
Lyons, Bob, 170
Lytel, Jimmy, 32

McCARTHY, Albert, 147
McDonnel, Rudy, 116
McGee, Howard, 198
McIntyre, Hal, 231-232
McKinley, Nina Mae, 195
McKinney, Bill, 69
MacPartland, Jimmy, 127, 128, 132
Manetta, Manuel, xvii

Manone, Wingy, 186, 195, 200
Marable, Fate, xvi, 55, 172, 183-184, 186, 261
Mares, Paul, 34, 121, 122, 123, 127-128
Marsala, Joe, 190
Marshall, Kaiser, 65, 197, 243
Martin, Sarah, 109-110, 114
Martinique, 4
Mascot, The, 18-19
Matlock, Mattie, 128
Matthews, Artie, 51
Matthews, Dave, 190
Matthews, Lewis, 208
May, Billy, 190
Mellers, Wilfred, 9, 32-33, 149-150
Melrose, Walter, 55-56, 58-59, 64-65
Metcalfe, Louis, 113-114
Meyers, Billy, 103
Mezzrow, Mezz, 152, 153, 195, 200, 201
Miles, Flora, 169
Miley, Bubber, 90, 107, 144, 145, 195
Miller, Eddie, 128, 229, 230
Miller, Punch, 200, 256
Milles, James, 63
Millinder, Lucky, 267
Mills, Irving, 267
Mitchell, George, 60-63, 88, 91, 93, 96, 190
Mole, Miff, 32
Monk, Thelonious, 202, 257, 273
Montgomery, Little Brother, 218
Moore, Fred, 80, 115, 242
Morden, Marili, 212, 214
Morgenstern, Dan, 211
Morton, Benny, 197
Morton, Jelly Roll, xi, xiv-xv, 18, 19, 26, 32-34, 38-76, 88, 104, 125-126, 147, 178, 189, 195, 206, 211, 214, 215, 228, 232, 233
    contradictory data on, 39-40
    death of, 75
    first recording date, 57
    musical influences on, 47-48
    recordings, 76
    religion of, 72
    snobbery of, 43
Moten, Benny, 216

Moynahan, J. S., 35
Mueller, Gus, 27, 28
Mulattoes, defined, 9
Murphy, Turk, 201
Murray, Don, 128-129
Music in a New Found Land (Mellers), 149-150
My Life in Jazz (Kaminsky), 195-196

NAPOLEON, Phil, 32
Negro-American culture, background of, 3-10
Nelson, Big Eye Louis, 21, 83, 141, 189, 209, 231, 233
Nelson, Dave, 112, 113
New Orleans
    ceded to Spain, 5
    general background data, xi-xvii
    history of, 4-10
    population figures, 5
    prostitution in, 15-19
    school segregation in, 42
New Orleans (movie), 199, 218-219
New Orleans Blue Book, 16-18, 45-46
New Orleans Jazz Foundation, 241
New Orleans Rhythm Kings, 121-135
New York Clipper, 21
New York Herald Tribune, 237, 243
Newhart, Bob, 251
Newton, Frankie, 138, 195-196
Nicholas, Albert, 69, 72, 85, 99, 101, 103, 104, 105, 139, 189, 196, 197, 249, 262, 264, 265, 268
Nixon, Teddy, 148
Noone, Jimmy, xiv, xv, 22, 85, 86, 105, 109, 121, 137, 170, 171, 188, 189-191, 199, 209, 212-214, 233, 247
    background of, 189
    death of, 190-191
Nunez, Alcide Yellow, 28

O'BANNION, Dion, 124
O'Brien, Floyd, 92
O'Hare, Husk, 125
O'Keefe, Jimmy, 112

Oliver, King, xiv, xvii, 19-23, 32-33, 34, 52, 58, 62, 64, 79-120, 121, 125, 167, 174-175, 178, 189, 192, 205-210, 225, 228, 232-235, 247, 256, 259-265
  background of, 81
  death of, 117-118
  influence on Armstrong, 169-170
  recordings, 118
Oliver, Stella, 81, 170
Olivier, Adam, 226-227
Ory, Kid, 61, 62, 75, 85, 86, 87-88, 103, 105, 171-172, 192-193, 199, 205-221, 236-237, 272
  background of, 207
  recordings, 220
Ostransky, Leroy, xiii

Page, Orin Hot Lips, 74, 197, 228
Paige, Billy, 103-104
Palao, Jimmy, 20, 87
Palmer, Jack, 111
Palmer, Roy, 19, 86, 206
Panassie, Hughes, 149, 230
Parenti, Tony, 186, 201
Parham, Tiny, 66, 211
Parker, Charlie, 70, 138, 158, 178, 198, 215, 222, 273
Parker, Daisy, 172, 176
Pasqual, Jerome Don, 23, 53, 172, 185
Payton, Dave, 187-188
Peavey, Sister Lottie, 240
Pecora, Santa, 64, 127, 131
Perez, Leander, 42
Perez, Manuel, 14, 80, 92, 141, 182
Perkins, Dave, 27
Peterson, Oscar, 271
Petit, Buddy, xv, 53, 86, 142, 162-163, 189, 225-226, 260
Petit, Joseph, 162
Pettis, Jack, 121, 122, 123
Peyton, Benny, 144, 146
Peyton, Dave, 100, 193, 211
Piazza, Countess Willie, 46-47, 109
Pichon, Walter Fats, 261, 262
Pickett, Tom, 12-13
Pickett, Ward, 72

Picou, Alphonse, 20, 97, 170, 231
Pinkett, Ward, 68
Piron, A. J., 20, 34, 85, 97, 109, 111, 181
Pleyel, Salle, 200, 201
Pollack, Ben, 121, 125, 132, 230
Ponce, Henry, 167-168
Porée, André, 1-2
Postom, Joe, 189
Potter, Jerry, 252-253, 254, 255
Powers, Ollie, xv-xvi, 23, 100, 176
Price, Sammy, 197, 228, 244
Prima, Louis, 132
Procope, Russell, 68
Prostitution, 15-19

Ragas, Henry, 28, 30-31
Rainey, Ma, 126, 205, 228
Rappolo, Leon, 121, 123, 124, 127-131
Ramsey, Frederick, Jr., 117, 214, 230, 231
Ravel, Maurice, 188
Record Changer, 16
Redd, Alton, 214, 236
Redd, Katie, 195
Redman, Don, 68, 71, 101-102, 103, 176, 265-266
Rena, Henry, 167
Rena, Kid, 231, 233, 256, 260
Rene, Henry, 260
Resnikoff, Mischa, 200
Rewèliotty, André, 159
Richards, Frank, 64
Roach, Max, 202
Robechaux, Joseph, 171
Robichaux, John, 227
Robinson, Alvin Zue, 55, 99, 170, 206, 209
Robinson, Bill, 65, 197
Robinson, J. Russell, 31
Robinson, Jim, 233
Rockwell, Tommy, 192
Rosenbaum, David, 239
Ross, Kid, 47
Rossiter, Will, 54
Rushing, Jimmy, 53
Russell, Alexander, 264
Russell, George, 257

Russell, Luis Carl, 100, 101, 102, 104, 107, 112-113, 173, 211, 261, 263, 264-266, 268, 273

Russell, Pee Wee, 132, 186, 195, 197, 265

Russell, William, xvi, 53, 189, 217, 228, 230, 231, 232, 234, 235, 236, 240-241

Rust, Brian, 22

Ryan, Jimmy, 196-197, 202

St. Cyr, Johnny, 23, 58, 82, 109, 172, 180, 183, 192-193

Sandburg, Carl, 188

Santo Domingo, 4, 5

Satchmo: My Life in New Orleans (Armstrong), 168

Saturday Evening Post, 35

Sbarbaro, Tony, 29

Scaate, Frank, 252, 254

Schaeffer, Gypsy, 45-46

Schenk, John, 218, 244

Schlitten, Don, 254

Schobel, Elmer, 66, 103, 121-122, 123, 124, 130

Schoffner, Bob, 104

Scobey, Bob, 237

Scott, Bud, 99, 100, 199, 212-214

Scott, Hazel, 269

Scott, Lannie, 252, 254, 255

Senter, Boyd, 64, 66

Shavers, Charlie, 138, 150, 151, 197, 271

Shaw, Artie, 188, 195-196, 247

Shearing, George, 271

Sherman, Joe, 269

Shields, Eddie, 130-131

Shields, Larry, 28-32, 35, 36

Shih, Hsio Wen, xvi

Shoffner, Bob, 105

Signorelli, Frank, 32, 36

Silver, Horace, 70, 271

Simeon, Omer, 58, 62, 68, 69, 103, 160, 189

Singleton, Margie, 186, 201

Singleton, Zutty, xv, 56, 74, 149, 164, 173, 178-204, 206, 211, 212-214, 218

Armstrong on, 187-188
background of, 180-181
recordings, 202-203

Sissle, Noble, 146-147, 148

Slaves
dances of, 6-9
music of, 3-4
religious supression of, 5

Smeck, Roy, 112

Smith, Bessie, 34, 107, 110, 121, 144, 179, 205

Smith, Charles Edward, 74

Smith, Harrison, 55, 65, 69, 72, 147

Smith, Mamie, 90, 244

Smith, Russell, 266

Smith, Willie the Lion, 72, 111

Snowden, Elmer, 107

Snyder, Frank, 123, 125

Solal, Martial, 137, 159

Souchon, Edmond, 10, 42, 82

Sousa, John Philip, xiii

Spain, 5

Spanier, Muggsy, 123, 132-133, 150, 197

Spargo, Tony, 29, 36, 200

Spencer, O'Neil, 148

Spikes Brothers, 54, 104, 206, 210

Spivey, Victoria, 202, 263

Stacy, Jess, 128, 186, 197

Stall, Lorenzo, 2-3, 11

Stearns, Marshall, 5, 10

Steele, Alphonso, 243, 244

Stein, Johnny, 28, 29, 32

Steiner, John, 127, 190

Stendehl, Bob, 245

Stevens, Ragbaby, 123

Stewart, Rex, 138, 266, 271

Stitzel, Mel, 64, 122, 125

Story, Sidney, 16

Story of Jazz, The (Stearns), 5

Story of the Original Dixieland Jazz Band, The (Brunn), 33

Storyville, 15-19, 45-47, 202
Armstrong on, 85, 168-169

Stovall, Don, 269

Streckfus, Joe, 173, 183-186

Stuart, David, 212, 231-234

Sullivan, Joe, 195, 197

Sunday Sun, 18-19

Swing That Music (Armstrong), 33-34, 230
Syncopation (movie), 199

TATE, Erskine, 23, 187
Tate, Harry, 212
Tatum, Art, 138, 195
Taylor, Billy, 73, 197
Taylor, Eva, 110, 145
Taylor, Jasper, 57
Teagarden, Jack, 132, 190, 262
Terassi, Lou, 201, 270
Terry, Clark, 185
Teschmacher, Frank, 127
They All Played Ragtime (Blesh and Janis), 44
Thomas, Evan, 229
Thomas, Joe, 197
Thomas, Kid, 261
Thompson, Bill, 269
Thompson, Kay C., 141
Thompson, Virgil, 237, 243
Time (magazine), 214
Tio, Lorenzo, Jr., 189
Tio, Lorenzo, Sr., 49, 82
Toledano, Ralph de, 231
Tough, Dave, 93, 178, 197
Traill, Sinclair, 111
Treat It Gentle (Bechet), 136
Trumbauer, Frankie, 186
Tucker, Ragtime Billy, 210
Tucker, Sophie, 110-111
Turner, Joe, 269

VAN ALSTYNE, Egbert, 48
Van Gelder, Rudy, 251-254
Venson, Eddie, 143
Venuti, Joe, 195
Vinson, Eddie, 20
Vodun (voodoo), 5, 6

WADE, Louis, 142, 143
Wallace, Sippie, 114
Waller, Fats, 69, 110, 111, 179, 197, 202, 211, 262-263
Washington, Dinah, 269
Washington, Fred, 206, 210
Waters, Ethel, 173, 179, 261
Watson, Loren, 262
Watters, Lu, 201, 232, 235-239

Webb, Chick, 65, 69, 244
Weber, Jack, 130
Weems, Ted, 186
Welles, Orson, 199, 212-214
Wells, Dickie, 195, 200, 201
Wellstood, Dick, 201, 202
Wettling, George, 178, 196, 197
Whaley, Wade, 53, 191, 212, 236
White, Lulu, 17-18, 48, 110, 171
White, Robert, 210
White, Sonny, 138
Whiteman, Paul, 92, 173, 183
Wiedhoft, Rudy, 64
Wiedoff, Rudy, 66
Wilber, Bob, 148, 150-158
Williams, Bert, xiv, 110
Williams, Clarence, xv, 38, 85, 107-112, 117, 126, 138, 142, 144, 145, 230, 262
    background of, 107-108
Williams, Cootie, 264, 271
Williams, Eugene, 217, 218, 231, 232, 234, 243, 244, 245
Williams, Fess, 65
Williams, Gene, 242
Williams, Guy, 63
Williams, J. Mayo, 126
Williams, Leon, 20
Williams, Mary Lou, 153
Williams, Ralph, 183
Williams, Sandy, 138, 151, 243
Williams, Spencer, xv, 110-111
Williams, Zack, 209
Wilson, Buster, 75, 212-214, 215, 218, 236
Wilson, Eudell, 180
Wilson, Teddy, 269
Wooding, Sam, 146
Wycliffe, John, 23
Wylie, Clarence, 236

YOUNG, Lee, 240
Young, Lester, 160, 197, 240, 257, 258
Young, Trummy, 220
Young, William, 258

ZENO, Henry, 170, 179
Ziegler, Elizabeth, 159
Zohn, Al, 237